Hermogenes and the Renaissance
Seven Ideas of Style

HERMOGENES
AND THE RENAISSANCE

Seven Ideas of Style

ANNABEL M. PATTERSON

PRINCETON UNIVERSITY PRESS

PRINCETON, NEW JERSEY

1970

Publication of this book has been aided by a
grant from the Humanities Research Council of
Canada, using funds provided by the Canada Council.

*PA 3998
H 8
A 52 L*

This book has been set in Linotype Granjon
Printed in the United States of America
by Princeton University Press

To Felicity and Jason and Anne and Tom
in lieu of many other things we might have done

Acknowledgments

I thank all those who have spent time and patience improving either my manuscript or my state of mind, including those anonymous readers, many of whose suggestions I have happily adopted, and especially John Chalker, Patricia Thompson, Millar MacLure, Denton Fox, George Kustas, and George Grube.

I am also grateful to Macmillan Co. for permission to quote *Ego Dominus Tuus, High Talk, Blood and the Moon, A Coat,* and *Coole Park and Ballylee* from *Collected Poems of William Butler Yeats*, copyright © 1963; Faber and Faber, Ltd., for permission to quote *A Mirror for Poets* from *Fighting Terms*, Thom Gunn, copyright © 1962; Random House, Inc., and Faber and Faber, Ltd., for permission to quote *Kairos and Logos* from *The Collected Shorter Poems 1930-1944*, W. H. Auden, copyright © 1945; Harcourt, Brace & World, Inc., for permission to quote *Courage Means Running*, William Empson, copyright © 1955; Alfred A. Knopf, Inc., for permission to quote *Bells for John Whiteside's Daughter* from *Selected Poems*, John Crowe Ransom, copyright © 1947; and John Murray, Ltd., and Houghton Mifflin Co., for permission to quote *Before the Anaesthetic*, John Betjeman, from *Collected Poems*, copyright © 1958.

ANNABEL M. PATTERSON

Contents

Preface

THIS BOOK takes as its starting point the historical fact that there was once a rhetorician by the name of Hermogenes of Tarsus, who flourished in the second century A.D., and whose work not only became the foundation of Byzantine rhetoric, but also caused considerable excitement during the European Renaissance. The influence of Hermogenes on Byzantium is just beginning to be charted, and is not part of our present concern; his influence in Europe has been either distorted or completely ignored by the majority of scholars, and at no time has there been a full assessment of how Renaissance writers and critics responded to his most mature work, the περὶ ἰδεῶν, or *Concerning Ideas*, which presents and analyzes Seven Ideas of style. This book is about those Seven Ideas, and their relevance to the rhetoric, poetics, and aesthetics of the Renaissance and thereafter.

Before going any further, as a precautionary measure, I shall quote the anonymous scholar who read this study for the Humanities Research Council of Canada, and gave the following wise definition of its necessary limitations:

> Any "influence study" may at best only argue a case and remain more or less convincing. It must ignore parallel influences and also those innumerable, indeterminate factors which allow that influence to be exerted. Any study of the influence of a specific rhetorical work confronts the problem that the rhetorical tradition was very extensive, thorough, and inclusive. Further, rhetorical tradition in schools was so thorough that any poet's use of rhetorical devices becomes a subconscious or "natural" activity. Finally, any "influence study" works against itself: the greater the influence, the less likely is any direct influence.

No one is more aware of these limitations than I am, though I doubt if I could have put them so well; and everything that follows about the influence of Hermogenes in the Renaissance is tentative by nature, as well as occasionally in tone. At the same time, much of the evidence about Hermogenes in the

Preface

Renaissance is to be found in matters of *fact*; and has, moreover, been sitting around waiting to be noticed for a remarkably long time.

The division of this book into seven chapters does not, unhappily, reflect the division of style into Seven Ideas. The first chapter is introductory and argumentative, setting out the grounds for serious consideration of the Ideas as a major influence in the Renaissance, and defining their relationship to the concept of decorum. The second chapter remains introductory, describing each of the Ideas in turn, and offering likely examples of their operation in practice. The remaining five chapters deal only with those Ideas which seem to have been of most value to Renaissance writers, and they are organized according to the major nondramatic genres of poetry: the Idea of Grandeur is investigated twice, first in relation to the high ode and canzone, and then in relation to formal verse satire; the Ideas of Beauty and Verity are seen in opposition to each other in the context of the sonnet and the sonnet sequence; the Idea of Speed is found virtually to define a new, minor genre—the temporal poem; and finally the Idea of Gravity, which is both the climax of the scheme and the acid test of its flexibility, is seen as the stylistic principle of Renaissance epic. The Ideas of Clarity and Ethos are given no special treatment because they are not closely related to the development of any particular genre, the first being the elementary requirement of all good writing, and the second being an assortment of substyles which were influential only separately, and not as a group.

Because *Concerning Ideas* is far from being merely a rhetorical textbook, there are distinguishable levels or degrees of its influence. At the primary level, there is the direct influence of the Ideas in the criticism of Scaliger, Minturno, and Tasso, or in the religious propaganda of Milton, or in the "flyting" between Thomas Nashe and Gabriel Harvey, or in George Herbert's theory of preaching. These authors indicate their debt to Hermogenes in a variety of ways, which range from lengthy descriptions of the Seven Ideas to a passing reference to Hermogenes by name. At the secondary level, the influence of the Ideas is seen as a necessary hypothesis to explain otherwise inexplicable characteristics and patterns of writing. At this level the Hermogenic Ideas of Beauty and Verity are deduced as structural principles in the sonnet sequences of Sidney and Shakespeare, and the sub-Ideas of Asperity and Vehemence are found to account for the style of Elizabethan verse satire. In both hypotheses the presence of the Ideas is deduced not only rhetorically, but also conceptually; the meaning of Verity is as important to Sidney and Shakespeare as its stylistic devices, which is but another way of saying that an "Idea of style" is very different from "a style."

Thirdly, and on a level which is a natural extension of this, the Seven Ideas as a whole are seen to be a conforming as well as a shaping influence in the Renaissance, in the sense that they take their place as part of a prevailing attitude of mind. They are a subtle and suggestive expansion of the Idea of the perfect orator as defined by Cicero in imitation of Plato's preexistent Forms or Ideas, the perfect orator who exists only in our minds as an aggregate of all the fine speakers we have ever heard, and whose total rhetorical ability is inevitably connected to his existence as a good man. They belong to the golden world of the intellect, which is best defined by Sir Philip Sidney in the *Defence of Poesie*, and in which the ideal orator and the peerless poet take their places beside the perfect courtier and the philosopher king in the utopian commonwealth. The attitude of mind which links together all these Ideas, rhetorical and otherwise, accepts with patience the gap between conceptual and actual achievement, in rhetoric as in all other arts and actions, and yet continues to draw from the ideal all its evaluative and analytical categories. So Castiglione, before describing the characteristics of the perfect courtier, remarks of his audience that "if with all this they can not compasse that perfection, such as it is, which I have endeavoured to expresse, he that cummeth nighest shall be the most perfect." So Sidney's realistic appraisal of what English poetry has actually achieved by the 1580's does not compromise his ideal of the "right poet," because he accepts the precept that though "our erected wit maketh us know what perfection is . . . yet our infected will keepeth us from reaching unto it." So Sir Thomas More concludes his own description of a Platonic commonwealth with an admission of human frailty which in no way compromises the idea: "So must I nedes confesse and graunt, that many thinges be in the utopian weal publique, which in our cities I may rather wisshe for then hoope after." And so Hermogenes described Seven Platonic Ideas of style in the knowledge that they would never be fully realized in practice, a knowledge which in no way compromises their usefulness as categories for the true understanding of style.

Nor is this attitude limited to self-confessed Platonists. George Puttenham begins his *Arte of English Poesie* (1580) with a scornful dismissal of what "the Platonicks with their Ideas do phantastically suppose," and then proceeds to set up as his major aesthetic principle the concept of decorum which, as he praises it, becomes indistinguishable from the concept of the "golden world." Decorum, like the Idea concept, transfers easily from one frame of reference to another, and is ultimately the same principle whether it is expressed in metaphysics, ethics, politics, or poetics, for it exists in "all good, comely, pleasant, and honest things, even to the spirituall objectes of the mynde." The Seven Ideas of Hermogenes, however, are even more closely analogous to the concept of decorum than other forms of idealism, for the last of the Seven Ideas, that of Gravity, is itself the principle of combining all the other Ideas into one harmonious relationship; and it is no coincidence that the Idea of Gravity is actually given the alternative name of Decorum by Johannes Sturm, Renaissance scholar and editor of *Concerning Ideas*. It is this principle of decorum within them, this "lovely conformitie, or proportion, or conveniencie" as Puttenham calls it, which ultimately justifies the Seven Ideas as a rhetorical scheme; for what more can one ask of a rhetorical scheme than detailed instruction in the parts of discourse, and downright insistence upon the unity of the whole. It was perhaps a happy accident of cultural history which caused this combination of values to become apparent in the sixteenth century. It would be a happy consequence if this predominantly historical study should re-invigorate the Ideas, and make them once again available for the flexing and understanding of style.

Hermogenes and the Renaissance
Seven Ideas of Style

As Xenophon showed the perfect Idea of
a good king in Cyrus, and Homer that of
a prudent general in Ulysses, and of a
brave man in Achilles, and Plato that
of a true philosopher in Socrates, so
Hermogenes showed, in Demosthenes, what
the true and perfect Orator ought to be.

Johannes Sturm

CHAPTER 1

"Imitation of Great Masters": *Decorum of Style*

HIC.   . . . Why should you leave the lamp
Burning alone beside an open book,
And trace these characters upon the sands?
A style is found by sedentary toil
And by the imitation of great masters.
ILLE.   Because I seek an image, not a book.

(William Butler Yeats, *Ego Dominus Tuus*)*

W E BELONG to a generation which has made mighty efforts to get inside the mind of the Renaissance and to fit together, whether out of envy, condescension, or pure heroic magnitude of mind, the pieces of a world picture so much neater than our own. But one of the more obvious sections of this pattern has not yet been properly investigated, and that is the whole area of stylistic decorum, the concept which controlled everything which we now regard, frequently with a derogatory glance, as technique. The work of Gregory Smith and Rosemond Tuve[1] in this area has been incidental to other matters and necessarily brief. Modern critics who are interested in technique have not gone back into decorum, but forward into linguistics; and what seems to have been omitted altogether is any relevant study of the ancient rhetorician to whom decorum was the most important of all criteria. This neglected rhetorician, neglected only since the seventeenth century, is Hermogenes of Tarsus, who made decorum apprehensible in terms of style, and by so doing became to the Renaissance an authority to rival Cicero and Quintilian.

* From *Collected Poems*, William Butler Yeats. Reprinted by permission of Macmillan Co.

[1] G. Gregory Smith, ed., *Elizabethan Critical Essays*, 1959. His introduction contains a section on decorum, pp. xli-xlvi, which emphasizes its role in the drama. Rosemond Tuve, *Elizabethan and Metaphysical Imagery*, 1947. Miss Tuve has a whole chapter on "The Criterion of Decorum," but her interest there lies mainly in relating "shocking" Metaphysical images to the decorum of the low style.

3

Decorum of Style

Hermogenes' Life and Works

Hermogenes of Tarsus lived during the second century A.D., and according to Philostratus was at the age of fifteen already so famous that Marcus Aurelius requested to hear his lectures.[2] Very little else is known about his life except that he had written several works of rhetoric by the time he was twenty, and that this early precociousness was followed by an equally premature and extreme senility; as one of his seventeenth-century editors puts it, he was "in pueritia senex: in senectute infans."[3] Legend has it that at his death his body was cut open, and his heart was found to be completely overgrown with hair.[4] His life is oddly paralleled by the fortunes of his rhetoric, which was rediscovered in Europe toward the middle of the sixteenth century, had some sixty years of considerable popularity, and gradually disappeared from view during the later part of the seventeenth century. Hermogenes has been virtually ignored by Renaissance scholars of our own century, partly because it has been assumed that his influence was limited to the schools and depended upon his *Progym-*

[2] For a summary of the biographical material, see L. Radermacher, "Hermogenes," in Pauly-Wissowa, *Real-Encyclopädie der classischen Altertumswissenschaft*, VIII, 861-881; H. Rabe, "Aus Rhetoren-Handschriften," *Rheinisches Museum für Philologie*, LXII (1907), 247-264. The most recent discussions of Hermogenes' place in the history of rhetoric are by W. Kroll, "Rhetorik" in Pauly-Wissowa, Supplementband VII, 1125-1128, and Dieter Hagedorn, *Zur Ideenlehre des Hermogenes*, 1964. Hermogenes the rhetorician is not to be confused with the heretical philosopher, Hermogenes "the painter," who probably lived at Antioch, and was the object of Tertullian's two treatises, *Adversus Hermogenem* [c. 207] and *De censu animae adversus Hermogenem* [c. 210]. See J. H. Waszink, tr., *Tertullian: The Treatise Against Hermogenes*, 1956.

[3] Gaspar Laurentius, ed., τέχνη ῥητορική, 1614, Sig. Pref. 4r.

[4] There was apparently a tradition that hairy hearts were a sign of the excessively hot temperament. See Levinus Lemnius, *The Touchstone of Complexions*, tr. Henry Newton, 1581. Lemnius explains that abundant heat makes men strong and courageous, subtle and crafty, industrious and politic, and hairy; and he relates a story told by Pliny of one Aristomenes Messianius, who having twice escaped from his enemies by means of extreme courage and cunning, was finally killed and cut open, and his heart was found to be overgrown with hair (p. 44). I owe this reference to Pat Vicari, University of Toronto.

4

Decorum of Style

nasmata, or exercises in Invention.[5] The other main reason, one suspects, is that his *Art of Rhetoric* (τέχνη ῥητορική) has never been translated into English.

The *Art of Rhetoric* consists of three major parts: περὶ στάσεων, *Concerning Status,* a treatise on the "status" or basis of arguments; περὶ εὑρέσεως, *Concerning Invention,* a loosely organized treatise in four books which deals with the structure of an oration and methods of ornamentation; and περὶ ἰδεῶν, *Concerning Ideas,* a treatise on style. The *Art of Rhetoric* also includes a fourth short work of sometimes questioned authenticity, περὶ μεθόδον δεινότητος, *On the Method of Gravity,* which is little more than a catalogue of rhetorical figures. These treatises are available today in the modern editions of Spengel, Walz and Rabe (all my references are to Rabe's edition, published in 1913), but the language barrier prevents them from being readily available. It was the discovery of Renaissance editions with Latin translations, as well as a series of translations and commentaries in Italian, which made this book not only possible but necessary; for the very existence of these editions and commentaries pointed to an interest in Hermogenes far beyond what had so far been allowed by the standard guides to Renaissance rhetoric. The view of Hermogenes, then, which is presented in this book is essentially that of the Renaissance editors and commentators, with judicious additions and corrections from the editions which are now standard; and wherever a classically trained eye detects dis-

[5] See, for example, W. G. Crane, *Wit and Rhetoric in the Renaissance,* 1937, which devotes several pages to the undesirable influence of the *Progymnasmata* on Erasmus and Sturm (pp. 69-71, 75-77), but mentions the *Art of Rhetoric* only once, in the bibliography; K. R. Wallace, in *Francis Bacon on Communication and Rhetoric,* 1943, mentions the fact that Hermogenes was studied in the universities, and that Whitgift, Master of Trinity College, apparently supplied Bacon with a text of Hermogenes (pp. 169-170), but nowhere indicates that he has heard of any text other than the *Progymnasmata;* C. S. Baldwin, in *Renaissance Literary Theory and Practice,* 1939, mentions the influence of the Ideas on the Italian critics Guilio Camillo and Bernadino Parthenio (pp. 55, 170-171), but describes that influence as though it were but another branch of topics or thematic exercises in Invention, like the *Progymnasmata* which Baldwin had previously translated in the first chapter of *Medieval Rhetoric and Poetic,* which was first published in 1928.

5

tortions of the original Hermogenic theory it will also, hopefully, discover the source of that distortion in some sixteenth-century need.

It is the purpose of this book to show that the interest in Hermogenes in the Renaissance focused not on the *Progymnasmata*, but on the most mature and original section of the *Art of Rhetoric*, the treatise about style which is called *Concerning Ideas*. In the two books of this treatise, Hermogenes analyzes discourse into Seven Ideas, or categories of style. The Seven Ideas are those of Clarity (σαφήνεια), Grandeur (μέγεθος), Beauty (κάλλος), Speed (γοργότης), Ethos (ἦθος), Verity (ἀλήθεια), and Gravity (δεινότης), with subsections thereof. Hermogenes illustrates his definitions of the Ideas by referring to Demosthenes, Plato, Herodotus, Thucydides, Xenophon, Isocrates, and also, significantly, to Homer and lesser poets. His constant emphasis on illustration to clarify precept was probably influential simply as a method among Renaissance critics like Minturno and Scaliger, but the most important aspect of the Ideas can be perceived simply by looking at their names, and recognizing their conceptual richness as compared to other stylistic schemes. By their names alone, Beauty, Speed, and Verity, for example, stimulate the imagination while they instruct. Any scheme based on high, middle, and low, on the other hand, invites a mathematical approach to style, and its conceptual basis is limited to the relationship between style and genre. "What is the nature of Speed?" is a far more interesting question than "How do I measure the height of a style?"

The main concern of this book, then, is to define the scope and influence of Hermogenic Ideas on the European Renaissance, and to show that they filled a great gap in the art, not of Invention, but of Persuasion. It is important to remember, at the outset, the earlier intellectual movement in which rhetoric was of primary importance, and the fact that the work of Hermogenes served for nine hundred years or more as the foundation of Byzantine rhetoric.[6] Whether it was because

[6] In an invaluable paper on "The Function and Evolution of Byzantine Rhetoric," 1 (1970), *Viator* (published by the University of California Press),

the extreme schematization of his work appealed to the Byzantine teachers, or because the potential Platonism of the Ideas suggested a Christian synthesis, rhetoric to the Byzantines meant primarily the rhetoric of Hermogenes. How it was transferred from Byzantium to Europe, one can only guess, but presumably the manuscripts came with the refugees from Constantinople to Italy, many of whom took shelter with the Medicis. There is at least one fifteenth-century manuscript of the *Art of Rhetoric* recorded in the library of Lorenzo de

---

George L. Kustas has distinguished four stages in the Hermogenic tradition in Byzantium. Each of these stages may be conveniently marked by one outstanding commentator. The first period extends in time from the third-century commentary by the philosopher Metropanes of Phrygia to the ninth century, and the major figure is that of Syrianus, a fifth-century Athenian scholar. With the closing of the Athenian school in 529, the tradition of commentary seems to have paused, having no visible influence on writers like Nicephorus and John of Damascus, though the rhetoric was probably still taught in the schools, and it was in the sixth century that the body of Hermogenes' work was divided into the sections now recognized. The second period of active influence, beginning in the ninth century, may have been stimulated by the Arab defeat in 868 and the systematic search for Greek manuscripts which followed it. The major figure of this second period is Photius, who was apparently the first of the Church Fathers to adapt Hermogenic concepts to Christian purposes, although, as Kustas points out, his extreme reliance on the critical *vocabulary* of the *Ideas* is not supported by a single reference to Hermogenes by *name*. (See also Kustas, "The Literary Criticism of Photius: A Christian Definition of Style," Ελληνικά, xvii [1960], 132-169). The effect is of Christianizing the rhetorician, in his absence, so to speak, by an eclectic use of the Ideas, those which are too violent for a Christian writer being ignored, and the others being identified as components of the perfect Christian rhetoric. The third period of influence shows at the same time a much more widespread knowledge of Hermogenes, and a dissolution of the Photian synthesis of pagan technique and Christian theology; the major figure is Psellus, who versifies the text of Hermogenes, but otherwise keeps it intact, unless there is some glaring inconsistency with Christian thinking. Instead of spiritualizing the Idea of Magnificence (δεμνότης) as Photius does, Psellus is content merely to change its primary subject matter, "of the gods," into the singular. Finally, the fourth period extends from the end of the twelfth century through the fourteenth, and the *Art of Rhetoric* once again becomes merely a text, to be elaborated and commented upon, even occasionally to be used as a weapon in polemic, but only in a rhetorical, not a metaphysical context; the chief exemplar of this approach is Maximus Planudes.

7

Medici.[7] Curiously enough, the Ideas apparently did not come to the attention of the Platonic Academy which developed under Lorenzo; at least, there is no evidence in the work of Ficino and Pico della Mirandola that they knew them, although they were later seized upon by Neoplatonists like Torquato Tasso and Fabio Paolini, and related *ex post facto* to the work of the Academy.[8]

The Ideas and Decorum

Whatever may have been the reasons for the Byzantine interest in Hermogenes, this whole section of the tradition is only introductory to our purpose. It serves to explain how the manuscripts survived from the second century A.D. to the beginning of the sixteenth, when they were first printed, along with some of the major Byzantine commentaries. But Hermogenes became important to the European Renaissance in a way which, as far as one can tell, has no precedent in his Byzantine history. In Byzantium, the ideas were assimilated to the concepts and needs of Christianity; in Europe, they were assimilated to the concept and needs of decorum. In Europe, the importance of the Ideas depends on the function of the Seventh Idea, that of δεινότης or Gravity, which is both a mighty style in its own right and, more importantly, an ideal of total eloquence by which all the other Ideas are rightly used. The concept of δεινότης as the right use of all other styles corresponds, without any forcing, to the Renaissance concept of literary decorum, and is indeed so identified by Sturm, one of the most famous editors and commentators on Hermogenes in the sixteenth century. And the fact that Her-

[7] R. R. Bolgar, *The Classical Heritage and Its Beneficiaries*, 1958, contains an appendix listing recorded fifteenth-century manuscripts of Hermogenes (p. 475). Bolgar shows that there were, for example, no less than nine manuscripts of the *Art of Rhetoric* in the Vatican Library by 1475.

[8] Torquato Tasso, in an undated dialogue, *Il Ficino, overo de l'Arte*, has Marsilio Ficino, as one of the speakers in the dialogue, arrive at a theory of artistic creativity in terms of Hermogenic Ideas. Fabio Paolini, in his *Hebdomades* (1589) ties together Ficino's theory of Orphic power acquired through harmony with the *anima mundi* and the Seven Ideas of Hermogenic oratory, which, by magical analogy with the seven spheres, he supposed to give the same power.

mogenes himself allowed δεινότης to stand for simultaneously the best, gravest style, and the right use of all styles, required a synthesis which Renaissance literary theory and practice were able to produce: the gravest style, and the right use of all styles—both are possible in an epic poem. Hermogenes himself had used the epics of Homer to illustrate his concept of δεινότης; and it is not surprising therefore that an age which saw the national epic as the culmination of international literary theory should be fascinated by δεινότης as the principle of epic style, and should require that no poet embark on an epic until he had mastered decorum.

The full treatment of δεινότης or Gravity as the best, gravest style, and also the principle of decorum in epic writing, will be deferred to the end of this book, as is appropriate for the last of the Seven Ideas. The rest of this introductory chapter will be concerned instead with decorum of style in a more general sense, as applicable to all genres and all details of literary technique; and it will also demonstrate how often, and how naturally, writers and critics of the late sixteenth century turned to Hermogenes as a guide to decorum of style. Finally, it will suggest some reasons for the gap in the art of Persuasion, and why it could be better filled by the Ideas than by any other rhetorical scheme.

Decorum of style is, of course, only a part of the much larger philosophical concept so elegantly defined in George Puttenham's *Arte of English Poesie* (1589). In true Renaissance manner, Puttenham comes at his subject by various etymological paths:

> The Greekes call this good grace of everything in his kinde, τὸ πρέπον the Latines [*decorum*] we in our vulgar call it by a scholasticall terme [*decencie*] our owne Saxon English terme is [*seemelynesse*] that is to say, for his good shape and utter appearance well pleasing the eye. . . . Now because this comelynesse resteth in the good conformitie of many things and their sundry circumstances, with respect one to another, so as there be found a just correspondencie betweene them by this or that relation, the Greekes call it

Decorum of Style

Analogie or a convenient proportion. This lovely conformitie, or proportion, or conveniencie, betweene the sence and the sensible hath nature her selfe first most carefully observed in all her owne workes, then also by kinde graft it in the appetites of every creature working by intelligence to covet and desire.[9]

In other words, Puttenham regards decorum not only as an organic unity which gives aesthetic pleasure, but as part of the total mysterious pattern of the universe which rational creatures can observe and desire to imitate.

Decorum of style, then, is but one aspect of the whole "lovely conformitie," and to place the patterns of language within the larger patterns of the universe was in itself an act of "decencie" and sometimes of devotion. The commentary of Sturm on the Ideas of Hermogenes actually makes such an analogy: as in the whole and superior man the first requirement "is sanity and lucidity, then a good-sized frame, then the beauty of members and features, then a matching speed and agility in action, then that all things be joined with virtue and probity, but a truthful, not a feigned virtue, and finally that all parts have proportion and decorum." So for a total eloquence Sturm says, Hermogenes required first Clarity, then Grandeur, then Beauty, then Speed, then Ethos, then Verity, and finally that Gravity which is itself decorum of style.[10]

Since Gregory Smith's and Rosemond Tuve's discussions of decorum, and more recently since Thomas Kranidas has gathered together an impressive array of Renaissance comments on

[9] George Puttenham, *The Arte of English Poesie*, ed. G. D. Willcock and A. Walker, 1936, p. 262. The italics here and throughout the text are in the original unless otherwise noted.

[10] All unidentified translations are mine. Johannes Sturm, ed., *Hermogenis . . . Partitionum rhetoricarum liber unus, qui vulgò de Statibus inscribitur . . .* (first part of the *Art of Rhetoric*), 1570, Bviir: "Debet enim in homine primò color esse sanus atque dilucidus: pòst magnitudo justa & usitata: membrorum deinceps atque lineamentorum pulchritudo, seu venustas: tum conveniens in actionibus celeritas et agilitas: tandem ut omnia sint cum virtutis atque probitatis studio conjuncta, sed virtutis verae, non simulatae: postremò omnia ista convenientiam debent habere atque decorum."

10

its use,[11] no one doubts that the term was of continuing interest to writers. One of the most revealing signs of how the term came to be at least on the tip of every poet's tongue is its use in the sixteenth century as an excuse for technical errors or clumsiness. Thus in the *Mirror for Magistrates* we have attempts by Baldwin and his fellow compilers to explain away the less metrically "regular" tragedies. Baldwin reports how the editorial committee of the *Mirror* listened critically to "The Blacksmith," in which there is considerable freedom of line length, and one of their number complained: "It is a pitie . . . that the meter is no better seing the matter is so good: You maye doo verye well to helpe it, and a littell fyling would make it formall."[12] But Baldwin, as editor-in-chief, replied that the author could have done that himself, had he wished, but instead had requested "that it may passe in such rude sorte as you have heard it: for hee observeth therein a double *decorum* both of the Smith, and of him selfe." And when they come to the tragedy of King James IV of Scotland, Baldwin remarks that "hee is paste mending, hee is to olde; for it seemes by the copy, that it was pende above fifty yeares agone." And again, "I like him (quoth one) the better: for if hee should bee otherwise, it would not well beseeme his person, nor the place whence he comes."[13] Here it is clearly understood, by mid-sixteenth-century writers, that verse which appears primitive to them can be accepted in terms of the decorum of primitive or uneducated speakers—an ignorant blacksmith, and a king who not only died two generations earlier but was a Scot to boot!

An engaging variant of the apologetic approach to decorum is introduced at the end of the century by the author of *Willobie his Avisa*, who, though working in a six-line octosyllabic stanza, at one point produces this:

> How can I love, how can I live,   8
> Whilst that my hart hath lost his hope,   8

---

[11] Thomas Kranidas, *The Fierce Equation: A Study of Milton's Decorum*, 1965, Chapter I.

[12] *The Mirror for Magistrates* (1559), ed. L. B. Campbell, 1938, p. 419.

[13] *The Mirror for Magistrates*, pp. 488, 483.

Dispaire abandons sweet reliefe,   8
My love, and life have lost their scope: 8
Yet would I live thy features to behold,   10
Yet would I love, if I might be so bold.   10

And in the margin we are told that "These verses exceed measure, to show that his affections keepe no compasse, and his exceeding love."[14] This replaces the decorum of crudity with that of unruly emotion, and its interest lies in the fact that it is not a rationalization after the event, as in the case of King James, who was "paste mending." It must be a deliberate variation introduced for the amusement or instruction of the reader, since, once noticed, it would have been easier to mend than to annotate; and its very smallness indicates the extent to which decorum of style branches out into the finest details of diction, meter, and rhythm.

This interpretation is borne out by the far longer and more suggestive comments by Thomas Watson about the relationship between emotional and metrical disturbances. The preface to the *Hekatompathia* (1582) leaves no stone unturned to win the indulgence of "the frendly Reader":

> I hope thou wilt in respect of my travaile in penning these love passions, or for pitie of my paines in suffering them (although but supposed) so survey the faultes herein escaped, as eyther to winke at them, as oversightes of a blinde Lover; or to excuse them, as idle toyes proceedinge from a youngling frenzie; or lastlie, to defend them, by saying, it is nothing *Praeter decorum* for a maiemed man to halt in his pase, where his wound enforceth him, or for a Poete to falter in his Poeme, when his matter requireth it. *Homer* in mentioning the swiftnes of the winde, maketh his verse to runne in posthaste all upon *Dactilus*: and *Virgill* in expressing the striking down of an oxe, letteth the end of his hexameter fall withall. . . . Therefore if I roughhewed my verse, where my sense was unsetled, whether through the nature of the passion, which I felt, or by rule of art, which

[14] *Willobie his Avisa or The true Picture of a modest Maide and of a chast and constant wife* (1594), ed. A. B. Grosart, 1880, p. 128.

12

I had learned, it may seeme a happie fault; or if it were so framed by counsell, thou mayest thinke it well donne; if by chaunce, happelie.

This is an important passage because it brings together explicitly the term "decorum," not only with the excuse of emotional disturbance, but also with the examples of expressive metrical variation so lovingly gathered from classical poetry by Renaissance critics. Watson's preface is also a useful answer to those who question the value of looking for decorous writing where the poet does *not* specify his intentions; as far as Watson is concerned, the decorum is truly felt whether it is arrived at "by chaunce, happelie," or whether it is in fact "framed by counsell." The whole passage shows how widely, in the late sixteenth century, decorum of style has been recognized as more than just a vague aim, and more than just a way of relating speech to character in the drama. It is seen instead as a complex art affecting all the poetic genres and requiring detailed study (the "sedentary toil" of the poem by Yeats which heads this chapter), while at the same time the large philosophical center of the concept remains intact.

George Puttenham, in his chapter on decorum in the *Arte of English Poesie*, tells us that he has written a whole book, *de Decoro*, on the double subject of decorous writing and decorous behavior.[15] The book is lost, but the fact that it was written indicates that the subject was far more comprehensive than Puttenham's treatment of it in the *Arte* would imply. The largest extant treatment of stylistic decorum is to be found not in English criticism of this period, but in Italian, in Minturno's *Arte Poetica* (1564) which contains a whole book on the subject. Minturno's treatment of decorum is worth looking at in some detail, because it shows how the Ideas of Her-

---

[15] Puttenham, *Arte of English Poesie*, p. 277: "And there is a decency to be observed in every mans action and behaviour as well as in his speach & writing. . . . Wherfore some examples we will set downe of this maner of decency in behaviour leaving you for the rest to our booke which we have written *de Decoro*, where ye shall see both partes handled more exactly."

13

mogenes fitted naturally into a full-scale analysis of the subject.

Early in the *Arte Poetica* Minturno repeats the Horatian commonplace that decorum consists in dramatic suitability of speech and behavior to character;[16] but it is in the third book that he really tackles the subject, the result being seven different kinds of decorum, of which the Seven Ideas form the seventh, and most important. The first is that of the Three Styles of Ciceronian rhetoric, high, middle, and low. Minturno makes no attempt to elaborate these, but proceeds to two categories which together would seem to make up the Horatian decorum of character. One is the decorum of style according to the *speaker* (his estate, his age, his profession, his rank); the other is the decorum of style according to the *auditor* (the speaker modifies his language according to the "estate, the power, the rank, the dignity" of the person he is addressing). The fourth category decides the character of style according to the "places" of rhetoric, and according to what is "useful," "honest," etc.[17] The fifth modifies style according to the emotions of the orator or the characters of whom he speaks; and the sixth is that of decorum according to Invention, Disposition, and Elocution, so that one's style varies according to whether one is beginning, narrating, dividing

[16] Antonio Minturno, *L'Arte Poetica* . . . *Con La Dottrina De'Sonnetti, Canzoni, & ogni sorte di Rime Thoscane*, p. 49. Gregory Smith believes that "Minturno's earlier work *De Poeta* (1559) shows nearly all the points of contact" between his criticism and that of the Elizabethans (*Elizabethan Critical Essays*, I, lxxxiii). However, it is the *Arte Poetica* of 1564 which would have been more relevant to Englishmen as poets rather than as critics, since, as the running title, *della Poetica Thoscana*, implies, it is largely concerned with the application of theory to poetic practice in the vernacular.

[17] Minturno defines this kind of decorum as being "secondo la Materia e la cosa istessa" (p. 427) and names only three kinds, that which is useful, that which is honest, and a mixture of the two. This seems to be a condensed version of that branch of the "places" or "topics" of rhetorical investigation which deals with the nature of a subject matter rather than its causal, temporal, or instrumental accidents. W. G. Crane, in *Wit and Rhetoric in the Renaissance* (p. 58), lists under this heading "whether or not a matter is manifest, just, lawful, profitable, possible, credible, proper, necessary, pleasant, easy, honest, safe, and consistent."

14

up the parts of a speech, or concluding with a peroration. The seventh and last category is that of decorum according to the Characters or Forms of speech. As Minturno says, there is a suitable form of speech for every different purpose, such as persuading, comforting, judging, attacking, disputing, or telling a tale, but he proposes to simplify matters by referring only to *the* Forms, or the Seven Ideas of Hermogenes. And whereas the first six kinds of decorum received from him a relatively brief treatment, Minturno devotes fifteen pages of commentary and illustration to the Ideas. The Three Styles of Cicero are dismissed in a brief sentence; it is clear that, for Minturno at least, the Seven Ideas provided a more interesting and effective scheme of stylistic choice.

Availability of the Ideas: European Editions and Commentaries

The fact that Minturno so calmly incorporates a discussion of the Seven Ideas into a vernacular poetics, with examples from the vernacular chosen by himself, indicates a considerable degree of familiarity among his audience with the rhetorical theories involved. How this situation was created can only be surmised, but that the *Ideas* were known is clear from the history of their publication. The whole *Art of Rhetoric* of Hermogenes had, as we have seen, been preserved during the Middle Ages as a result of its importance in Byzantine rhetoric, and was first edited by Aldus Manutius in 1508, along with the Byzantine commentaries of Syrianus, Sopatrus, and Marcellinus. After this, new editions appeared steadily all through the sixteenth century, sometimes of the whole work, sometimes of the parts singly. In 1569 there appeared an edition by Franciscus Portus, professor of Greek at Geneva, with a preface which apologizes for yet another edition of Hermogenes, in view of the fact that there have already been Aldine, Florentine, French, and German editions. Portus' preface is worth quoting at length as an indication of contemporary interest in Hermogenes, who shares the edition with Aphthonius and Longinus, but is given the lion's share of the introduction:

As far as Hermogenes is concerned, many indeed are Rhetoricians both Greek and Latin, but no one will easily discover which of them wrote more accurately than he about the Status of [judicial] causes and the Forms of an oration: nor who divided more diligently than he the "questions" and "bases" of causes, nor handed down a better method for dealing with them. And Aristotle in the third book of his Rhetoric scarcely touched on the Forms of an oration themselves. . . . Hence arose Hermogenes, and advised by these few hints, as if from a tiny spring, sent down seven perpetual rivers of water: I mean those seven forms of oratory, from which he then derived many other streams, and so irrigated that part of Rhetoric, that students of eloquence, who wish to judge the writings of others, or to create themselves, or to write as closely as possible to the old standards and those of the most approved authors, will receive great profit thereby.[18]

There is no doubt in Portus' mind as to which part of Hermogenes' *Art of Rhetoric* is the most characteristic and the most important; it is the *Concerning Ideas*, the "seven perpetual rivers of water" which have flowed into the rhetorical country and made it fruitful.

It is not entirely clear which of the editions prior to his own Portus is referring to, other than the *editio princeps*, the Aldine

---

[18] Franciscus Portus, ed., *Apthonius, Hermogenes, & Dionysius Longinus, . . . opera industrique illustrati atque expoliti*, 1570:

Quod ad Hermogenem attinet, multi quidem sunt Rhetores tum Graeci tum Latini, sed qui accuratius eo scripserint de Statu causarum & Formis orationis, neminem facilè reperietis: nec qui diligentius quaestiones statusque causarum diviserit, aut methodum eas tractandi tradiderit. Ac de formis ipsis orationis Aristoteles in tertio Rhetoricorum vic pauca haec attigat: . . . Hinc orsus Hermogenes iisque paucis monitus, quasi ex fonte parvulo, septem ferè perpetuos aquarum rivos deduxit: septem (inquam) illas orationis formas . . . , ex quibus plures alios deinde rivulos derivavit, atque ita partem istam Rhetorices irrigavit, ut studiosi eloquentiae, qui aliorum scripta judicare, aut ipsa facere, vel scribere velint quae ad normam veterum et probatissimorum authorum proximè accedant, maximos inde proventus sint percepturi.

edition of 1508.[19] There had been two French editions, one from the press of Christian Wechel in Paris, of which the part containing *Concerning Ideas* came out in 1531; and another Paris edition from the press of Jacob Bogardus in 1544-45. By a German edition, Portus may have been referring to the Strassburg edition from the press of Josias Richel, of which the part containing *Concerning Ideas* came out in 1555. The Florentine edition was presumably that recorded by Rabe as being published in 1515 by the press of Philip Giunta. Portus himself was immediately followed by the Strassburg scholar Johannes Sturm, who seems to have had something to do with the earlier Strassburg edition, and who later produced his own divided edition of the *Art of Rhetoric*, with a Latin translation and massive commentary. His edition of *Concerning Ideas* in 1571 is likely to have been one of the most influential in England because Sturm was well known there and a close friend of Roger Ascham; Ascham's *Scholemaster* contains several laudatory references to Sturm, and quotes approvingly a remark from the text of *Concerning Ideas*.[20]

The fact that there were seven sixteenth-century editions of the *Art of Rhetoric*, and that Portus' edition came out with an apology for further supplying an already well-filled market, points to a considerable demand for texts. But the Renaissance interest in Hermogenes is documented even more convincingly by the very large number of translations of and commentaries on his works, and especially on *Concerning Ideas*. As early as 1538 Antonio Bonfine produced an extremely

---

[19] For details of this and all editions subsequently mentioned, see the bibliographies.

[20] Roger Ascham, *The Scholemaster*, in *Elizabethan Critical Essays*, I, 25: "And trew it is that *Hermogenes* writeth of *Demosthenes* that all formes of Eloquence be perfite in him" (περὶ ἰδεῶν I, I). Ascham's section on Imitation includes three admiring references to Sturm (pp. 13-14, 21, 25), and Gregory Smith, in annotating the reference to Hermogenes, remarks that "Sturm's very popular edition of Hermogenes, the rhetorician, was probably the quarry for most of the references to that writer" (p. 355). L. V. Ryan, in *Roger Ascham*, 1963, p. 26, draws attention to a letter Ascham wrote in 1538 to a friend, thanking him profusely "for certain commentaries on the rhetorician Hermogenes."

lucid Latin translation of the whole *Art of Rhetoric* (*Hermogenis Tarsensis, Philosophi, ac Rhetoris acutissimi, de Arte rhetorica praecepta*). His title indicates the Renaissance belief that the theory of the Seven Ideas of style, as a branch of the Platonic theory of Ideas, entitles Hermogenes to the title of "philosopher." The same is true of the Latin translation in 1550 by Natalis Conte, which has an almost identical title. In 1570-71 Sturm's Greek edition appeared with Latin translations and commentaries. In 1590 Gabriele Zinano included in his *Sommarii Di Varie Retoriche Greche, Latine, Et Volgari* a condensed paraphrase of *Concerning Ideas* in Italian; and in 1594 and 1608 there appeared the two editions, both posthumous, of Guilio Camillo Delminio's Italian translation of *Concerning Ideas* and *On the Method of Gravity*. Finally in 1614 Gaspar Laurentius produced a new Latin translation to accompany his edition, a translation which was twice reprinted in Venice during the seventeenth century.

The importance of translations from 1538 onwards shows that interest in Hermogenes went far beyond that of classical scholarship; and this is confirmed by the various works of *literary criticism* which incorporate description of and commentary on *Concerning Ideas*. It is here that the focus of interest on the Ideas, rather than on other parts of Hermogenic rhetoric, becomes most apparent. In 1558, for example, there appeared the seven-book Rhetoric of Antonius Lullius, which purports to explain "not only the whole of Hermogenes himself, but also whatever of the Art of Speaking has been handed down from the rest of the Greeks and Romans," or so the title claims! Lullius was obviously an extremely learned and cultured man, and he included a vast amount of information about classical rhetoric (as well as Renaissance scholarship, literature, and painting) in his encyclopedic work; but his main inspiration remains Hermogenes. From the Seven Ideas he took the structure of his own work, which has seven books: Book VI, "De Ideis," explains at length what Hermogenes meant by each of the first six Ideas, with much additional commentary and explanation; Book VII, "De Decoro," is a massive expansion of the principle of decorum embodied in the last of the Seven Ideas. Here Lullius divides his subject matter according to the three great categories of Renaissance ontology—philosophy, or everything speculative; history, or everything factual; and poetry, or everything imaginative— and shows how writers in each category can benefit by knowing which of Hermogenes' Ideas to use.

Shortly after the appearance of Lullius' Rhetoric there were published three different "poetics" which include a description of the Seven Ideas, as though there were a sudden wave of interest in the relevance of the Ideas to poetry rather than to oratory. In 1560 there was Bernadino Parthenio's *Della Imitatione Poetica*, which describes the Ideas in Italian, with examples from Latin poetry. In 1561 there was Julius Caesar Scaliger's enormous *Poetices Libri Septem*, which devotes its fourth book to the Seven Ideas, again with examples from Latin poetry. In 1564 there came Minturno's *Arte Poetica*, of which enough has already been said. And these are followed by a second wave of treatises which do not give descriptions of the Ideas to the ignorant, but rather *assume knowledge* of them when they discuss individual problems of criticism. This is the most useful evidence of all to show the rapidly diffusing influence of *Concerning Ideas*. The list is impressive:

1560 Guilio Camillo Delminio, *Discorso sopra l'Idee di Hermogene.* (Compares the Three Styles of Cicero to the Seven Ideas, and then subdivides the Ideas into Sentences, or subject matter based on the different passions, with illustrations from both Virgil and Petrarch)

c. 1570 Pietro Pagano, *Discorso . . . sopra il secondo sonetto del Petrarca.* (Defines the style of this sonnet as Hermogenic Magnificence or σεμνότης)

Franciscus Portus, *Commentarius in Longinum.* (Interprets the Sublime of Longinus as being the Magnificence of Hermogenes)

1582 Torquato Tasso, *Lezione . . . sopra il sonetto "Questa*

19

vita mortal" di Monsignor Della Casa. (Defends Della Casa's use of the Magnificent style in this sonnet)

1585 Orazio Ariosto, *Risposte ad alcuni luoghi del dialogo dell'epica poesia del Signor Cammillo Pellegrino.* (Explains the literary quarrel over Ariosto and Tasso as a failure to comprehend the different Ideas within which their respective epics were written, Tasso having chosen to work mainly with the Idea of Magnificence, and Ariosto with that of Clarity)

1588 Battista Guarini, *Il Verrato.* (Defends the genre of tragicomedy as a mixed genre in terms of Hermogenes' theory of a mixture of Ideas)

1589 Fabio Paolini, *Hebdomades.* (Discusses the Seven Ideas as a means of giving oratory Orphic power, in terms of Neoplatonic magic and by identifying the Ideas with the seven planets)

1594 Torquato Tasso, *Discorsi del Poema Eroico.* (Discusses the Platonic Idea of an epic poem, and of an epic hero, and analyzes style in terms of the Seven Ideas)

1598 Camillo Pellegrino, *Del concetto poetico.* (Analyzes sonnets of Petrarch in terms of the Ideas)[21]

1600 Faustino Summo, *Discorsi.* (Contains an attempted rebuttal of Guarini's *Il Verrato* on the merits of tragicomedy, and attempts to deny the authority of Hermogenes on this matter)

I do not suppose that this list, impressive though it is, is exhaustive. There is a hint of a still earlier interest in Hermogenic theory as applied to poetics in Robortello's *In librum Aristotelis de arte poetica explicationes* (1548),[22] which anticipates Tasso's

---

[21] I have not seen the undated manuscript of Pagano's *Discorso* (B.M. Add. 33, 470), the *Commentary on Longinus* attributed to Portus, or Pellegrino's *Del concetto poetico.* In all three cases the information comes from Bernard Weinberg's *A History of Literary Criticism in the Italian Renaissance,* 1961, I, 187-188, 242.

[22] See B. Hathaway, *The Age of Criticism: The Late Renaissance in Italy,*

argument that the epic hero should be, not an individual, but a Platonic Idea of heroic virtue, and which also cites Hermogenes as an authority. But it is not the length of such a list alone but also its breadth (the variety of topics so discussed) that indicate considerable critical interest in the Ideas in Italy at a time when the prestige of Italian literature and criticism was at its height. It clearly demonstrates that there was a renaissance in Hermogenes (as a guide to the poet, as well as the orator), which took place toward the end of the sixteenth century, and which was analogous, on a smaller scale, to the rediscovery of Aristotle's *Poetics.*

The Ideas in England

On probability alone, this interest would have filtered into England to some extent, given the caliber of the critics who were incorporating Hermogenes into their arguments and the importance of those arguments to the development of vernacular poetics. We know that Minturno and Scaliger were influential in England,[23] and can reasonably assume that the poets who admired Tasso's *Gerusalemme Liberata* would have been anxious to read about his theories of style. And though there is virtually no parallel criticism in England in terms of the Ideas, there are comments by English writers which indicate familiarity with Hermogenes. There is the disparaging remark by Bacon in the *Advancement of Learning* in which he characterizes an age of pedantry as one in which Sturm could "spend such infinite and curious pains upon Cicero the Orator and Hermogenes the Rhetorician,"[24] a disparaging remark, to be sure, but nevertheless showing some knowledge of Sturm's editions. Gabriel Harvey applies the word "curious" to the Hermogenic tradition in *Against*

1962, pp. 145-146: "Robortelli [sic] was not reluctant to identify the poet's method [of universalization] with that used by Xenophon in the *Cyropaedia* . . . pointing out that Cicero had determined in his *Orator ad Brutum* that Plato had also embraced this method . . ." thus linking Hermogenes' Ideas of style with the Ideas of a perfect orator and a perfect king.

[23] See Gregory Smith, *Elizabethan Critical Essays,* I, lxxxiii-lxxxvi.

[24] Francis Bacon, *Works,* ed. J. Spedding et al., 1876-1883, III, 284.

Thomas Nashe, in which he berates Nashe for the wild form-lessness of his speech, and complains that he will not learn from the authorities; "neither curious *Hermogenes,* nor trim *Isocrates,* nor stately *Demosthenes,* are for his tooth."[25] Nashe returns the compliment with interest in *Have With You to Saffron Walden* (1596), giving with elephantine irony examples of Harvey's "right varnish of elocution, not varying one I tittle from the high straine of his harmonious phrase, wherein he puts downe Hermogenes with his *Art of Rheto-rique.*"[26] Richard Rainolde, in his preface to *A Booke called the Foundacion of Rhetorike* (1563), states that "No man is able to invente a more profitable waie and order, to instructe any one in the exquisite and absolute perfeccion, of wisedome and eloquence, then *Aphthonius, Quintilianus* and *Hermogenes.*"[27] And halfway through the next century, there is George Herbert's comment in *A Priest to the Temple* (1652) that the ideal country parson is "not witty, or learned, or eloquent, but Holy. A Character, that *Hermogenes* never dream'd of, and therefore he could give no precepts thereof."[28]

Of these comments, at least those of Nashe and Herbert indicate familiarity with the *Art of Rhetoric* of Hermogenes and his theories of style as distinct from exercises in Invention, while Herbert shows knowledge of the Ideas, or Characters, as they were sometimes called. But the best evidence of all that English writers must have known of the Ideas is found in the most obvious place, and yet one which seems

[25] Gabriel Harvey, *Against Thomas Nashe,* in *Elizabethan Critical Essays,* II, 277. See also Harvey's acid comment to Edmund Spenser in 1580 that many of the "pregnantest and soonest ripe Wits" at Cambridge are proving to be "of Hermogenes mettall for al the world," i.e. precocious when young and foolish when mature. (*Three Proper, and wittie familiar Letters* in Edmund Spenser, *The Prose Works,* ed. Rudolf Gottfried, 1949, p. 461.)

[26] Thomas Nashe, *Have With You to Saffron Walden,* in *Works,* ed. R. B. McKerrow, 1958, III, 91.

[27] Richard Rainolde, *A Booke called the Foundacion of Rhetorike,* 1563, fol. Aiii v. This is a translation of Reinhardus Lorichius' annotated edition of Aphthonius' *Progymnasmata,* and therefore the remark about Hermogenes in the preface may refer only or primarily to his *Progymnasmata.*

[28] George Herbert, *A Priest to the Temple or, The Country Parson,* in *Works,* ed. F. E. Hutchinson, 1941, p. 233.

to have been ignored—the statements of the educators. As early as 1531, Elyot in *The Governour* distinguishes the teaching of Invention, which he sees as part of dialectic, from the teaching of Persuasion, and assigns to the first the *Topics* of Cicero, and to the second the work of Quintilian or Hermogenes:

> After that xiv. yeres be passed of a childes age, his maister if he can, or some other, studiouslye exercised in the arte of an oratour, shall firste rede to hym some what of that parte of logike that is called *Topica*, eyther of Cicero, or els of that noble clerke of Almaine, which late floured, called Agricola: whose warke prepareth invention. . . . Immediately after that, the arte of Rhetorike wolde be semblably taught, either in greke, out of Hermogines, or of Quintilian in latine, begynnyng at the thirde boke, and instructyng diligently the childe in that parte of rhethorike, principally, whiche concerneth persuation . . .
>
> (*The Governour*, I. x.)

Elyot is thus recommending some part of the τέχνη ῥητορική of Hermogenes to be included in the education of a fourteen-year-old; since his emphasis is on Persuasion, this would almost certainly have included the περὶ ἰδεῶν.[29] Then, in 1549, there was a statute of Edward VI, appointing for the first time a professor of dialectic and rhetoric at both Oxford and

---

[29] Elyot's suggestion that the τέχνη ῥητορική of Hermogenes and the *Institutia Oratoria* of Quintilian are parallel works is echoed by the statement in the *Real-Encyclopädie* that "In der Tat lehrt ein Vergleich mit Quintilians *Institutio*, das sie in einem inneren Zusammenhang stehen: περὶ τῶν στάσεων entspricht dem dritten und siebenten Buch der Institutio, περὶ εὑρέσεως allenfalls dem vierten bis achten, περὶ ἰδεῶν bringt die Stillehre wie die Letzten Bucher Quintilians" (p. 869). As already mentioned, the περὶ τῶν στάσεων is a treatise on the "status" or basis of arguments, and the περὶ εὑρέσεως, *Concerning Invention*, is a loosely organized treatise in four books dealing with the structure of an oration and methods of ornamentation. Either would be a reasonable alternative to Quintilian's treatment of the same subjects; but compared with the last book of the *Institutio Oratoria*, which also deals with the concept of the ideal orator and the distinctions between different styles, the περὶ ἰδεῶν is much more comprehensive and more satisfying.

Decorum of Style

Cambridge, and laying down that such a professor "is to lecture in the Elenchi of Aristotle, the topics of Cicero, in Quintilian, or Hermogenes."[30] Not long after this Gabriel Harvey was exhorting the students at Cambridge, who had presumably left the *Progymnasmata* behind them in their grammar schools, to pass through the pleasant but enclosed gardens of Talaeus and other contemporary rhetorics, and to enter the vast plains of the greatest Greeks and Romans: "to begin with, Cicero, and Quintilian, and Aristotle, and Hermogenes, and also, if there is time, Demetrius Phalereos and Dionysius of Halicarnassus."[31] Later on in this public lecture (published under the title of the *Rhetor* in 1577) Harvey issues an ironical warning against the oversophistication for which Hermogenes is sometimes blamed, and then promptly offers to take upon himself the title of Pseudo-Hermogenes![32]

[30] See *Statutes for the University and Colleges of Cambridge*, 1840, p. 7; *Statuta Antiqua Universitatis Oxoniensis*, ed. Strickland Gibson, 1931, p. 344.

[31] Gabriel Harvey, *Rhetor, vel duorum dierum Oratio, De Natura, Arte, & Exercitatione Rhetorica*, 1577:

> Ad vos redeo, carissimi Auditores: quos primùm velim in amænissimis Audomari hortulis educari, utpotè omnibus Aquilarum, Luporum, Capellarum, aliorumque brutorum Rhetorum Latibulis, in quibus tamen plaerique deliscunt, longè commodioribus, atque suavioribus: deinde, si lubet, & si otium est, expatiari in xisto, & immensos illos, amplissimosque latinorum, ac Graecorum campos; in primisque Ciceronis, & Quintiliani, Aristotelis, & Hermogenis, &, si vacat etiam, Demetrii Phalerei, Dionisiique Halicarnassæi magnifica, & sumptuoso praedia, & rebus multis ornata non necessariis, sed tamen, ad speciam, atque pompam, gloriosis, peragrare.
>
> (fol. H2r)

[32] Gabriel Harvey, *Rhetor*:

> . . . ut ne in Hermogenis illius . . . infinitam, et ambitiosam nimis ματαιοτεχνίαν incumbatis; de quo literis proditum est, adeo eum fuisse in sua arte oculatum, atque curiosum, ut in una, eademque periodo sexcentas se figuras, atque subtilitates Rhetoricas deprehendere posse gloriaretur. Ex qua ferè ματαιοπονία, cùm alii iampridem non pauci laborarunt, homines alioqui neutiquam despiciendi; tum hodie nimis profecto ubique multi, & multò sanè plures, quàm unquam antea: in primisque ii, quos Harveius vester & Philograecos solet, & Pseudoargentinenses nominare: ego hoc tempore Pseudo-hermogenes non inscitè usurparim . . .
>
> (fol. M3v)

[Lest you incline towards that infinite and too ambitious vain art of

This goes a long way to explaining the use of Hermogenes in the Nashe-Harvey "flyting," and suggests that Harvey was one of the authorities on Hermogenic rhetoric, which, if true, would certainly have had some effect on Edmund Spenser, whose mentor he became. There is also a reference to Hermogenes in Puttenham's *Arte of English Poesie*, under the section on decorum, which is both a compliment to his fame and a reminder of his senility:

And if they be spoken by a man of account, or one who for his yeares, profession or dignitie should be thought wise & reverent, his speeches & words should also be grave, pithie & sententious, which was well noted by king *Antiochus*, who likened *Hermogenes* the famous Orator of Greece, unto these fowles in their moulting time, when their feathers be sick, and be so loase in the flesh that at any little rowse they can easilie shake them off: so saith he, can *Hermogenes* of all the men that ever I knew, as easilie deliver him from his vaine and impertinent speeches and words. (p. 265)

Finally, there is the statement by Milton himself in *Of Education* (1644) that the mature student should acquire, as the summit of his education, a "gracefull and ornate Rhetorick taught out of the rule of Plato, Aristotle, Phalereus, Cicero,

---

Hermogenes . . . by which literature was betrayed, he being so perceptive and curious in his art that he boasted that he could discover in one and the same period six hundred figures and rhetorical subtleties. On account of this virtually useless endeavour, many have been set to work, not only long ago, and those by no means men to be despised, but also, certainly, too many everywhere to-day, and many more forsooth, than ever before: particularly those whom your Harvey used to call Hellenophiles and Pseudo-Argentinians: I at this time will knowingly take upon myself the title of Pseudo-Hermogenes.]

The tone of this passage is rather curious also, being partly humorous, partly self-defensive. It looks as though Harvey, who was often attacked for his own pedantry, is using irony on his students to try and break down their resistance to the details of rhetorical instruction. According to W. S. Howell, *Logic and Rhetoric in England 1500-1700*, 1961 p. 178, Harvey was appointed praelector in rhetoric at Christ's College, Cambridge, in the spring of 1574.

Hermogenes, Longinus." Milton's list of authorities is given in what to his day would have been the chronological order, but his unwillingness to state a preference here must be balanced by his frequent use of Hermogenic terms in his other prose pamphlets, including his attack in the *Apology for Smectymnuus* (1642) on all ignorant clergymen who do not "know how to write, or speak in a pure stile, much lesse to distinguish the *ideas,* and various kinds of stile."[33] We thus have three educators, two of them closely associated with Cambridge, assuming that a study of Hermogenes, at a higher level than the *Progymnasmata,* was an essential part of a full education in rhetoric; and we actually find this assumption written into the curricula of the universities by a royal statute.

The Attraction of the Ideas

We have now accumulated a considerable body of evidence that the Seven Ideas of Hermogenes were both of interest and influence in Italy and England at the end of the sixteenth century and the beginning of the seventeenth. What remains to be done here is to suggest some of the reasons why this interest should have developed, and what literary and critical needs were filled by discovery of the Ideas.

THE NEED FOR SPECIFIC INSTRUCTIONS

As a beginning, we have the testimony of Franciscus Portus in the preface to his edition that it was the methodical nature of the Hermogenic scheme and the amount of detail it contained which made it invaluable to "students of eloquence." According to Portus, one cannot name another rhetorician, Greek or Latin, who "wrote *more accurately* than he about the Status of causes and the Forms of an oration"; unlike Aristotle, who merely drops a few hints, Hermogenes defined not only "seven perpetual rivers" of style, but also many offshoots and rivulets of the main streams to delight the discriminating mind. It is true that the approach of Hermogenes

---

[33] John Milton, *Of Education,* in *Works,* IV, 286; *Apology for Smectymnuus,* III, 347. Here, and in all subsequent quotations from Milton, *Works* designates the Columbia edition (New York: Columbia Universty Press, 1931).

sometimes led, as in Bacon's comment in the *Advancement of Learning*, to the reproach of oversophistication; but it is also true that neither Cicero, Quintilian, Demetrius, nor the author of the *Rhetorica ad Herennium* offer the same breadth of stylistic choice and analysis. In place of the Three Styles of Cicero and Quintilian and the four of Demetrius, Hermogenes offers Seven Ideas, subdivided to make a total of sixteen styles; and he further defines those styles or substyles under the heading of eight Parts, which not only describe the style but are also the elements needed to reproduce it. Thus each Idea has a certain Sentence, or subject matter; Method, or principle of organizing that subject matter; Diction; Figures, or appropriate list of schemes and tropes; Members, or use of junctures to create phrases and periods of different length; Composition, or texture of vowels and consonants; Cadence; and Number, or rhythm generally. It is the orderly description of these Parts which would probably have appealed both to writers and critics, not just because the Renaissance mind loved schematization, as indeed it did, but also because the apprentice writer, like the bride who is learning to cook, needs precise measurements and step-by-step instructions. It is not very helpful to be told by Puttenham, for example, that a high style is "advaunced by choyse of wordes, phrases, sentences, and figures, high, loftie, eloquent, & magnifik in proportion" (p. 152). It *is* helpful to be told by Hermogenes and his commentators that the Idea of Magnificence is achieved by a firm and stable rhythm, without consonantal harshness or hiatus, by the resonance of long vowels, particularly the long *A* and *O*, by a greater proportion of nouns than verbs, and by the figures of *rectitudo*, metaphor and allegory. This is the kind of detail provided by the scheme of the Seven Ideas, and it is the kind of detail which could provide a writer initially with confidence in the recipe, and ultimately with confidence to do without it.

THE FAILURE OF THE THREE STYLES

The generalizations about high style quoted above from Puttenham's *Arte of English Poesie* are characteristic of rhetorics based on the Three Styles of Cicero. On the other hand, we have evidence that Minturno in his *Arte Poetica* emphasized the fact that for him the Seven Ideas were a more satisfactory way of approaching stylistic decorum than were the Three Styles. Why he should switch his allegiance in this way is worth some exploration. It has, of course, long been realized that there are several problems inherent in the concept of the Three Styles, problems which are partly a result of their origin. According to Hendrickson's very acceptable theory, the middle style is not really intermediate at all, but rather derives from the intricate Gorgian rhetoric of Isocrates, and was merely inserted, by a kind of rationalization, between the two styles distinguished by Aristotle as the objective (low) and the nonobjective (high).[34] The result of this artificial placing can be seen in Cicero's description of the middle style in the *Orator*; somewhat uneasily, he defines it as "akin to both the others, excelling in neither, partaking in both, or, *to tell the truth, partaking in neither*."[35] The problems of this artificial grouping are compounded by the fact that different names for the first and third style carry different connotations, and indeed suggest that there are really more than three styles involved. Cicero at various times calls the first style "gravis," "grandiloquus," and "vehemens," names which are not synonymous; but there is an even greater gap between the names for the third style, "subtile," "tenue," or "humile." The nuances of "tenue" are those most frequently indicated by the classical treatises, which define the third as a spare, functional, and somewhat cunning style; but in the Renaissance it is clear that many critics, among them Puttenham, Wilson, Minturno, Tasso, and Milton, accepted instead the connotations of "humile," or a simple, "base" style. The archetypal description of such a style is that given by Puttenham in the *Arte*

[34] G. L. Hendrickson, "The Origin of the Three Characters of Style," *American Journal of Philology*, xxvi (1905), 286.

[35] *Orator* v. 20-22: "Est autem quidem interjectus inter hos medius et quasi temperatus nec acumine posteriorum nec fulmine utens superiorum, *vicinus amborum, in neutro excellens, utriusque particeps vel utriusque, si verum quaerimus, potius expers . . .*" (My italics)

of English Poesie, where he calls it a "low, myld, and simple maner of utterance, creeping rather than clyming, & marching rather then mounting upwardes, with the wings of the stately subjects and stile" (p. 152); and without such a concept it is impossible to understand the tone of Renaissance pastoral.[36]

Uncertainties about the nature of the Three Styles were undoubtedly not only felt but compounded by those who began to work out their implications for the literary genres. Being concerned with oratory rather than poetry, Cicero and Quintilian do not go beyond the relation of the Three Styles to the three *officia oratoris*: to persuade, to delight, to teach. Critics who wished to work out generic decorum could, of course, refer to Aristotle's *Poetics*, from which they could be sure that the high style was appropriate to epic and tragedy, and that comedy was subordinate to both. But since Aristotle only mentions other genres in passing, it remained up to the individual to erect his own hierarchy of genres, either on an Aristotelian principle of ethical usefulness, or on some other, such as Tasso's rating in terms of verisimilitude.[37] This led to con-

[36] The importance of this view of the Three Styles has recently been greatly underestimated by Wesley Trimpi, in *Ben Jonson's Poems: A Study of the Plain Style*, 1962, largely because he is concerned to identify the third of the Three Styles with the neoclassical "plain Style" of Ben Jonson and the seventeenth century. But to ignore the "humile" aspect means, in effect, ignoring the whole theory of Renaissance pastoral, by which a poet deliberately exercised his early talent in the decorously simple speech of shepherds, before trying his hand at anything more complicated. In any case, Ben Jonson himself clearly accepts the connotation of "humile," in a passage from the *Discoveries* which Trimpi does not quote:

> Some men are tall, and bigge, so some Language is high and great. Then the words are chosen, their sound ample, the composition full, the absolution plenteous, and powr'd out, all grave, sinnewye and strong. Some are little and Dwarfes: so of speech it is humble, and low, the words poore and flat; the members and *Periods*, thinne and weake, without knitting, or number. The middle are of a just stature. There the Language is plaine, and pleasing: even without stopping, round without swelling; all welltorn'd, compos'd, elegant, and accurate. (Ben Jonson, *Works*, ed. C. H. Herford and P. Simpson, 1965, VIII, 625).

[37] See Weinberg, *History of Literary Criticism in the Italian Renaissance*, II, 1030-1031, on Tasso's *Risposta* (1586). Weinberg quotes Tasso's state-

siderable disagreement as to which genres should be assigned to the second and third styles; even comedy is uncertain, being sometimes associated with the middle style, sometimes with the low. And if Aristotle's preoccupation with the high genres was one source of confusion, another was created by a different but equally venerated authority, that of Virgil. During the Middle Ages critics like John of Garland discovered that an analogy could be drawn between the Three Styles of Cicero and the three achievements of Virgil. Thus the *Aeneid*, the *Georgics*, and the *Bucolics* could stand as examples of the high, middle, and low styles, respectively.[38] What such critics presumably did not realize is that this analogy directly contradicts the Ciceronian principle of decorum, which assigns pleasurable material to the middle style, and informational material like the *Georgics* to the third.

The third major disadvantage of the Ciceronian scheme of styles is inherent in its developed structure of two extremes and a mean. This produced rigidity, since extremes cannot mix with each other, nor can they meet in the mean if the mean is not really intermediate; and it also produced, among Renaissance critics, an unhelpful tendency to heap all the weight of commentary on the high style, to define the low by its opposite, and the middle by vague remarks about an intermediacy which it

---

ment that "tutti i poemi habbiano qualche fondamento della verità, chi piu, e chi meno, secondo che piu, e meno participano della perfettione." He then sums up Tasso's argument as follows:

It is on the basis of this ingredient of truth that Tasso establishes his hierarchy of the genres. Some poems have no foundation at all in truth: eclogues, woodland fables, marine stories, books about battles. These are the worst. Almost as bad are comedies and pastorals, since the actions which they represent are not true; only the cities and countries where they take place are real. Somewhat better are the poems, sometimes in these same genres, in which some of the persons are also real. Both tragedy and the heroic poem, being based upon the truth, are at a high level of excellence and close to perfection. As for his own *Gerusalemme*, it is not a history . . . but rather a poem based upon history and legend; to these it adds elements of allegory, of verisimilitude, and of the special kind of truth that comes to it through its context of Christian faith.

[38] This arrangement, known as part of the "wheel of Virgil," is described in E. Faral, *Les Arts poétiques du XIIe et du XIIIe siècle*, 1924, p. 87.

did not really have. An illustration of this tendency can be seen in Tasso's *Arte Poetica* (1587), where the triple scheme is expanded by matching the three styles with three parts of discourse: *concetti*, which includes both the subject matter and its development in rhetorical figures; *parole*, or choice of vocabulary; and *composizione*, which covers all patterns of sound.[39]

	Magnifico	*Mediocre*	*Umile*
	epic, tragedy	lyric	
concetti:	grand subjects, "come di Dio, del mondo, degli eroi, di battaglie"	beauty	ordinary concepts, ordinary people
	such figures as amplification, hyperbole, reticence, prosopopeia		
parole:	diction composed of native words, foreign borrowings, onomatopoeia, and poetic mutations		common and native words only
composizione:	long phrases, long periods, capacious stanza forms, dense consonantal texture	sweet sound	brief periods and phrases, few conjunctions, natural word order

As might have been expected from an epic poet, Tasso concentrates on the high style to the point at which the other two are dismissed as being concerned merely with "ordinary concepts, ordinary people." And, as we shall see later, even his remarks about the high style reveal the weakness of the scheme in which he claims to operate, since in order to arrive at the necessary amount of detail he has had to incorporate advice

[39] Torquato Tasso, *Discorsi Dell'Arte Poetica, E in particolare sopra il Poema Eroico* in *Opere*, 1823, xii, 237-241. This early work, published in 1587 and said to have been written "in gioventù," was later revised and expanded into the *Discorsi del Poema Eroico* of 1594. The earlier version shows no trace of influence by Hermogenes, the later shows considerable influence.

taken partly from Demetrius, and largely from Hermogenes.[40]

These, then, are some of the problems which, at this distance, one can see were attached to the scheme of the Three Styles: confusion about their nature, and a suspicion that there were really more than three styles involved; scanty or contradictory classical guidance on the matching of style to genre; a certain rigidity of structure, and a resulting critical tendency to ignore both middle and low in favor of the high, at least during the sixteenth century when the high style was still the ultimate goal of most poets. The Seven Ideas, on the other hand, more

[40] Torquato Tasso, *Lezione . . . sopra il sonetto "Questa vita mortal" di Monsignor Della Casa,* in *Opere* XI, 45:

> Di vari scrittori, vari caratteri, o idee, o forme che vogliam dirle, di stile sono state costituite, perchè Demetrio Falereo . . . quattro ne pone. Una delle quali chiama magnifica, e veemente l'altra, umile la terza, e l'ultima florida, o ornata. Molto più ne mette Ermogene nel suo libro delle idee, che sono l'idea chiara, la grande, la bella,[la velocità], la morata, la vera, e la grave e altre poi ad alcune di queste ne sottopone. Cicerone ultimamente nel suo Oratore tre ne costituisce, all'una delle quali di sublime dà nome, di umile, all'altra, e di temperata alla terza. Ma quale sia la miglior di queste visioni, rimettendo per ora all'altrui guidicio, chiara cose è che quella forma, che magnifica da Demetrio, grande da Ermogene, e sublime da Cicerone vien detta, è una medesima.

> [Of the various writers, various Characters, or Ideas, or Forms, I would say, of which style is constituted, Demetrius Phalereus has set out four, one of which he called magnificent, another vehement, the third base, and the last flowery or ornate. Hermogenes in his book on the Ideas set forth many more, which are the Idea of Clarity, Greatness, Beauty [Speed], Ethos, Truth, and Gravity, and other subcategories of these. Finally Cicero in his *Orator* set up three, to one of which he gave the name Sublime, to the other Base, and to the third Mean. But which is the better of these views, I leave it to the judgment of others to decide, since it is clear that that Form which Demetrius called Magnificent, Hermogenes called Grandeur, and Cicero called Sublime are one and the same.]

> The four styles of Demetrius mentioned by Tasso come from the περὶ ἑρμηνείας, the treatise *On Style* originally attributed to Demetrius of Phalerum and for convenience still attached to his name. See, for example, G.M.A. Grube, *A Greek Critic: Demetrius on Style*, 1961. The four styles described by "Demetrius" are the plain (ἰσχνός), the grand (μεγαλοπρετής), the elegant (γλαφυρός), and the forceful (δεινός). In effect his scheme is that of the Three Styles of Cicero, with an additional style of forcefulness or vehemence added for use where controlled grandeur is not enough.

than satisfied the need for additional styles—perhaps to the point of making some duplications. Flexibility is built into their structure, partly because they overlap somewhat—Speed and Vehemence share the same rhythms, for example—which makes it possible to modulate from one Idea to another. Moreover, the Ideas all have distinguishable but complementary aims. According to Sturm, the aim of Clarity is that the audience should understand what is said, whereas Grandeur is designed to impress them with what is said. Beauty is designed to give pleasure, Speed to avoid boredom, Ethos helps to win over the audience by allying them with the speaker's customs and character, and Verity persuades them he is speaking the truth. Finally Gravity, or Eloquence as Sturm prefers to call it, stirs up the audience, and they are carried away by the completeness of the performance, not only to accept what they have heard, but to act upon it.[41] In other words, the Seven Ideas cooperate to achieve the total oratorical effect, and the more of them that can be combined in a single oration or poem, the greater the effect. Minturno's commentary on the Ideas contains the final marginal comment that the poem "which has most Forms, is most perfect" (p. 443).

It is clear from this that the three *officia oratoris* of Cicero and Quintilian (to teach, to please, and to move to action) are all contained and expanded in the aims of the Seven Ideas,

[41] Johannes Sturm, *Scholae In Libros Duos Hermogenis De Formis Orationum Seu Dicendi Generibus*, bound with *Hermogenis . . . de dicendi generibus sive formis orationum libri II*, 1571, but with separate pagination. Unless otherwise noted, all subsequent page references to Sturm will indicate this work, which is the commentary which accompanies his edition and translation of *Concerning Ideas*.

Hæ septem formæ differunt inter se quadam proprietate seu fine. Perspicuitas adhibetur intelligentiæ causa: ut bene intelligatur quod dicitur. Magnitudo, ut animo, et auribus satisfaciat: hoc est, ut rei intellectæ nihil desit. . . . Pulchritudo voluptatis causa. . . . Celeritas ad vitandum fastidium. . . . ἦθος proprium est personarum, & adhibetur ad conciliandum. . . . Veritas adhibetur probandi & persuadendi gratia. δεινότης motus causa, decori et aptitudinis, ut ita dicam, ut concitemus animos, sed concitemus decorè & honestè, ut res, personæque requirunt: ut in omnibus locis & partibus faciat suum officium Orator (p. 21).

just as it will later be clear that any advice given under the Ciceronian scheme of style is also contained and expanded in the descriptions of the Ideas. But the fact that in the Hermogenic scheme the aims are essentially *complementary*, immediately solves most of the problems of generic decorum. Any genre may admit a mixture of styles, and the greater the genre, the more styles it will admit; while the rigid matching of style to genre, as in the Wheel of Virgil, is no longer desirable or possible.

One can be reasonably sure that this flexibility was another important reason for the popularity of the Ideas in the late sixteenth and early seventeenth century. It was, after all, a period which was developing new genres such as tragicomedy, which would not fit into any scheme of decorum in which styles are kept separate and modulations between them discouraged. As an example of how the inherent flexibility of the Ideas was put to use, there is Battista Guarini's defense of tragicomedy in *Il Verrato*, already mentioned as one of the significant documents of the Hermogenic revival:

> [That Magnificence and Simplicity can mingle] is not my doctrine . . . but that of Hermogenes, famous artificer of style; speaking of that fine mixture achieved by Demosthenes and Xenophon and Plato, he says that styles mingle together like colors, and just as white and black, which are opposites, form a third color, which he calls φαιόν and we call gray, so opposing forms of speech create mixtures which make the oration beautiful and outstanding . . . according to the example of man himself, he who is as a whole very different from all other animals, and yet is very like them in being mortal, while in having intellect and reason he has something in common with the Gods.[42]

[42] Battista Guarini, *Il Verrato* (1588), in *Opere*, 1737, II, 276:

Nè questa è mia dottrina . . . ma di Ermogene, famoso artifice degli stili; favellando egli delle vaghe, e belle misture, che hanno fatto, e Demostene, e Senofonte, e Platone, dice che gli stili si mescolano insieme a guisa dei colori, e che siccome dal bianco, e dal nero, che sono tanto contrarii, si forma un terzo colore, ch'egli chiama φαιόν, e fosco diremo noi, così dalle contrarie forme del dire nascono i misti, che vaga, e ragguardevole

Decorum of Style

This analogy between mixed Ideas and the sliding scale of the Great Chain of Being is but one more example of the context of thought in which the Seven Ideas found their natural home; the nonwhimsical delight in aptness, symmetry, cosmic "convenience," the coming together of apparently disparate things into a single, satisfying concept of decorum. Again and again what is practical for the writer to know blends into something which is intellectually comforting. It is important that in this part of *Il Verrato* (p. 274), Guarini sets Hermogenes as an exponent of stylistic flexibility against his opponent's authority Demetrius, whose scheme is made to seem rigid by contrast; but more significant still is the fact that he chooses to support a point of practical criticism by bringing out the big guns and defending tragicomedy in terms of the compromise status and precarious intellectual dignity of man.

THE ATTRACTION OF PLATONISM

This brings us to the third and final reason, or suggested reason, for the renaissance of the Seven Ideas. It lies in their implicit Platonism, and the implications of this for the development of Renaissance aesthetics. Although the actual origin of the Ideas is apparently to be seen in discussions of the virtues of style, beginning with Theophrastus, and although "idea" can be used in such discussions merely as a synonym for "character" or "style," there is no doubt that the Seven Ideas of Hermogenes came to be associated with the Ideas or Forms of Platonic philosophy, and were thus capable of being assimilated into Neoplatonic theories of various kinds. The reason for this may have been partly that Hermogenes so often refers to Plato's dialogues in exemplifying his own Ideas; but it must also have developed from Hermogenes' opening remarks in *Concerning Ideas*, in which he states that he does not intend to describe the characteristic styles of Demosthenes or Plato or any other orator, but rather

---

rendono l'orazione, . . . dandone l'esempio dell'uomo, il qual tutto'nsieme è molto differente da tutti gli altri animali, ma nell'esser mortale è però simile a molti, e nell'aver intelletto e ragione con gli Iddii alcuna cosa comune.

35

what is the essential nature (ὁποῖόν τί ἐστι) of Magnificence, Simplicity, Asperity, and the other Ideas (*Opera*, p. 215). Hermogenes uses the term "idea" to mean both "characteristic style" and "essential nature"; but a clear example of how this passage could be read in a Neoplatonic manner is seen in the commentary of Sturm, who remarks:

> There are two kinds of Forms, which are called Ideas in a Platonic sense. One of these is . . . not perceived by any of our senses, neither seen by our eyes nor heard by our ears . . . the other is . . . that which is seen, read, heard: the Demosthenic oration, the Platonic dialogue, the speeches of Aeschines, Lysias and other similar orators are of this kind. The orator ought always to have these two kinds of Forms placed before his eyes for imitation . . . . But the first kind is deduced from the second; and we see what kind of words and conceptual frameworks Demosthenes used, and from this we deduce the imperceptible ideal: because [his style] is almost that of the perfect Orator. But Hermogenes handed down precepts about the first kind . . . *from which we realize that Hermogenes was not only a Rhetorician, but also a Philosopher, and a Platonic philosopher at that*: according to his own words . . .[43]

Cicero himself, Sturm reminds us, gives an excellent account of the Platonic theory of eloquence when discussing the perfect

[43] Sturm, *Scholae . . . De Formis Orationum*, pp. 11-12.

Formarum autem duo sunt genera, quae Platonica voce Ideae vocantur. quorum alterum est ἀορατόν : quod nullo sensu percipitur: nec oculis cernitur, neque auribus hauritur . . . alterum est ὁρατόν, ἀνάγνορον, ἀκουρόν, quod videtur, legitur, auditur: cuiusmodi est oratio Demosthenis, sermo Platonis, orationes Aeschinis, Lysiae, & aliorum similium oratorum. Haec duo genera formarum orator in imitando semper ab oculos posita habere debet: . . . Sed à posteriore initium est sumendum: & videmus Demosthenes, quibus generibus verborum & sententiarum utitur, & ab hoc accedendum est, ad illud ἀορατόν : quod penè est perfectissimi Oratoris. Hermogenes autem traditurus est praecepta de primo illo genere. . . . Ex quibus verbis intelligimus, *Hermogenem fuisse non solùm Rhetorem, sed etiam Philosophum & Platonicum Philosophum*: siquidem ipsius verbis utitur. Ego, inquit, non institui indicare, cuiusmodi sit oratio Demosthenis, aut Platonis: sed dicam de universo dicendi genere. (My italics.)

orator, and demonstrates how easily Platonic idealism can blend with rhetorical theory:

> . . . with our minds we conceive the ideal of perfect eloquence, but with our ears we catch only the copy. These patterns of things are called ἰδέας or Ideas by Plato, that eminent master and teacher both of style and thought; these, he says, do not "become"; they exist forever, and depend on intellect and reason; other things come into being and cease to be, they are in flux and do not remain long in the same state. Whatever, then, is to be discussed rationally and methodically, must be reduced to the ultimate form and type of its class.[44]

In other words, for the purpose of rational consideration, one must abstract from the variable phenomena of unideal eloquence the forms of ideal eloquence as the mind conceives them. And, as Sturm points out, the Idea of the perfect Orator, as defined by Cicero and made possible by Hermogenes, is no different in kind from any other Idea: for "as Xenophon showed the perfect Idea of a good king in Cyrus, and Homer that of a prudent general in Ulysses, and of a brave man in Achilles, and Plato that of a true philosopher in Socrates, so Hermogenes showed, in Demosthenes, what the true and perfect Orator ought to be" (p. 21). These "patterns of things" may never be found in actuality among fallible human beings; and yet the existence of the Idea consoles both the artist who abstracted it and the audience who admire it for the normal imperfection of their lives.

A fascinating example of how this concept was absorbed into Renaissance literary theory is found in the prose of Torquato Tasso. In the *Discorsi del Poema Eroico* (1594) Tasso

---

[44] Cicero, *Orator*, II. 8:

. . . perfectae eloquentiae speciem animo videmus, effigiem auribus quaerimus. Has rerum formas appellat ἰδέας ille non intellegendi solum sed etiam dicendi gravissimus auctor et magister Plato, easque gigni negat et ait semper esse ac ratione et intellegentia contineri; cetera nasci occidere fluere labi nec diutius esse uno et eodem statu. Quicquid est igitur de quo ratione et via disputetur, id est ad ultimam sui generis formam speciemque redigendum.

distinguishes between the Ideas of natural things, which exist in the Divine Mind, and the Ideas of works of art, which exist within the human intellect:

> The Idea therefore of artifacts is formed after consideration of many artifacts; many of which are not perfect, but the better they are, the nearer one approaches the Idea. Therefore when I have to demonstrate the Idea of the finest heroic poem, I do not have to propose as an example a single poem, even if it were more beautiful than others, but rather to show, by gathering together beauties and perfections from each, how the total effect could be ultimately beautiful and perfect.[45]

In other words, by applying the theory of Ideas to the practical problem of defining heroic poetry, Tasso is able to avoid the limitations of Aristotelian criticism, which depends on the existence of masterpieces for the development of a theory of genres and rules of excellence. Not being bound by the limitations of any existing heroic poem, even if it is the best of its kind, Tasso is able to speculate as to the nature of the absolute heroic poem, which may never be written. There is also a much longer discussion of the same concept incorporated into an undated dialogue of Tasso's, *Il Ficino, overo de l'Arte*, in which he has Marsilio Ficino and Cristoforo Landino discussing the theory of Ideas in relation to works of art in general. In rather laborious dialectic, Tasso puts into the mouth of Ficino the same distinction between the Divine Ideas and those in the mind of the artist:

> It is necessary that in the [artist's] mind there exist in advance the exemplary forms of all things, but in the Divine

[45] Torquato Tasso, *Discorsi del Poema Eroico*, in *Opere*, XII, 9:

L'idea dunque delle cose artificiali è formata dopo la considerazione di molte opere fatte artificiosamente; nelle quali tuttavolta non è l'ottimo, ma quella è migliore, che più le s'avvicina. Dovendo dunque io mostrar l'idea dell'eccellentissimo poema eroico, non debbo proporre per esempio un poema solo, benchè egli fosse più bello degli altri, ma raccogliendo le bellezze, e le perfezioni di ciascuno insegnare come egli si possa fare bellissimo e perfettissimo insieme.

Mind substances only; however . . . there are no Divine Ideas of artificial things: but in the mind of the artificer, in the opinion of Aristotle again, there are the artificial proportions of the things created, as Syrianus says in Book XII of his *Metaphysics*; and these we call Ideas: and so Marcus Tullius named the Forms of speech in his *Orator*, and Hermogenes also.[46]

Tasso has thus combined the authorities of Cicero (in the passage from the *Orator* already cited), Aristotle, Syrianus (one of the Byzantine commentators on Hermogenes), and Hermogenes himself to arrive at a Neoplatonic theory of artistic creativity, by which any work of art is preceded by its perfect conception in the mind. Moreover, despite the distinction between Divine Ideas and artistic Ideas, a union between the two is provided by the existence of the supreme art, that of poetry. For:

One can affirm absolutely that before any poem, whether it be Greek, or Italian, or Hebrew, or another language, there was the art and the harmony of poetry, born perhaps simultaneously with our soul, which was composed by God of harmonious numbers and musical proportions. . . . And it is no marvel that poetry is natural to the human soul, if God himself, by whom we were created, is a poet; and the divine art, by which he made the world, is as it were the art of poetry; and his poem is the Heaven, and the whole world, to which highest and sweetest concord human ears are perhaps deaf and closed . . .[47]

[46] Torquato Tasso, *Il Ficino, overo de l'Arte*, in *Opere*, VII, 255:

È necessario che nella mente siano avanti le forme esemplari di tutte le cose, ma nella mente divina le sostanze solamente; perchè delle cose artificiose non sono le divine Idee: ma nell'anima de l'artifice, per opinione d'Aristotile ancora, sono le ragioni artificiali delle cose operate, come dichiara Siriano nel XII. de la Metafisica, e queste da noi sono chiamate idee, e così chiamò Marco Tullio quella del suo Oratore, ed Ermogene le forme del parlare.

[47] Tasso, *Il Ficino*, p. 463:

Laonde si può assolutamente affermare, che prima d'alcun poema, o

Thus by the possession of innate Ideas of harmony the mind of the poet is related to that of God, while at the same time the concept provides a valuable distinction between artistic intentions and results, and a valid excuse for the poet who fails to produce, or the critic who fails to cite a perfect example of, say, the heroic poem.

One can see a very similar application of the Ideas in Sir Philip Sidney's *Defence of Poesie* (1595), where the logical basis of the defense is just this, that poetry, rightly conceived, can create a better moral universe, a golden world corresponding not to actuality, but to the Ideas in the mind of the poet; nor should one judge it by its products alone:

> . . . for any understanding knoweth the skill of the artificer standeth in that *Idea* or fore-conceit of the work, and not in the work itself. And that the poet hath that *Idea* is manifest, by delivering them forth in such excellency as he hath imagined them. . . . Neither let it be deemed too saucy a comparison to balance the highest point of man's wit with the efficacy of Nature; but rather give right honour to the heavenly Maker of that maker, who having made man to His own likeness, set him beyond and over all the works of that second nature: which in nothing he showeth so much as in Poetry, when with the force of a divine breath he bringeth things forth far surpassing her doings . . .[48]

Sidney, like Tasso, is making the concept of the Ideas serve two apparently contradictory ends. By insisting on the "force of a divine breath" in the poet he justifies every attempt of the poet to create an ideal world of the imagination; and at

---

greco, o italiano, o ebreo, o d'altra lingua, fosse l'arte e la ragione del poetare, nata peravventura insieme con l'anima nostra, la qual fu da Dio composta di numeri armonici e di musiche proporzioni. . . . E non è meraviglia che la poesia sia naturale ne gli animi umani, se Dio medesimo, da cui furono creati, è poeta; e l'arte divina, con la quale fece il monde, fu quasi arte di poetare; e poema è'l Cielo, e'l mondo tutto, al cui altissimo e dolcissimo concento sono peravventura sordi e rinchiusi gli orecchi de' mortali . . .

[48] Philip Sidney, *Defence of Poesie* (1595), ed. G. Shepherd, 1965 (under the alternative title of *An Apology for Poetry*), p. 101.

the same time, when looking at the actual products of that endeavor, genre by genre, he has to admit that very few, if any, of them, live up to that ideal. In both Sidney and Tasso, as in the Florentine Neoplatonists they followed, the Ideas of creativity are central to the placing of poetry higher on the intellective ladder than Plato himself would have allowed, so that its works become not a reflection of a reflection of reality, but a step closer to reality as the "erected wit" conceives it. In both, moreover, the definition of an Idea of poetry or of a kind of poem provides a bridge from theory to practice, and a basis for practical criticism in terms of that Idea. Sidney, of course, does not mention Hermogenes by name. But since this section of the *Defence* is largely a paraphrase of the first book of Scaliger's *Poetices*, it seems reasonable to assume that he would also have read the fourth book, where Scaliger applies the Seven Ideas of Hermogenes to poetic theory.[49]

It is important to remember, however, that at no time during the Renaissance are aesthetics discussed in isolation from ethics, and any valid theory of imagination always carries with it the implicit context of moral action. Sidney's poet is superior to the philosopher and the historian in his power to move his audience to virtue, to extend *gnosis* into *praxis*. It is not surprising, therefore, to find the golden world of Ideas being used more directly as the basis of action in Castiglione's *Courtier*, where ethics and aesthetics merge to create the Idea of a beautiful life. Like Tasso in *Il Ficino*, Castiglione uses Cicero's remarks on the Ideas in oratory as a precedent for the

[49] The clear debt to Scaliger is conveniently indicated in the notes to Shepherd's edition of the *Defence*, pp. 155-158, and he also suggests analogies for the passage on the Ideas from Pico, Ficino, and Fracastor. None of the passages cited by Shepherd, however, is nearly so close in meaning or in phrasing as that from Tasso's dialogue, *Il Ficino*, which Sidney might conceivably have seen while he was in Italy. In particular, the phrase which introduces Sidney's statement on the Ideas ("Neither let this be jestingly conceived, because the works of the one be essential, the other in imitation or fiction; for any understanding knoweth . . .") sounds like a direct response to Tasso's distinction between "le sostanze" in the Divine Mind and "le cose artificiose" in the mind of "L'artifice."

Idea of the perfect Courtier, and he defends himself against overrealistic critics:

> Others say, bicause it is so hard a matter and (in a maner) unpossible to finde out a man of such perfection, as I would have the Courtier to be, it is but superfluous to write it: for it is a vaine thing to teach that can not be learned. To these men I answere, I am content, to err with Plato, Xenophon, and M. Tullius, leaving aside the disputing of the intelligible world and of the Ideas or imagined fourmes: in which number, as (according to that opinion) the Idea or figure conceyved in imagination of a perfect commune weale, and of a perfect king, and of a perfect Oratour are conteined: so is it also of a perfect Courtier. To the image wherof if my power could not draw nigh in stile, so much the lesse paynes shall Courtiers have to drawe nigh in effect to the ende and marke that I in writing have set beefore them. And if with all this they can not compasse that perfection, such as it is, which I have endevoured to expresse, he that cummeth nighest shall be the most perfect.[50]

Like Tasso in the *Del Poema Eroico*, and Sidney in the *Defence of Poesie*, Castiglione is using the Idea concept as a protection for limited achievers. As Tasso perceives that the Idea of the perfect epic is only formed by consideration of many epics which are not perfect, "but the better they are, the nearer one approaches the Idea," and as Sidney admits that though "our erected wit maketh us know what perfection is . . . yet our infected will keepeth us from reaching unto it," so Castiglione consoles himself and his readers with the reflection that "he that cummeth nighest shall be the most perfect." One can never even describe the perfect Courtier with certainty and completeness, but only with debate and by approximation. It is for this reason that the *Courtier* is a work of fiction with dramatic characters presented in working tension (despite the relaxed connotations of "pastime"), and the Idea of the Courtier is arrived at only as the consensus of

[50] Thomas Hoby, tr., *The Book of the Courtier*, in *Three Renaissance Classics*, ed. B. A. Milligan, 1953, p. 249.

many suggestions. And although there are moments of vision when the Idea is apprehensible, as in Bembo's speech on the nature of Platonic Love, they are indicated rather than presented, and the vision is carefully distanced before it is complete, because, as Bembo says, Platonic Love (or any other Idea) "will not have his secretes discovered any farther . . . and therefore it is not perhaps lawfull to speake any more of this matter."[51]

It is this personal humility in the face of the ideal which, being common to Tasso, Sidney, and Castiglione, we may reasonably suppose to be a characteristic of the "Renaissance mind," if indeed there is such a thing. And it is perhaps, finally, this humility which accounts for the revival of the Seven Ideas of Hermogenes toward the end of the sixteenth century. We have tried three possible explanations for this revival (two of them essentially practical, and the third essentially metaphysical), which demonstrate how the needs for practical instruction in poetry, practical criticism of poetry, and philosophical justification for poetry can be made to meet. The conclusion can best be stated in terms of the poem by Yeats with which this chapter began. Those who found the Ideas helpful in their detailed instructions, and who believed in "sedentary toil" and "the imitation of great masters," and those who found them fascinating for their Platonism were probably as closely related as Yeats's two personae; for the Ideas are simultaneously the "image" and the "book."

[51] *The Courtier*, pp. 615-616.

CHAPTER 2

"The Seven Capital Stars": Descriptions of the Seven Ideas

Hacks in the Fleet and nobles in the Tower.
Shakespeare must keep the peace, and Jonson's thumb
Be branded (for manslaughter), to the power
Of irons the admired Southampton's power was come.
Above all swayed the diseased and doubtful queen:
Her state canopied by the glamour of pain.
. . .
Here moved the Forms, flooding like moonlight,
In which the act or thought perceived its error.
The hustling details, calmed and relevant.

(Thom Gunn, *A Mirror for Poets*)*

THE "Forms" in Thom Gunn's *Mirror* are not specifically those of poetry or oratory, but they should probably include them. His poem is about the contrast between the facts of life in the late sixteenth century, "violent . . . and evil-smelling," and the astonishing ability of its poets to create ideals and abstractions of unfactual things, such as permanence and magnanimity. It is only taking the *Mirror* slightly out of context to apply it to the Seven Ideas, or Forms, or Characters of style, which are abstractions of a studied control over detail never to be reached in fact by any orator or poet.

The Seven Ideas defined by Hermogenes are Clarity (σαφήνεια), Grandeur (μέγεθος), Beauty (κάλλος), Speed (γοργότης), Ethos (ἦθος), Verity (ἀλήθεια) and Gravity (δεινότης). As the table shows, there is some difference of opinion among the commentators about the translations of some of the Greek words, and therefore the main variations are presented side by side, with the translations chosen for this study in the last column. The descriptions of the Ideas themselves are necessarily rather dense, and therefore include occasional "illustrations" from Renaissance poetry which, at this

* From *Fighting Terms*, Thom Gunn. Reprinted by permission of Faber and Faber, Ltd.

HERMOGENES	STURM	SCALIGER	MINTURNO	DELMINIO	PATTERSON
1. σαφήνεια	Claritas	Claritas	Chiara	Chiarezza	Clarity
2. μέγεθος:	Magnitudo:	Magnitudo:	Grande:	Grandezza:	Grandeur:
σεμνότης	Gravitas	Gravitas	Magnifica	Gravitate	Magnificence
τραχύτης	Asperitas	Asperita	Aspra	Asprezza	Asperity
σφοδρότης	Vehementia	Vehementia	Agra	Vehemenza	Vehemence
ἀκμή	Vigor	Hilaritas	Gagliarda	Vigore	Vigor
λαμπρότης	Splendor	Illustre	Splendida	Splendore	Splendor
περιβολή	Circumductio	Circumductio	Ricca	Circonduttione	Circumlocution
3. κάλλος	Pulchritudo	Pulchritudo	Ornata	Bellezza	Beauty
4. γοργότης	Celeritas	Velocitas	Volubile	Prestezza	Speed
5. ἦθος:	Moratum:	Moratum:	Costumata:	Costume:	Ethos:
ἀφέλεια	Simplicitas	Humilitas	Humile	Semplicitate	Simplicity
γλυκύτης	Suavitas	Suavitas	Soave	Dolcezza	Sweetness
δριμύτης	Acutum	Acutum	Soltile	Acrimonia	Subtlety
ἐπιείκεια	Modestia	Modestia	Modeste	Mansuetudine	Modesty
6. ἀλήθεια	Veritas	Veritas	Vera	Veritate	Verity
7. δεινότης	Eloquentia or Decorum	Gravitas	Grave	Graviate or Severitate	Gravity

stage in the argument, are mainly designed to clarify the distinctions between the different styles; though they may also contribute, by internal evidence, to a sense of the pervasive influence of the Ideas.

1. *Clarity*

Clarity is simultaneously a separate style, and a quality of all good writing, that which makes an oration or poem intelligible. Hermogenes subdivided the Idea according to the two chief sources of intelligibility, diction and syntax; the first category of Clarity is Purity (καθαρότης), which ensures a diction within every man's grasp, and the second is Lucidity (εὐκρίνεια), which ensures a straightforward organization of the argument. In each case, one of the eight Parts of analysis has become dominant in the definition of the Idea, so that Purity is recognizable chiefly by its Diction and Lucidity by its Method.

The diction of Purity is essentially normal, avoiding long, harsh, or otherwise difficult words, such as foreign importations. Puttenham was in effect advising Purity when he remarked in the *Arte of English Poesie* that "this part in our maker or Poet must be heedyly looked unto, that it be naturall, pure, and the most usuall of all his countrey" (p. 144). Its Sentence or subject matter is so general as to be indescribable, the only requirement being that it not be abstruse. The only Figure mentioned is that of *rectitudo* (ὀρθότης), or the consistent use of only nominative and vocative cases, as opposed to *obliquitas* (πλαγιασμός), or the use of oblique cases, genitive, dative and ablative. Purity shares with Lucidity short Periods and Members which are well within the grasp of the untrained ear, and a rhythm or Number which is smooth in order to avoid distraction from the sense, rather than to give pleasure to the audience. Lucidity, in fact, is only distinguished as a separate category by its Method, which is logical, putting first things first, and avoiding all inversions and suspensions, and by its *Figura*, which includes partition, enumeration, and simple recapitulation (the structural supports of the ideal undergraduate essay).

Description of the Seven Ideas

There is nothing particularly original in any of this, as far as the recommendations themselves are concerned, with one exception. Aristotle had initiated the discussion by calling σαφήνεια the chief virtue of style (*Rhetoric*, III. 2). In Theophrastus it becomes one of the four virtues (hellenism, clarity, propriety, and ornamentation) and all subsequent discussions are based on his theory.[1] Cicero in *De Oratore* (III. 49) redefines the Theophrastian virtue in Latin terms. Quintilian has a long and careful discussion of the subject, also based on Theophrastus, in which he distinguishes between different kinds of "propriety" of diction and lists the main causes of obscurity (*Institutio Oratoria*, VIII. 2). It was Quintilian's discussion of deliberate obscurantism which influenced the arguments of the Pléiade against certain types of obscurity, as, for example, in the ninth chapter of Jacques Peletier's *Art poétique* (1555).[2] And yet although it is supposedly Quintilian who was the main source of Ben Jonson's remarks on style in the *Discoveries*, it is surely from Hermogenes that he takes his remarks on Clarity: "Pure and neat Language I love, yet plaine and customary."[3] Jonson also states:

> For Order helpes much to Perspicuity, as Confusion hurts.
> *Rectitudo lucem adfert: obliquitas et circumductio offuscat.*
> We should therefore speake what wee can, the neerest way.[4]

[1] See George Kennedy, *The Art of Persuasion in Greece*, 1963, pp. 273ff.

[2] See R. J. Clements, *Critical Theory and Practice of the Pléiade*, 1942, pp. 84-121.

[3] Ben Jonson, *Discoveries*, in *Works*, ed. C. H. Herford and P. Simpson, 1965, VIII, 620.

[4] Ben Jonson, *Works*, VIII, 624. Rosemond Tuve cites these remarks of Jonson's in her discussion of "*clarté* or *chiarezza*" (*Elizabethan and Metaphysical Imagery*, 1947, pp. 30-33) and objects rather perversely, it seems to me, to a simple opposition between these terms and obscurity, seeing them as standing rather for a kind of luminous fitness of image: "To ask for the aesthetic quality of *clarté*, then, is not to ask for a special type of style. And although Jonson talks about 'pure and neat language,' and Sidney about

The vocabulary here is not to be found in Quintilian, but in the Latin translations and commentaries on the Idea of Clarity, and there is no mention in Cicero or Quintilian of the opposition between the figures of *rectitudo* (ὀρθότης) and *obliquitas* (πλαγιασμός) which comes straight from Hermogenes.

The description of Clarity in the Hermogenic formulation may also have appealed to Jonson because it puts a greater stress on the organization of material than does the section in Quintilian's *Institutio*, partly because there the subject had been treated earlier (in the fourth book) under the heading of Narration. What is really different, however, about Hermogenic Clarity is its place in the scheme. It is all very well for Quintilian to state that Clarity is the first essential of good style; this does not prevent it from becoming somewhat submerged in the vast structure of his work. In Theophrastus, it takes second place to the virtue of hellenism, and of his successors only Dionysius of Halicarnassus makes Clarity a separate style or a separate virtue within his scheme. Hermogenes, on the other hand, reinforces its primary position by making it the first of the Seven Ideas, that which must be mastered before the others are attempted. By making it the first of the Seven Ideas, Hermogenes has at the same time emphasized how fundamental is Clarity in the development of style, and also how it is possible to go beyond it. This is what Milton means when he attacks the uneducated clerics of his own time by observing how few there are "among them that know how to write, or speak in a pure stile, much lesse to distinguish the *ideas*, and various kinds of stile."[5] To understand the role of Clarity we should remember the analogy made by Sturm between this Idea and sanity in man, a prerequisite of humanity;[6] or perhaps one could say that Clarity takes the same

---

language not too abstract and generalized, and Minturno about language 'non humilis, non abiecta,' all three seem to recommend a kind of luminous immediacy, a formal *clarté* . . ."

[5] John Milton, *An Apology for Smectymnuus*, in *Works*, III, 347.

[6] Johannes Sturm, ed., *Hermogenis . . . Partitionum rhetoricarum liber unus. qui vulgò de Statibus inscribitur*, 1570, Bvii. (This is the first part of Sturm's four-volume edition of the *Art of Rhetoric*.) Sturm remarks here

place in the education of a writer that Holiness does in Spenser's view of the education of a Christian gentleman, a prerequisite of all meaningful states of being, and yet distinguishable from them, and occasionally not the purpose.

In other words, Clarity in Hermogenes is both the basis of all mastery of style, and a separate style with its own identity. Hermogenes had pointed to that separate identity by using sections of well-known orations as illustrative of Clarity. Minturno is doing the same thing when he illustrates the diction of Purity ("con parole communi senza molta diligenza locata," p. 429) by quoting the first few lines of Petrarch's Sonnet LXI:

> Benedetto sia'l giorno, e'l mese, e l'anno,
> E la stagione, e'l tempo, e l'hora, e'l punto,
> E'l bel paese, e'l luoco, ov'io fui giunto
> Da' duo begli occhi, che legato m'hanno . . . (*sic*)

In the mind of the reader, this sonnet readily becomes a symbol of the separate existence of Clarity; and it is only a short logical step from this to criticism which finds the Idea of Clarity characteristic or uncharacteristic of a particular writer or a particular poem. Thus in the fourteenth century there was a literary quarrel between two Byzantine followers of Hermogenes, Theodore Metochites and Nicephorus Choumnos, the former defending his own lack of Clarity on the grounds that his aim was the Idea of Gravity or δεινότης;[7] and in the sixteenth century in Italy, during another literary quarrel, Orazio Ariosto could claim that the *Orlando Furioso* could only be fully appreciated by realizing that it was written according to the Idea of Clarity. It was therefore folly to apply to the *Orlando* standards of epic writing derived from a poem written according to a different Idea, and to compare it unfavorably with Tasso's *Gerusalemme Liberata*, written according to the Idea of Magnificence.[8]

---

that as "in homine primò color esse sanus atque dilucidus," so Hermogenes perceived that Clarity must be the prerequisite and foundation of style.

[7] G. L. Kustas, "The Function and Evolution of Byzantine Rhetoric," I (1970), *Viator*; Igor Ševčenko, *Etudes sur la polémique entre Théodore Métochite et Nicéphore Choumnos*, 1962, p. 57.

[8] Orazio Ariosto, *Risposte ad alcuni luoghi del dialogo dell'epica poesia del*

Description of the Seven Ideas

It is possible to follow Minturno's method here, and yet with a little more decorum, by choosing an "example" of Clarity from an English poet who, unlike Petrarch, would have had ample opportunity to become acquainted with the Ideas. Samuel Daniel not only went to Oxford, where, as we have seen, he could have attended lectures on Hermogenes, but he also, by his own account, visited Italy, and met Battista Guarini, whose *Il Verrato* uses Hermogenes as an exponent of flexibility in style.[9] Daniel wrote a poem to Sir Thomas Egerton, Lord Keeper of the Great Seal, congratulating him on his responsibility for Equity in the country, in which he in effect characterizes Equity as clarity and Law as obscurity. Law is described as that

---

Signor Cammillo Pellegrino, in Torquato Tasso, *Opere*, x, 244-246: ". . . l'uno ch'è l'Ariosto, proposto di usar nel suo poema il carattere, ovver l'idea dello stile chiamata da Ermogene dilucidità, dove l'altro, cioè il Tasso, ha avuto in mira di servare l'idea, o forma dello stile magnifico: le quai due forme, essendo poco meno che dirittamente opposte, chi non vede ch'egli è vanità il farne paragone per cavar da loro poi maggior lode più dell'altro scrittore?"

[9] For Guarini's use of Hermogenes as an authority on flexibility of style, see Chapter 1, n. 42. The fact that Daniel met Guarini in Italy, and spent enough time with him to have at least some discussions about literature, was pointed out by Alexander Grosart (*The Complete Works of Samuel Daniel*, 1, xviii-xix), and depends on the evidence of Daniel's dedicatory sonnet to *Il Pastor Fido*, when it appeared in Fanshawe's translation in 1647. The sonnet in question reads:

> I do rejoyce learned and worthy Knight,
> That by the hand of thy kinde Country-man
> (This painfull and industrious Gentleman)
> Thy deare esteem'd *Guarini* comes to light:
> Who in thy love I know tooke great delight
> As thou in his, who now in England can
> Speake as good English as Italian,
> And here enjoyes the grace of his owne right.
> *Though I remember he hath oft imbas'd*
> *Unto us both the vertues of the North,*
> *Saying, our costes were with no measures grac'd,*
> *Nor barbarous tongues could any verse bring forth.*
> I would he sawe his owne, or knew our store,
> Whose spirits can yeeld as much, and if not more.
>
> (*Works*, 1, 280; my italics)

Which so imbroiles the state of truth with brawles,
And wraps it up in strange confusednesse,
As if it liv'd immur'd within the walls
Of hideous termes, fram'd out of barbarousnesse
And forren customes, the memorialls
Of our subiection, and could never be
Deliv'red but by wrangling subtilty.
. . .

It's falshood that is intricate and vaine,
And needes these labyrinths of subtlenesse . . .

Whereas, under Equity, truth is restored to its natural state,
where:

> . . . it dwells free in the open plaine,
> Uncurious, Gentle, easie of accesse;
> Certaine unto it selfe, of equall vaine,
> One face, one colour, one assurednesse . . .[10]

There could scarcely be a better image in style of the opposition between clarity and obscurity, rectitude and obliquity, the "open plaine" and the labyrinth; and Daniel's poem is the more interesting because its subject matter is one of the three great sources of oratorical style—the law courts, and the peculiar nature of justice.

2. *Grandeur*

Once the orator or poet has mastered the art of Clarity he is capable of tackling those elements of the second Idea, μέγεθος or Grandeur, which produce obscurity. Greatness is subdivided into six lesser Ideas or categories, which work together to make up the grand style, as the Seven Ideas cooperate with each other to make a single ideal of eloquence. Sturm, as usual, is the commentator who provides the most in the way of a rationale for these divisions. According to him, the first requirement for Grandeur is the choice of deeply serious subject matter, and the first category of Greatness (σεμνότης) is therefore that in which Sentence is primary, although it

---

[10] Samuel Daniel, *Works*, I, 191-198.

also has a characteristic Diction, Number, and other parts as well. Sturm calls this first category Gravity, but Minturno translates it as Magnificence, a better name because it helps to avoid confusion with the Seventh Idea. To the basic seriousness of Magnificence there may be added the copiousness and impressive syntactical control of Circumlocution ($\pi\epsilon\rho\iota\beta o\lambda\acute{\eta}$), the necessary urgency of Asperity ($\tau\rho\alpha\chi\acute{\upsilon}\tau\eta s$), when the orator is on the attack; gleams of figurative and decorative brilliance by the use of Splendor ($\lambda\alpha\mu\pi\rho\acute{o}\tau\eta s$); strength and virility, from Vigor ($\dot{\alpha}\kappa\mu\acute{\eta}$); and sharpness to strike and wound, when necessary, by Vehemence ($\sigma\phi o\delta\rho\acute{o}\tau\eta s$).[11] A desirable and powerful obscurity may appear under several of these headings, since Magnificence may have a mysterious or occult subject matter, Vehemence may confuse the logical issue, and Circumlocution, with its involved syntax, is the very opposite of Clarity.

Under these six headings detailed instructions for writing in a grand but flexible style can be found—a style which can be, as occasion requires, sonorously dignified, passionately excited, or even violently abusive, and which can treat of the best of men and actions as well as of the worst. In this way, Greatness both incorporates the powers of the High Style of Cicero and the grand and forcible styles of Demetrius, and

[11] Sturm, *Scholae . . . De Formis Orationum*, 1571, pp. 116-117:

Necesse est enim ut illa magnitudo habeat $\sigma\epsilon\mu\nu\acute{o}\tau\eta\tau\alpha$ gravitatem: quae maximè spectatur in sententiis, de Deo, de immortalitate animorum . . . Sed gravitas ista non debet esse jejuna & exanguis, verùm copiosa, referta, & sententiis exaggerata: igitur ad eam gravitatem, $\pi\epsilon\rho\iota\beta o\lambda o\nu$, orationem circumductam accedere necesse est. hanc verò non decet esse mollem & tardam, ut istud flumen sedatè fluat, verùm ut profluat, et currat . . . necesse est igitur in copia orationis, uti $\tau\rho\alpha\chi\acute{\upsilon}\tau\eta\tau\iota$, asperitate. quae non debet esse tenebrosa, opaca: sed oportet habere $\lambda\alpha\mu\pi\rho\acute{o}\tau\eta\tau\alpha$, splendorem: ut etiam in densitate silvae lumen appareat: . . . Splendor ille non debet esse senilis, sed virilis & juvenilis: ut oratio habeat $\dot{\alpha}\kappa\mu\grave{o}\nu$ vigorem, robur virile: . . . Sed istud robur eiusmodi debet esse: ut non solùm aures feriat, verùm animum quoque vulneret, e reum vinculis quasi constringat: . . . Ergo in magnitudine orationis requiritur $\sigma\phi o\delta\rho\acute{o}\tau\eta s$, acrimonia & vehementia, ad docendum, conciliandum, permovendum.

also solves the ethical question raised by Puttenham in the *Arte of English Poesie* as to whether the high stylist may decorously "reporte the vanities of *Nero*, the ribaudries of *Caligula*, the idlenes of *Domitian*, & the riots of *Heliogabalus*" (p. 151). In fact, the six categories of Greatness seem to divide in half on an ethical basis, since Asperity, Vehemence, and Vigor are all styles of reproof or blame, and Magnificence, Splendor, and Circumlocution are styles or qualities of praise. Once again Minturno is able to illustrate without hesitation from the sonnets, canzones, and "Triumphs" of Petrarch; but since there is substantial reason to think that English poets knew the Idea of Grandeur and made good use of some of its recommendations, the reader is asked to wait for examples until Chapter 3, which deals with the styles of praise, and Chapter 4, which deals with the styles of reproof.

3. *Beauty*

As the function of Grandeur is essentially to impress the audience, that of κάλλος or Beauty is essentially to give pleasure. Minturno compares its function to that of the blood vessels in the body ("come il corpo per lo sangue diffuso nelle vene acquista gratia," p. 435), an infinitely wide and delicate coverage which diffuses warmth and color through the whole structure. It is thus not a matter of occasional "beauties," and its scope is much greater than that of the occasional line or purple passage. Some of the commentators accept only that part of the Hermogenic definition of Beauty which is generalized; Scaliger, for example, defines it as proportion and harmony, "for where the parts are in proportion, the body is beautiful" (p. 445). Sturm's commentary is particularly suggestive for two reasons. In the first place he gives reasons for using the alternative name of Accuracy (ἐπιμέλεια) for this Idea, the theory behind the name being that in Nature there is a true beauty, neither painted nor meretricious. It is the duty of the writer to preserve this beauty with all the accuracy of which he is capable, and it is in this light that the exquisitely smooth composition and ornamentation of the Idea should be

53

understood.[12] This is different from Sidney's defense of the poet's golden world, and perhaps a more convincing argument if used defensively, since the poet does not claim to improve upon fallen Nature, but merely to preserve what she gives in the honeycomb of his talent. Secondly, Sturm points out that the Idea of Beauty corresponds to the "floridum" or flowery style used by Isocrates, and thus to the Gorgian rhetoric which became the middle of Cicero's Three Styles (p. 245). Like the middle style, the function of Beauty is only to give pleasure, but unlike the middle style, its function is cooperative with that of Clarity, Grandeur, and the other Ideas, making it in a very real sense the sugar coating on the improving pill.

Beauty uses an elegantly polished Diction, but avoids long, difficult, or awe-inspiring words. Whereas Magnificence uses an even rhythm for the sake of dignity, and Clarity does so to avoid distraction from the sense, Beauty elevates smoothness of Number into its most characteristic virtue, and seeks above all things a smooth sweet flow of sound. Similarly, whereas Circumlocution is marked by its use of the figures of complex syntax, which demand alertness in the audience and command its respect, Beauty is marked instead by figures which are audibly pleasing, emotionally moving in a mild way, but not intellectually demanding, such as *epanastrophe* or *epanaphora*.

Beauty is not clearly distinguishable from part of the fifth Idea, Ethos, which has as one of its subcategories Sweetness, or γλυκύτης. Hermogenes himself concentrates on the style of Beauty and the subject matter of sweetness, which is approximately all Grecian mythology, especially in its most beautiful moments, such as the birth of Venus (Rabe, p. 330), but the

[12] Sturm, *Hermogenis . . . de dicendi generibus sive formis orationum libri II*, p. 244:

Hanc formam Graeci κάλλος, nominant: quia pulchritudo ista debet esse conjuncta cum honestate: non debet esse cerussa, aut fuco meretricio ac cersita: sed à natura accepta, studio & diligentia conservata, virtutibus autem ornata: & hinc, propter diligentiam in conservando, ἐπιμελεια, vocatur. Tametsi enim pulchritudinem nobis natura largiatur: tamen cura atque diligentia conservatur.

commentaries give almost identical descriptions of Beauty and Sweetness, and Sturm even gives the same list of ten Figures for both, which is not found in the original. Both Beauty and Sweetness, for the Renaissance, are appropriate styles for matters of love. Minturno had illustrated the various categories of Grandeur by reference to Petrarch's Triumphs of Death, Fame, Time, and Eternity, but when he comes to Beauty he illustrates by citing the first thirty lines of the *Triumph of Cupid*. And Torquato Tasso devotes the sixth book of the *Discorsi del Poema Eroico* to a defense of the Idea of Beauty in epic poetry in order to justify the mingling of love and war, and the presence of the enchantress Armida as love's chief representative in the otherwise martial *Gerusalemme Liberata*.

The English Renaissance poems to which the Idea of Beauty most obviously applies are similarly poems of love, the "sweet sugared sonnets" of the Elizabethans. The style of those sonnets will be explored in detail in Chapter 5, along with their stylistic opposites, the "truthful" sonnets of Sidney and Shakespeare; for it is now clear that what has until now been labeled as anti-Petrarchanism in Sidney and Shakespeare can be more fully explained in terms of the Hermogenic Idea of Verity, which is opposed to Beauty. But in order to show now what the Idea of Beauty would have looked and sounded like in English poetry, we can find an "example" on the same principles as before, by decorous wisdom after the event. Edmund Spenser, being directly exposed to the Ideas, we may assume, through his friendship with Gabriel Harvey (who called himself Pseudo-Hermogenes), was also, obviously, influenced by Tasso. And since Tasso sees the Venus-figure of Armida as representing the Idea of Beauty in his own epic, there is no more appropriate analogy than the passage in *The Faerie Queene* II, where Spenser introduces his own version of Armida in the figure of Acrasia, and defines her nature by the loveliest, if most suspect, of all his lullabies to the intellect:

The whiles some one did chaunt this lovely lay;
Ah see, who so faire thing does faine to see,

In springing flowre the image of thy day;
Ah see the Virgin Rose, how sweetly shee
Doth first peepe forth with bashfull modestee,
That fairer seemes, the lesse ye see her may;
Lo see soone after, how much more bold and free
Her bared bosome she doth broad display;
Loe see soone after, how she fades, and falles away.

So passeth, in the passing of a day,
Of mortall life the leafe, the bud, the flowre,
Ne more doth flourish after first decay,
That earst was sought to decke both bed and bowre,
Of many a Ladie, and many a Paramowre:
Gather therefore the Rose, whilest yet is prime,
For soone comes age, that will her pride deflowre:
Gather the Rose of love, whilest yet is time,
Whilest loving thou mayst loved be with equall crime.

(II, xii, 74-75)

The smoothness of this, the liquids, the alluring repetitions,
all relate to Sturm's comment that the Idea of Beauty requires
a relaxed mind ("animum sedatum" p. 248), a state in which
the young knight Verdant is only too obviously to be found!
It is also intriguing to consider what connection there might
be between Sturm's concept of the crystallizing effect of the
Idea on the true beauty of Nature, and the unnatural state of
arrest in Acrasia's bower, where Nature has been dangerously
taken over by Art, and stasis implies not preservation but its
opposite.

4. Speed

In striking contrast to these concepts of arrest and crystalli-
zation is the Idea of Speed (γοργότης), also translated as
velocity or volubility. Scaliger is interpreting it in the most
general way when he describes it as "that which makes a
speech seem lively and mobile" (p. 447), and Sturm speaks
of it in terms which suggest flowing water—Speed makes style
a living river instead of a standing pool (p. 4). But again,
Speed is clearly also a specific style with its own techniques.

Sturm and Delminio, for example, provide careful lists of the appropriate Figures as they appear in Hermogenes, while Minturno and Parthenio concentrate on the appropriate length and consonantal texture of the Diction. Hermogenes also recommends trochaic rhythms and tetrameter Members, a suggestion which had considerable implications for poetry.

It is Minturno who provides the best guide to an understanding of what the Idea of Speed would have meant to a Renaissance poet, because he not only illustrates from poetry, rather than oratory, but he also draws attention to the possibilities of using Speed for figurative effect. He illustrates the techniques of speedy writing by referring to Petrarch's *Triumph of Time*, focusing on the central and figurative line "Per la mirabil sua velocitate" (p. 437), and thus gives the key to a whole group of subjects which could appropriately be handled under the Idea of Speed. There is a potential relationship between poems on the passage and power of Time, poems of *carpe diem*, and poems of battle where speedy action is essential and mortality a preoccupation. All three kinds were highly popular in England in the late sixteenth and early seventeenth centuries, and some of the most successful have become traditions. Nothing could be more appropriate as an "example" of Speed than Marvell's *To his Coy Mistress*, and everyone knows that audible image of "Times winged Charriot hurrying near." However, it may add something to our understanding of Marvell's poem to see how its short lines, its trochaic rhythm, and its cunning enjambments are the signs, not just of Marvell's own brilliance, but of a minor genre of speedy poems, which will be investigated more carefully in Chapter 6.

5. *Ethos*

The fifth Idea is the least satisfactory to deal with, since at first sight it seems to be neither a style, nor a quality, nor a concept, but rather an ill-assorted collection of styles. Both Minturno (p. 438) and Sturm (p. 284) associate Ethos with the dramatic decorum of character. Sturm distinguishes between two kinds of Ethos, one which "pertinet ad Scriptores

Comoediarum & Tragoediarum: & decorum poëticum," but about which Hermogenes left no instructions: and another which has little to do with poetry but is the business of the orator, who has to win the sympathy of the audience for himself or his client. However, as the descriptions evolve, it becomes apparent that the four subcategories of Ethos, Simplicity (ἀφέλεια), Sweetness (γλυκύτης), Subtlety (δριμύτης), and Modesty (ἐπιείκεια), do after all have some relevance to poetry, and it also appears that they have an underlying unity of purpose. As its name would indicate, the Idea of Ethos is related to Cicero's distinction in the *Orator* between the ethic and pathetic topics:

> One, which the Greeks call ἠθικὸν or "expressive of character," is related to men's nature and character, their habits and all the intercourse of life; the other, which they call παθητικὸν or "relating to the emotions," arouses and excites the emotions: in this part alone oratory reigns supreme. The former is courteous and agreeable, adapted to win goodwill; the latter is violent, hot and impassioned, and by this cases are wrested from our opponents.[13]

In the Hermogenic Idea, the ethical topic has been subdivided into four styles, each of which is either "expressive of character," or "adapted to win goodwill," or both. Moreover, Cicero's description of the pathetic topic is relevant to the Idea which follows, that of Verity, which is expressive not of character but of the emotions, as well as to Vehemence, a category of Greatness to which Verity is closely related.

The first category of Ethos, Simplicity, is expressive of character in the sense that it is appropriate to the affairs of women, children, shepherds and other rustic characters, who are sim-

---

[13] Cicero, *Orator*, XXXVII. 128:

Quorum alterum est, quod Graeci ἠθικὸν vocant, ad naturas et ad mores et ad omnem vitae consuetudinem accommodatum; alterum quod idem παθητικὸν nominant, quo perturbantur animi et concitantur, in quo uno regnat oratio. Illud superius come, jucundum, ad benevolentiam conciliandum paratum, hoc vehemens, incensum incitatum, quo causae eripiuntur. (I have used the translation by H. M. Hubbell [Loeb edition], 1939.)

ple but honest (*Opera*, pp. 322-323). It is here, in fact, that we have an equivalent for the third of the Three Styles, when treated as the *genus humile*. The classical genres and authors mentioned in connection with Simplicity confirm this, for Minturno says explicitly that "this kind of speech is appropriate to the Comic and Bucolic Poets" (p. 438), presumably because Hermogenes mentions Menander, and quotes from the *Idylls* of Theocritus. Apart from this limitation of subject matter, Simplicity is achieved by using the Diction, Composition, and Number of Clarity, although Parthenio differs here, insisting that it uses an even simpler Diction and syntax (p. 227). Sturm also stands out from the other commentators by dividing Simplicity into two kinds, one which is rustic and inferior, and a superior kind which is concerned not with innocence and foolishness, but with "igni, aqua, pane, vino, domo, coniuge, liberis" (p. 288), or, in other words, with the fundamentals of living.

Having mentioned the "Comic and Bucolic Poets," Minturno does not illustrate Simplicity from Italian poetry; if we were to illustrate from English poetry, the most reasonable source would be Spenser's *Shepheardes Calender*, though there is nothing in the *Calender* which cannot fully be explained by the models cited by E. K. It would be hard, however, to illustrate Sturm's superior kind of Simplicity from Renaissance pastoral, which is either too artificial or too dogmatic about the values which it represents, values which in any case are not as fundamental as fire and water, bread and wine, wife and children. However, one *can* see an adequate expression of this Idea in the poetry of Robert Herrick, whose sense of decorum was as academic as anyone's, but who had actually experienced "the Countries sweet simplicity"[14] at first hand. Herrick knows, on the one hand, what gives "our Numbers Euphonie, and weight . . . when a Verse springs high, how understood/To be, or not borne of the Royall-blood,"[15] and applies this knowledge when writing a formal

[14] Robert Herrick, *A Country life: To his Brother, M. Tho: Herrick*, in *Poetical Works*, ed. L. C. Martin, 1956, p. 34.

[15] Herrick, *To his honoured and most Ingenious friend Mr. Charles Cotton*, p. 297.

or a mock-formal ode. On the other hand, he can write with simple conviction of *His Content in the Country*:

> Here, here I live with what my Board,
> Can with the smallest cost afford.
> Though ne'r so mean the Viands be,
> They well content my Prew and me.
> Or Pea, or Bean, or Wort, or Beet,
> What ever comes, content makes sweet:
> Here we rejoyce, because no Rent
> We pay for our poore Tenement:
> . . .
>
> We blesse our Fortunes, when we see
> Our own beloved privacie:
> And like our living, where w'are known
> To very few, or else to none.

After Simplicity comes Sweetness, which, as already said, is usually subsumed under or confused with the Idea of Beauty, insofar as it is concerned with gratification of the senses and of providing the element of *dulce* which makes the *utile* palatable.

However, this approach to Sweetness is only part of what Hermogenes originally intended, and in fact constitutes the fourth of five categories which he sets out quite clearly according to their subject matter. The other four categories are not as fully illustrated by the Renaissance commentators, but their conceptual implications were much more important for the development of Renaissance criticism. This is particularly clear in the commentary of Antonius Lullius (1558). The first category of Sweetness is that of pure fable, such as the loves of Venus, or, as Lullius adds, the *Metamorphoses* of Ovid. The second category is that of near-fable, such as stories of the Trojan war, or "among us, stories of Roland or Amadis of Gaul, and the like."[16] The third category is when some fabulous matter is intermingled with fact, as in Herodotus; and the fifth category is when an otherwise factual work contains

---

[16] Antonius Lullius, *De Oratione Libri septem*, 1558, p. 477.

fictional speeches to bring the characters alive, or when natural or inanimate objects are given human emotions. Pastoral poetry, of course, is recognized as the natural home of prosopopoeia, since the shepherd can seldom engage in dialogue unless he be echoed by his surroundings, and both Lullius and Sturm leap to illustrate this last category of Sweetness from the *Bucolics* of Virgil. But the real interest of these categories comes from their underlying assumption that Sweetness and fiction go together, and that one can create a hierarchy of written works, in which the amount of Sweetness decreases in proportion to their increasing factuality. The effect is similar to that produced by Hermogenes in his descending scale of Magnificent subjects, but it was possibly of even more relevance to Renaissance critics like Tasso and Sidney, faced as they were with the task of evaluating works of literature according to their truth. The instincts of Lullius give us a guide to theirs, and as he places the *Chanson de Roland* and the *Amadis* in the second category, along with stories of the Trojan war, he anticipates many of the arguments of the later part of the century as to the place of the romances in the hierarchy of genres.

The third kind of Ethos, Subtlety, is the nearest equivalent within the Hermogenic scheme of the *genus tenue* of Cicero. Subtlety is described by Minturno as that style in which "humble material . . . is given some sharpness, and acutness" (p. 439). Subtlety departs somewhat from the common usage, accepting tropes like metonymy, metaphor, and irony, such as are used by comedy, satire, and epigram. Minturno insists, however, that bluntness, roughness, and coarseness have no place in this style, which uses wit and point, the rapier rather than the ax. Similarly Sturm defines it as "the biting and nipping kind of speech," but its jokes and allusions must not appear unmannerly to the audience, especially if that audience is a judge (p. 320).

Finally, the fourth category of Ethos is Modesty, which more than any other is supposed to ingratiate the speaker or poet with his audience. It is more useful to the orator than the poet, especially useful at the beginning of an oration.

Modesty is achieved mainly by self-protective figures of thought. Although Hermogenes has no section on the modest "Figura" as such, Minturno gathers from his discussion a list of figures in which the modest speaker builds up others and diminishes himself, anticipates objections, corrects and interrupts himself, and expresses doubt of his own opinion (pp. 439-440). The modest speaker is frequently heard to say, "It seems to me . . ." Although Modesty is mainly a matter of oratory, and of forensic oratory at that, it has one important application to poetry, for it is connected with the poetic invocation; as Parthenio puts it, it is only modest to say that "all high and sublime matters are not of one's own begetting, but proceed from the Gods and the Muses" (p. 236).

Modesty is also to be found, of course, in any poetry which apologizes for lack of skill, though it would be hard to distinguish Hermogenic Modesty from the familiar *captatio benevolentiae* or the modesty topos so fully documented by Curtius.[17] Minturno cites as an example Petrarch's Sonnet XX, the antecedent of many tongue-tied poems in English:

> Vergognando talor ch'ancor si taccia,
> Donna, per me vostra bellezza in rima,
> ricorra al tempo ch' i' vi vidi prima,
> tal che null'altra fia mai che mi piaccia;
> ma trovo peso non da le mie braccia,
> né ovra da polir colla mia lima;
> però l'ingegno, che sua forza estima,
> ne l'operazion tutto s'agghiaccia . . .

[Ashamed that through me, Lady, your beauty is still unsung, I recall the time when I first saw you, such that no other could give me so much pleasure. But the weight I find binds my arms, and prevents my file from polishing the work. Therefore my talent, which knows its own strength, becomes completely frozen in this endeavor.]

The other aspect of Modesty which Hermogenes spends some time discussing is its relationship to Vehemence. Essen-

17 E. R. Curtius, *European Literature and the Latin Middle Ages*, 1953, pp. 83-85.

tially Modesty is opposed to Vehemence, and indeed Gaspar Laurentius translates it as *Moderata*; but the modest or moderate speaker, provided that he does so obliquely, can use Vehemence and still not be condemned for it. He may say, for example, "Do not be angry with me: for I shall say nothing against you, you wicked man!" And it is worth noticing that Milton, whose knowledge of the Ideas has already been indicated, pauses in the *Apology for Smectymnuus* to attack his opponent for an unwarranted use of the word "modest" in the title of his tract:

> Whereas a modest title should only informe the buyer what the book containes without furder insinuation, this officious epithet so hastily assuming the modesty which others are to judge of by reading, not the author to anticipate to himself by forestalling, is a strong presumption that his modesty set there to sale in the frontispice, is not much addicted to blush. A surer signe of his lost shame he could not have given, then seeking thus unseasonably to prepossesse men of his modesty. And seeing he hath neither kept his word in the sequel, nor omitted any kind of boldnesse in slandering, tis manifest his purpose was only to rub the forehead of his title with this word *modest*, that he might not want colour to be the more impudent throughout his whole confutation.
>
> (*Works*, iii, 289-290)

The whole of Milton's *Apology* could be described as an attack on the style of his opponent, and a defense of his own; and considering that shortly after this passage Milton refers to "The aptest *Ideas* of speech to be allow'd . . . by the rules of best rhetoricians," it seems only reasonable to deduce that the "modesty" he is defending from abuse belongs to the Hermogenic Idea of Ethos. As we shall see in Chapter 4, the Idea that Milton regards as most suitable for polemic is that of Vehemence, which is opposed to Modesty; so his objection to the title of *A Modest Confutation* would seem to be that his opponent names his tract after one Idea but writes according to a different and opposing one. Milton himself, by contrast, is willing to admit his Vehemence, and further justifies its use on the grounds of his own ethical integrity.

The essentially Aristotelian concept which Milton here invokes, that the speaker's own ethos is inevitably part of his effect on his audience, helps to explain the grouping of these four minor styles, however arbitrary it may at first appear, in the Hermogenic scheme. Simplicity, Sweetness, Subtlety, and Modesty all render the speaker agreeable to his audience and convince them that he is basically a decent fellow: not too complicated (Simplicity); indulgent of their taste for the *dulce* as well as the *utile* (Sweetness); witty, of course, but never offensive (Subtlety and Modesty); in fact, one of themselves.

6. *Verity*

In some ways the style of Modesty leads naturally to the sixth Idea, which is, like Modesty, recognized as a literary stance taken up deliberately in order to achieve certain results; and yet they are distinguished by the difference between Ethos and Pathos, since Pathos deals not with permanent manifestations of character but with the impermanent responses to events which we call emotions. Verity, explicitly connected with Pathos in the commentary of Sturm (p. 343), is expressive of anger, fear, pity, and "similar perturbations" largely by being a mirror image of the tale of the Emperor's Clothes. Verity pretends to be naked, but it is not really so. Unlike Modesty, it is allowed to proclaim itself. Verity carefully avoids the appearance of any kind of polish or preparation, but it does so by using well-recognized rhetorical Figures like *apostrophe, aposiopesis, merismus,* or *diaporesis,* and by using the short Members and broken rhythms of Vehemence, to which Verity is related. Hermogenes distinguishes between the two main emotions of anger and grief, hard and soft, the expression of anger bringing Verity very close indeed to Vehemence, whereas grief obviously requires a softer Diction. But Minturno points out that at all cost soft and pleasing rhythms are to be avoided, since they will suggest artifice, and therefore in its use of rhythm, as also in its basic assumptions, Verity is in opposition to Beauty.

There is also a minor subcategory of Verity, βαρύτης or Weightiness, to which none of the Italian commentators seem to pay any attention, perhaps because it has a limited function and limited devices. It is appropriate only when the orator reproaches his audience for not treating him according to his deserts, and its main devices are irony and pretended doubt. It would seem that Hermogenes has here overindulged his delight in subdivision, since there is nothing to prevent this kind of reproach from being part of the seemingly candid, highly emotional relationship between orator and audience which Verity itself defines.

On the face of it, at least, it would not be surprising to find that Verity became for the Renaissance one of the most significant Ideas. It became part of the vocabulary of the eternal debate as to whether truth of content must be compromised by elegance of form, and the sincerity of the speaker by rhetorical skill. When the Hermogenic terms first became part of this debate as it particularly affected Christianity, it was, as G. L. Kustas has pointed out,[18] the Idea of Simplicity (ἀφέλεια) rather than the Idea of Verity (ἀλήθεια) by which the Church Fathers justified the lowly style of the New Testament; and they found comfort in the fact that Simplicity was said, both by Hermogenes himself and by pseudo-Aristides, to be the defining style of the Socratic dialogues of Plato. The personality of Socrates himself, and the intellectual humility expressed by dialectic, were similarly appropriated to the new Christian ideal, in which children, women, shepherds, and fishermen become both the teachers and the dominant images, and the last, in any classical theory of genres, become first. However, when it is removed from a strictly Christian context and the emphasis on humility becomes less important than the need for persuasion, the Idea of Simplicity as a vehicle of truth can be replaced by the Idea of Verity itself.[19]

[18] G. L. Kustas, "Late Greek Rhetoric: A.D. 200-550," unpublished paper given at the Pontifical Institute, University of Toronto.

[19] Compare Lullius, *De Oratione Libri septem*, p. 467: "Et redemptoris

Verity is especially useful in any situation where, while artfully professing one's own sincerity, one seeks to disparage the more obvious artifice of another's style. In the περὶ ἰδεῶν itself Verity is set up in opposition to the style of Isocrates, who is said to have used a highly ornamental style "because he was more interested in Beauty, and Diligence, than in probability, and Verity."[20] This opposition, which appeared as a significant feature of the thinking of the Pléiade, found its way into English poetry of the Renaissance in that genre in which sincerity of emotion was most to the point—the lyrics and especially the sonnets of love. And there, in the sonnets of Sidney and Shakespeare, the debate seems to take shape, not only in the Hermogenic vocabulary, but also in the same context of Platonic idealism in which the Ideas themselves were defined. Finally, in the poetry of George Herbert, the Idea of Verity is assimilated also to the Christian ideals of simplicity and humility, Herbert being too much a craftsman to be satisfied with Simplicity alone.

7. *Gravity*

When we come to δεινότης, the seventh and last Idea, the Renaissance commentaries diverge. For Minturno, who sees it as "proprio dell'Heroico Poeta" (p. 442), and for Parthenio, who sees it as the style of extreme premeditation, depending on circumlocution and rotund periods (p. 243), there seems to be agreement, and it is difficult to see how their commentaries distinguished between the last of the Ideas and the second, Grandeur, taken as a whole.

Scaliger, on the other hand, defines Gravity instead as a general sense of harmony and proportion, and Sturm prefers

---

nostri: Amen amen dico vobis. neque alio dicendi genere constat sermo CHRISTI, qui hoc ingenuo et simplici, ut omnibus hominibus, & maximè pauperibus & parvulis spiritu evangelizaret, quorum est regnum coelorum." [And these words of our Lord are an example of Simplicity, Amen, amen, I say to you. Nor does the speech of Christ admit of any other style, Christ who was ingenuous and simple to this extent, that he sent his spirit out to all men, and especially to the poor and meek, of whom he was the heavenly king.]

[20] *Opera*, ed. Rabe, p. 301.

to translate it as Eloquence, which suggests a larger concept, achieved mainly by decorum, the right use of everything, and in an earlier treatise he actually identified the seventh Idea with the concept of decorum itself: "oportet omnia ista facere decorè, quod decorum vocatur δεινότης ut omnia decorè fiant."[21] The cause of these divergent opinions is to be found in Hermogenes himself, since he begins by discussing the older meaning of δεινότης as that which is awesome or terrifying, and proceeds to the more universal meaning adopted by Scaliger and Sturm. As Chapter 7 of this book will show, a resolution between these two approaches is possible, not in the canzones of Petrarch which Minturno uses as illustrations of Gravity, but within the much larger limits of epic, which both requires a style which is "proprio dell'Heroico Poeta," and can also contain that mixture of Ideas which is necessary for δεινότης conceived as decorum.

These, then, are the Seven Ideas of Hermogenes, as they appear both in the original and through the filter of Renaissance commentary, where they are sometimes condensed and often imaginatively expanded. Parthenio condenses, Sturm expands vastly with learned detail, Scaliger stops to quarrel about the proper interpretation of the Hermogenic terms, Lullius pauses to discuss Flemish painting, and Minturno inevitably changes the character of the Ideas by applying them to vernacular poetry. But by combining them all, a modern reader can get a fairly accurate notion of what the Seven Ideas meant to the Renaissance; and a reader of the sixteenth or seventeenth century, having studied the original while at the university, would not have been led astray by the idiosyncrasies of any commentary he happened to read.

When Minturno is asked by his companion in the *Arte Poetica* which of the Ideas have the most currency among his contemporaries, he replies that the most important are Gravity,

---

[21] Johannes Sturm, *Scholae in Partitiones rhetoricas Hermogenis*, bound with *Hermogenis . . . Partitionum rhetoricarum liber unus. qui vulgò de Statibus inscribitur*, 1570, the first part of Sturm's four-volume edition of Hermogenes' *Art of Rhetoric*.

Magnificence, Sweetness, Ethos, and Speed, and that the three styles of reproof, Asperity, Vehemence, and Vigor, are also much in use. To make the same assessment of English poetry requires at least as much confidence as Minturno obviously possessed, as well as a sense, which he did not possess, of the difference between necessary and unnecessary hypotheses. There are certain features of English poetry in this period which require knowledge of the Ideas of Hermogenes as a necessary ingredient for total understanding: the appearance of a certain kind of lofty ode, for example, is partly accounted for by the positive styles of Grandeur, especially Magnificence; the peculiar development of Elizabethan verse satire is largely explained by the negative styles of Grandeur, especially Vehemence; the preoccupation of some sonneteers with statements and styles of sincerity falls into perspective in the light of the Ideas of Beauty and Verity; the techniques of poems of *carpe diem* are easier to explain by reference to the Idea of Speed; and finally the mixture of styles in a number of epic poems can be explained by the last of the Seven Ideas, Gravity or decorum, which blends all the others into an organic and persuasive whole.

CHAPTER 3

"High Talk": *Canzone and Ode*

Where are the kings who routed all confusion,
The bearded gods who shepherded the spaces,
The merchants who poured gold into our lives?
Where the historic routes, the great occasions?
Laurel and language wither into silence;
The nymphs and oracles have fled away . . .

(W. H. Auden, *Kairos and Logos*)*

E RICH AUERBACH, in *Literary Language and Its Public*, has
admirably defined the decay of high style and the sublime
in late Latin antiquity and the early Middle Ages, and then
its rediscovery in the vernacular and the *dolce stil nuovo* of
Dante.[1] He attributes the decay of the lofty style partly to
pedantry and overrhetorical emphasis, partly to the lack of
any truly sublime subject matter, since Christianity, under
the influence of Augustine, had become indissolubly linked
with the *genus humile*. This chapter on the styles of praise
and the Idea of Grandeur in Hermogenes is also written at a
time when high style is out of fashion, and yet must deal with
the Renaissance assumption that high style is a highly desirable
thing—the ultimate achievement of all serious writers. Accus-
tomed as we are now to a poetic of intense moments rather
than "great occasions," it is hard to respond to the details of the
Idea of Greatness, and harder still to understand what greatness has to do with such minutiae. And yet the details can
give precise information about the difference between a lofty
and a light ode, for example, which is sometimes more instructive than either an historical or emotional approach to
the genres.

It has already been remarked that the six categories of
Grandeur divide in half according to whether they deal in

* From *The Collected Poetry*, W. H. Auden. Reprinted by permission of
Random House, Inc., and Faber and Faber, Ltd.

[1] Erich Auerbach, *Literary Language and Its Public*, tr. Ralph Manheim,
1965, passim.

praise or blame, with positive or negative examples of virtue. In this chapter we are to examine more closely the three positive categories, Magnificence, Splendor, and Circumlocution, which were originally described by Hermogenes in terms of laudative oratory, but which are readily transferred into the sphere of poetics, a transfer which Hermogenes himself anticipated by referring incidentally to Homer, Pindar, and the structure of a Pindaric ode.[2] And we shall examine styles in terms of their possible influence on the development of "praising" poems in English, though Minturno's examples from Italian poetry serve again as a useful introduction.

It is clear from the text of the περὶ ἰδεῶν that Magnificence or σεμνότης is intended to stand as the foundation of Hermogenic high style, for it is under this heading that he describes the subject matter or Sentence for which high style is appropriate, whereas Splendor and Circumlocution are seen as additional ways of producing Grandeur, not, however, to be used consistently. The subject matter of Magnificence is carefully subdivided by Hermogenes into four kinds, hierarchically arranged. The first deals with the philosophical or theological nature of the immortal Gods, but not with fabulous or anthropomorphic aspects of deity, which would be regarded as ornamental, and therefore come under the heading of Sweetness. The second deals with Nature itself, with the causes of things, such as the four elements, and especially with the great natural movements of the earth, the sea, or the heavenly bodies. The third deals with those aspects of human nature which ally men with the Gods, with Reason, Justice, or the other virtues. The fourth deals with magnificent human action, especially with battles of various kinds.

Put all four together, and the result very roughly corresponds with the subject matter of the grand style of Demetrius ("a great and notable battle on land or sea, or when there is talk of the heavens, or of the earth")[3] and equally roughly with the subject matter of the high style of Cicero, as it appears, for

[2] *Opera*, ed. Rabe, 1913, p. 292.
[3] *A Greek Critic: Demetrius on Style*, tr. G.M.A. Grube, 1961, p. 80.

70

example, in George Puttenham's formulation in the *Arte of English Poesie*: "The matters therefore that concerne the Gods and divine things are highest of all others to be couched in writing, next to them the noble gests and great fortunes of Princes, and the notable accidents of time, as the greatest affairs of war and peace" (p. 152). The difference lies in Puttenham's omission of Natura as a lofty subject, and in the less orderly progression of subjects. There is a trace of hierarchy in Puttenham, but not the same clear steps toward or away from the absolute. A poet who understood Magnificence could judge his own poetic strength, and then choose to write of God, or of his vice-regent Natura, or of his diffused image in man, or mere human heroism; and the very definition of the hierarchy would have provided a warning against the presumption of Icarus, who flew too high. It is clear that poetry can embrace all four kinds of Magnificent subject matter: on the epic scale, Dante's *Paradiso* would be an example of the first, the *Sepmaines* of Du Bartas an example of the second, the *Faerie Queene* of the third, and the *Gerusalemme Liberata* of the fourth, while *Paradise Lost* might reasonably be said to have combined all four. And within the smaller limits of the lofty ode, the first Sentence is treated in hymns, the second, as we shall see, becomes the conceptual basis of epithalamia and funeral elegies, the third becomes the subject matter of encomia, and the fourth of triumphal odes.

The Figures recommended for the achievement of Magnificence are merely those already suggested for Clarity, *rectitudo* and *adjudicatio*, though a judicious use of metaphor is required (under the heading of Diction) and Sturm, interestingly enough, adds allegory. The instructions for creating a Magnificent diction, however, are both extremely full and extremely important, since they contain recommendations *not* found in any of the other major rhetorics. The first of these is Hermogenes' insistence that resonance is achieved not merely by a liberal use of diphthongs and long vowels (as Demetrius also pointed out),[4] but specifically by use of the Greek vowels

[4] Grube, p. 79.

A and ω, which quite literally fill the mouth with sound. This is a recommendation calmly adapted by Scaliger for Latin poetry, and by Parthenio, Minturno, Dolce, and Tasso for Italian,[5] using the nearest phonetic equivalents. The second unusual recommendation is that a Magnificent diction should be made up largely of nouns, pronouns, and other parts of speech serving as nouns, and should avoid verbs as far as possible. Hermogenes cites a magnificent sentence from Thucydides which uses only one vowel, and Sturm even goes so far as to say that "quò rariora sunt verba, eò gravior est oratio" (p. 134). Parthenio comments that a sense of amplitude is provided by "the names of Gods, of famous men, of cities, of peoples, of provinces, of kingdoms, of mountains, of rivers" (p. 191), thus making his own remarks into a recognizable epic device, the catalogue.

The recommendations for the Magnificent members, cadences, composition, and number, when combined, describe a rhythm which is above all firm and stable, with reasonably short phrases, but without harsh collisions of sound. Hermogenes recommends as the ideal cadence nouns which are not less than three syllables long; but Minturno apparently did not feel that this could be translated into Italian terms, and replaced it by the statement that Magnificence is heard "quando le voci sono di poche syllabe" (p. 431). Similarly Parthenio interpolates the statement that "it is not only the length of words which gives the composition dignity, but also those which are only one syllable long" (p. 195).[6]

---

[5] Julius Caesar Scaliger, *Poetices Libri Septem*, 1561, p. 208: "Igitur vocales grandisonae sunt, A, & O." See also: Bernadino Parthenio, *Della Imitatione Poetica*, 1560, p. 191: "Le gonfiate & sonore sono quelle, che hanno pienezza della a, overo dello o, secondo Hermogene." Ludovico Dolce, *Osservationi Nella Volgar Lingua*, 1550, fol. 94r: "Dirò solamente, che si come tra le vocali, l'A, et l'O hanno maggiore sonorità." Torquato Tasso, *Discorsi del Poema Eroico*, 1594 (in *Opere*, 1823), XII, 145: "Quantunque il concorso dell'I, non faccia così gran voragine, o iato, come quello dell'A, e del'O, per cui sogliamo più aprir la bocca." Minturno does not make the same statement explicitly, but clearly implies it by the examples he gives of Magnificence in Petrarch (*Arte Poetica*, p. 431).

[6] Parthenio, *Della Imitatione Poetica*, p. 195: "Ne solamente la lunghezza

The Members or phrases of Magnificence should not be very long, because, as Delminio says, shorter phrases match the decisiveness or determination of the style (p. 12). The long breathing spans which we tend to associate with high style, partly thanks to Milton, are therefore not part of this basic Magnificence, but can be added to it by the supplementary style of Splendor. Splendor is to be used whenever the orator or his audience is particularly convinced of the splendor of his subject, and it deals not with facts but with qualities, not with narration but with amplification. Splendor, even more than Magnificence, is the style which takes its time, and holds the audience in awed suspension. Like Magnificence, it is opposed to Speed, as well as to Asperity and Vehemence, which as Tolkien's Treebeard would have said, are the media of "hasty folk." Splendor comes into being when the orator or poet pauses to provide for the visual imagination with fine descriptions, or for the ear with long phrases and periods, as Parthenio says, "quando più lunghi, tanto più splendidi" (p. 212). And, as Lullius says, "the subjects of splendor are filled with things precious either by nature or the value we put on them, such as Light, gold, jewels" (pp. 443-444), a remark worth remembering when we come to consider the imagery of the Elizabethan ode.

---

delle voci questo oprano nella compositione della dignità, ma anchora quelle che sono di una sillaba sola, massimamente se sono poste nel mezzo dopò un dattilo." And he quotes, or rather misquotes, in illustration a line from the *Aeneid* XII. 48: "Quam pro me curam geris, hanc precor, optime." Virgil's effective use of monosyllables for emphasis and retardation was fully commented upon during the Renaissance; presumably any critic would have wished to include some reference to Virgil's technique, as Parthenio does here, in a description of a grave or magnificent style. But beyond this, the question of how cadence affected gravity of style was of obvious interest to Renaissance poets, since it affected theories of rhyme. The respective qualities of masculine and feminine rhymes are discussed in Samuel Daniel's *Defence of Ryme*, Sir John Harington's preface to his translation of the *Orlando Furioso,* and Puttenham's *Arte of English Poesie*; and it is clear that the majority opinion, from which Harington, for obvious reasons, dissents, is that double or feminine rhymes in English are essentially light or frivolous in effect.

Finally, for a full description of a lofty style of praise, we need one more element which is not found in either Magnificence or Splendor, and that is syntactical involvement. This is provided by the style of περιβολή or Circumlocution, usually found with a Magnificent subject, but occasionally appearing in connection with other Ideas. Circumlocution comes into being when subjects are treated not simply, but accompanied by all their accidents of genus, species, cause, time, place, instrument, and so on, and this is done, not straightforwardly, but by inversion and digression, with lesser things before greater, and all sorts of other devices designed to keep the audience intellectually on their toes. Circumlocution is distinguished by its Method and its Figures, which are those producing syntactical complexity or intellectual agility, such as *antithesis, parenthesis, hypothesis,* and *epanalepsis.* Hermogenes makes a particularly significant remark about *epanalepsis* (a form of repetition in which the elements are linked over a considerable distance): the intellectual reach needed to keep the parts in relationship is the same as that which relates the strophe and antistrophe in an ode.

In order to see what relevance these recommendations for creating a high style of praise might have had for Renaissance poetics, it is sensible to turn first to Minturno's commentary in the *Arte Poetica*, where he illustrates Magnificence, Splendor, and Circumlocution from the canzones, "Triumphs" and sonnets of Petrarch. Minturno's examples have to be supplemented with cautious interpretation, because he does not state *what* it is in a chosen passage that attracted his attention, and also because he sometimes uses a single line to indicate that the reader should refer to the passage which that line introduces.

Minturno describes Magnificence as the style which is identified by "chosen words, which resound fully and deeply, and with serviceable composition, not however achieved with too much care, which seems affected . . . and without harsh concurrence of letters, and without languid hiatus, *and with cadences and rhythms which are stable, and firm.*"[7] He does

---

[7] Minturno, *Arte Poetica*, pp. 430-431: "La Magnifica poi . . . sì fà trat-

not mention specifically the Hermogenic recommendation for use of the long *A* and *O*, though it is implied by the phrase "che pienamente, & altamente risonino," and confirmed by the examples he chooses, which are these:

Quando ad un giogo, & in un tempo quivi	*Triumph of Chastity*, 1.
Dapoiche morte triomphô nel volto	*Triumph of Fame*, 1.
Una Donna più bella assai che'l Sole	Canzone cxix, 1.

... Beati spirti, che nel sommo choro
Sì troveranno, ò trovano in tal grado,
Che sia in memoria eterna il nome loro.
O felice colui, che truovo il guado
Di questro alpestro, e rapido torrente,
C'hà nome vita, ch'à molti è sì à grado. (*sic*)

Triumph of Eternity, 43-48.

It seems perfectly clear that by choosing these lines Minturno is defining resonance in the same terms as Scaliger when he states that "vocales grandisonae sunt, A. & O. . . . In verbo igitur, *cano*, utraque illustris: plus enim ibi audis, quàm si dicas: Canus" (p. 208).

It is impossible to say with certainty what else Minturno intended his audience to notice about the first three illustrations, and whether they were intended to go further than the first line in each case. But the passage from the *Triumph of Eternity* is an exceedingly interesting choice for two reasons. It is not the opening of the poem, and it is clear that Minturno could not possibly have drawn attention to the opening lines, which deny momentarily the conceptual basis of Magnificence. Having just passed through the experience of the preceding *Triumph of Time*, the poet begins by saying, "Da poi che sotto'l ciel *cosa non vidi/Stabile, & ferma* . . ." Minturno had described Magnificence as being marked by "posamenti, i

---

tando cose grandi . . . con scelta di parole, che pienamente, & altamente risonino, e con acconcia compositione, non però fatta con tanta studio, che paia affettata, . . . e senza aspro concorso di lettere, e senza languido incontro di vocali, e con posamenti, i numeri de' quali sieno stabili, e fermi."

75

numeri de' quali sieno *stabili, e fermi,*" and he was certainly
aware of the cosmic stability assumed by the four levels of
Magnificent Sentence. He chooses therefore not the opening
of the *Triumph of Eternity*, which still reflects the fear of the
triumph of Time, but rather the passage where the poet
recognizes the possibility of attaining permanence within flux.
It is also noticeably a passage of direct praise; the poet praises
the man who has found the ford in the swift and alpine river
that we call life. And it is therefore in direct contrast to the
lines which immediately follow, which are in the opposite
mode of blame, and which Minturno in fact chooses as an
illustration of Vehemence:

> Misera la volgare e cieca gente
> [Che pon qui sue speranze in cose tali,
> Che'l tempo le ne porta sì repente!
> O veramente sordi, ignudi, & frali . . .]

Instead of praising the blessed spirits who have seen their
way clear to eternity, Petrarch here attacks the crude and
blinded race who place their hope in temporal things, and
he does so with the harsher consonants and uneven rhythms
characteristic of Vehemence. Minturno's example of Magnificence is therefore valuable not only in itself, but by contrast
with what comes before and after it, and because of these
contrasts we can see that it is both form and content which
guide his choice.

When Minturno comes to describe and illustrate Splendor,
he emphasizes the descriptive brilliance and impressive amplification of the style, and again his illustrations call for some
measure of interpretation. Presumably the opening lines of
the *Triumph of Time* ("De l'aureo albergo con l'aurore in-
nanzi/Si ratto . . .") stand on their own merit as a splendid
and shining metaphor. However, when Minturno cites two
comparatively unimpressive lines from the *Triumph of Death*,
"Cosi rispose: & ecco da traverso/Piena di morti tutta la campagna . . ." he surely intends us to read on and complete the
splendid *ubi sunt* passage thus introduced:

76

Così rispose; ed ecco da traverso
piena di morti tutta la campagna,
che comprender nol puoprosa né verso:
da India, dal Cataio, Marrocco et Spagna.

. . .

Ivi eran quei che fur detti felici,
pontefici, regnanti, imperadori:
or sono ignudi, miseri e mendici.
U'sono or le ricchezze u' son gli onori?
e le gemme e gli scettri e le corone,
e le mitre e i purpurei colori?[8]

Even more interpretation is required for the inclusion of Canzone xxiii ("Nel dolce tempo de la prima etade") under the heading of Splendor, since the opening line appears to be simple and straightforward in the extreme. However, as the poem develops, the states of mind experienced by the poet are described as physical transformations, first into a green laurel rooted helplessly by a stream, then into a lamenting swan, then a blind rock, then a fountain of tears, and finally a deer running desperately from pursuing hounds. It is presumably the pictorial and metaphorical nature of this canzone which seemed splendid to Minturno, the "nova figura" in which emotions are made visible reminding us of his statement that Splendor uses "l'imitatione, & rappresentatione delle cose, che si trattano, e . . . figure tali di parlare, che forza elle habbiano, e splendore, onde la cosa dia chiaramente à vedere" (p. 43). But this canzone also recalls (though Minturno does not mention it) the Hermogenic recommendation that the phrases and periods of Splendor be exceptionally long, since it has the longest stanza in the entire *Rime*, a stanza of twenty lines, of which all but one are hendecasyllables.

---

[8] [Thus she replied. And lo, from side to side, the whole plain was filled with the dead, more than prose or verse can tell, from India, Cathay, Morocco, Spain. Here now are they who were called fortunate, popes, rulers and emperors. Here are they naked, poor and beggarly. Where are now their riches? Where are their honors? And their gems, and scepters, and their crowns, and the mitres with purple dyes? *Rime, Trionfi e Poesie Latine*, ed. F. Neri, 1951.]

Although the stanzas of this canzone are splendid in their proportions, the syntax is relatively straightforward, as promised in the opening lines ("Canterò . . . Poi seguirò . . ."). It makes an excellent contrast to the canzone Minturno picks as an example of the chief device of Circumlocution, which is syntactical involvement, or what he calls "implicando le Membra":

> O aspettata in ciel beata e bella
> anima che di nostra umanitade
> vestita vai, non come l'altre carca,
> perché ti sian men dure omai le strade,
> a dio diletta, obediente ancella,
> onde al suo regno di qua giù si varca,
> ecco novellamente a la tua barca,
> ch'al cieco mondo à già volte le spalle
> per gir al miglior porto,
> d'un vento occidental dolce conforto;
> lo qual per mezzo questa oscura valle,
> ove piangiamo il nostro e l'altrui torto,
> la condurrà de' lacci antichi sciolta
> per dritissimo calle
> al verace oriente ov'ella è volta.[9]

It is necessary to quote, as Minturno does, the whole first stanza of this canzone, because it is not until the end that the syntactical suspension is resolved, and there appears the completed metaphor of the soul as a ship receiving new wind for her sails in the eastward voyage toward the "true Orient." Here, then, we have the Italian counterpart of the control which produced the opening periods of *Paradise Lost*, by

[9] [O blessed and beautiful spirit, awaited in heaven, who goes clothed in our humanity, and with no other burden, so that henceforth the road may be less hard for you, chosen by God, his obedient servant, from whence you may cross to his kingdom from the one below, behold again your boat; she has already turned her back on the dark world to go to a better harbor, comforted by a soft West wind, by which, through the midst of this dark vale where we weep our own wrongs and those of others, she is guided swiftly out of the old snares, through the straightest passage, to the true Orient whither she is turned. Canzone xxviii]

which, as Minturno puts it, "we interfold and involve the discourse so that no part can stand by itself" (p. 435).

We have now seen how an Italian critic, known to have had some influence in England, could take poems by one of his greatest national poets and declare them to be examples of the three positive categories of the Idea of Grandeur, although it would have been virtually impossible for Petrarch himself to have been *influenced* by the Ideas, which remained in manuscript until 1508. Minturno's method is obviously to treat the Ideas as merely descriptive terms when applied to Petrarch, but terms which can then become instructive and formative, both in themselves and by the added power of Petrarch's "example." Our own method, in this and the following chapters, differs from Minturno's in that we shall be looking for examples of the Ideas in action *only* in poems where there is a reasonable presumption that the author would have learned of Hermogenes at the university, and perhaps had his interest revived since then by criticism such as Minturno's. As a method, however, it is, finally, no more verifiable than Minturno's, since it has to depend almost entirely on internal evidence.

Minturno's choice of the canzones and "Triumphs" of Petrarch provides a lead to English poems of analogous genre. We shall come back to the "Triumphs" later; as far as the canzone is concerned, it is clear that Italian critics of the Renaissance regarded it as their national equivalent of the classical ode. Tasso, for example, remarks firmly that the canzone "risponde all'ode Greca o Latina."[10] And it would take little reflection to perceive the further analogy between the Idea of positive Grandeur and the lofty classical ode as represented by Pindar. In England it is clear that there was the same fusion of lofty ode and canzone. Michael Drayton, in presenting his own *Odes* (1619) to the public, defines the genre in terms of Pindar, Horace, and Anacreon, but he also invokes, with equal respect, the name of Petrarch as an authority on the ode.[11] Drayton in his Preface does not claim to have achieved

[10] Tasso, *La Cavalletta ovvero della Poesie Toscana* in *Opere* VII, 308.
[11] Drayton, *Works*, ed. J. W. Hebel, 1931—41, II, 346.

anything as lofty as a Pindaric ode, preferring to classify his own productions as mixed, or Horatian odes. Nevertheless his collection includes the *Sacrifice to Apollo*, which, though not Pindaric in form, is decidedly lofty in style and content. He begins by stressing the inspired and esoteric nature of poetry, the worship of Apollo:

> Priests of Apollo, sacred be the Roome
> For this learn'd Meeting: Let no barbarous Groome,
> > How brave soe'r he bee,
> > Attempt to enter;
> > But of the Muses free,
> > None here may venter;
> This for the *Delphian* Prophets is prepar'd:
> The prophane Vulgar are from hence debar'd.[12]

And he then goes on to define a high style which would be equally appropriate for a heroic ode or an epic poem, and which is seen as part of the votarist's achieved skill:

> Or if the deeds of HEROES ye rehearse,
> Let them be sung in so well ord'red Verse,
> > That each word have his weight,
> > Yet runne with pleasure;
> > Holding one stately height
> > In so brave measure,
> That they may make the stiffest Storme seeme weake,
> And dampe JOVES thunder, when it lowd'st doth speake.

The style which Drayton describes here is virtually identical with the description of the Magnificent style given by Minturno, the style in which one speaks "con scelta di parole, che pienamente, & altamente risonino . . . e con posamenti, i numeri de' quali sieno stabili, e fermi." Though it could be argued that Drayton's requirements for such a style are vague enough to derive from any formulation for the high style, it is nevertheless interesting that he chooses to stress the firmness and stability of rhythm which is characteristic of Magnificence, rather than the ornamental and impressive

---

[12] Drayton, *Works*, II, 357.

Diction which is emphasized, for example, by the *Rhetorica ad Herennium*.[13]

Where Drayton indicates his knowledge of the canzone by referring to Petrarch as an authority on the ode, Edmund Bolton makes that indication in the title of his *Canzon Pastorall in honour of her Majestie*, which appeared in *England's Helicon* (1600). It stands out from most of the other poems in that pastoral anthology like an oak in a meadow because of its monumental firmness both of rhythm and statement:

> Loe Matron-like the Earth her selfe attires
>   In habite grave,
> Naked the fields are, bloomelesse are the brires,
>   Yet we a Sommer have,
> Who in our clime kindleth these living fires,
>   Which bloomes can on the briers save.
> No Ice dooth christallize the running Brooke,
> No blast deflowres the flowre-adorned field,
> Christall is cleare, but cleerer is the looke,
> Which to our climes these living fires dooth yeild:
>   Winter though every where
>   Hath no abiding heere:
> On Brooks and Briers she doth rule alone,
> The Sunne which lights our world is always one.[14]

Here language, like "the Earth her selfe," has taken on the "habite grave," with its firm pace, wide vowels, many diphthongs, and great negations which are really affirmations. "No blast deflowres the flowre-adorned field" because the splendor of

---

[13] *Rhetorica ad Herennium*, tr. Harry Caplan (Loeb edition), IV, 11: "In gravi consumetur oratio figura si quae cuiusque rei poterunt ornatissima verba reperiri sive propria sive extranea ad unam quamque rem adcommodabuntur, et si graves sententiae quae in amplificatione et commiseratione tractantur eligentur, et si exornationes sententiarum aut verborum quae gravitatem habebunt." [A discourse will be composed in the Grand style if to each idea are applied the most ornate words that can be found for it, whether literal or figurative; if impressive thoughts are chosen, such as are used in Amplification and Appeal to Pity; and if we employ figures of thought and figures of diction which have grandeur.]

[14] *England's Helicon* (1600), ed. Hugh MacDonald, 1962, p. 17.

the Elizabethan sun is strong enough to withstand the cyclical process of Nature, while at the same time the stability of the throne is an image of that of the cosmos: "The Sunne which lights our world is alwayes one." If this ode or canzone is a pastoral, it is only because its means of praise are taken from natural processes, since its style is undoubtedly loftier than is usual in pastoral. It might with equal justification have been titled a "Magnificent Ode in honour of her Majestie," since not only is the style the essence of that which is firm and stable, but the conceptual framework is that of the second Sentence of Magnificence, Nature, the causes of things, and the movements of the earth and the heavenly bodies.

To develop this line of approach by the use of contrast, we can compare two English odes which share the same parentage. According to Ringler, the "first formal epithalamium" in English is Dicus' marriage song in Sidney's *Arcadia*;[15] it is a very rough translation of an epithalamium in Gil Polo's *Diana Enamorada*, a poem which was also translated by Bartholomew Young.[16] It is immediately clear from a comparison of the two versions that Sidney's ode is more solemn in sound than Young's. Sidney's ode begins:

> Let mother earth now decke her selfe in flowers,
> To see her ofspring seeke a good increase,
> Where justest love doth vanquish Cupid's powers,
> And warr of thoughts is swallow'd up in peace
>   Which never may decrease
>   But like the turtells faire,
>   Live one in two, a well united paire,
>   Which that no chaunce may staine,
> O Himen long their coupled joyes maintaine.

There is no question that this is more impressive than Young's first stanza:

> Let now each meade with flowers be depainted,
> Of sundrie colours sweetest odours glowing:

[15] *Philip Sidney, Poems*, ed. W. A. Ringler, Jr., 1962, p. 411.
[16] Bartholomew Young, tr., *Diana of George of Montemayor*, 1598, pp. 468-470.

Roses yeeld foorth your smels, so finely tainted,
Calme windes, the greene leaves moove with gentle
    blowing:
    The christall rivers flowing
    With waters be increased:
And since each one from sorrowes now hath ceased,
(From mournefull plaints and sadnes)
Ring forth faire Nymphs, your joyfull songs for gladness.

Both poets were obviously aiming for a background of natural peace and harmony, when increase is possible; but where Sidney's style supports the image of a peace (and a marriage), which is firm and stable, Young's prettier images and feminine rhymes produce the image of a peace which is languorous. The difference is admirably symbolized in the two refrains, Bolton merely asking the participation of Nature in a lyric act, Sidney on the contrary invoking the power of Nature, in the person of the marriage god, not only to create, but also, significantly, to "maintaine." Both Sidney and Bolton, in contrast to Young, conceive of Nature's function in these odes to be not ornament, but power, the power which actually regulates the "great occasions." Thus Young merely askes that "each meade with flowers be depainted," but Sidney calls on "mother earth" to "decke her selfe in flowers," and Bolton asserts that "Matron-like the Earth her selfe attires/In habite grave." And the odes of Sidney and Bolton, in contrast to Young's, are therefore conceptually stabilized by what their authors, had they paused to consider it, would have known to be the second level of the Magnificent Sentence.

Especially when its subject is death or marriage, the lofty ode in England at this period seems to draw on this concept of Nature, since the order of her cycles is equally relevant to consolation and celebration. Spenser's November elegy for Dido in the *Shepheardes Calender* (1579) gains additional power from its placing in the dead season of the year, and its implicit contrast with the much lighter April ode to Elizabeth. Spenser has in the November ode, which according to E. K. is superior in "reach" to the other eclogues, combined the three

methods by which Nature can be seen as comforting in time
of loss. The first is pathetic fallacy, by which "The faded lockes
fall from the loftie oke," as if, E. K. explains, "Nature her
selfe bewayled the death of the Mayde." The seasonal November weather is forced into participation with the poet's grief
in a way that is aesthetically soothing but finally unsatisfying.
The second is the cyclical consolation, a more mature position
also gathered from the observation that November must follow
April, since, as E. K. comments upon the emblem, "by course
of nature we be borne to dye, and being ripened with age, as
with a timely harvest, we must be gathered in time, or els of
our selves we fall like rotted ripe fruite fro the tree." This
consolation is also incomplete, because, unlike the flowers of
the field which return the following year, the poet knows that
"vertues braunch and beauties budde,/Reliven not . . ." unless,
in the third approach, the natural cycle is transcended, and
the imagination moves to Elysian fields where the grass is
unchangeably green. These three approaches to the natural
cycle, aesthetic, philosophic, and religious, which are explicit
only in the November ode, point forward to the transcending
of time and Nature in the *Mutability Cantos*, while at the
same time they explain the structure of Spenser's *Calender*.
Spenser concludes the *Calender* with a "square poem"[17] in
which he states the nature of his own achievement.

[17] The relationship between Spenser's envoy in the *Calender* and the
definition of a "square" poem by Puttenham in the *Arte of English Poesie*
was pointed out by Maren-Sofie Røstvig in *The Hidden Sense*, 1963, p. 91:
"The envoy is a particularly pleasing example of numerical construction in
the manner suggested by Puttenham when he defines a square poem as one
whose lines are equal to the number of syllables in the line. Puttenham
argues that this poetic figure implies constancy . . . and on turning to the
envoy we find that the poet here expresses his conviction that his poem
will outlast time, and that he does so by means of twelve twelve-syllable
lines." Despite the fact that Miss Røstvig's book often displays the most uncritical use of numerological theories, there does seem to be a real likelihood
that Spenser consciously "squared" the envoy to the *Calender*, and that
its statement bears some relation to Puttenham's statement (p. 100) that the
square "for his inconcussable steadinesse [is] likened to the earth." It is interesting to compare with this Tasso's numerological defense of the Italian
octave, which is also a square, although not in Puttenham's sense: "Oltre

Loe I have made a Calender for every yeare,
That steele in strength, and time in durance shall
  outweare:
And if I marked well the starres revolution,
It shall continewe till the worlds dissolution . . .

By mastering the poetic and human implications of the annual
cycle he has achieved stability within flux, and, until time is
transcended, the poetic achievement itself stands for that
which is firm and stable. As E. K. puts it in his comment
upon the December emblem, "all thinges perish and come to
theyr last end, but workes of learned wits and monuments of
Poetry abide for ever."

These concepts, which are still partly embryonic in the
Shepheardes Calender, receive their full expression, both in
form and content, in Spenser's *Epithalamion*, which has been
shown to be intricately constructed on the pattern of twenty-
four hours, and the movements of sun and moon which create those hours.[18] Spenser actually invokes, as primary hand-
maids of his bride, the "fayre" hours:

> Which doe the seasons of the yeare allot,
> And al that ever in this world is fayre
> Doe make and still repayre . . .

Within this slow-moving, midsummer poem he is able to
give full emphasis to the continuity implied in the rituals of
marriage. At high noon, he brings his bride "up to th'high
altar, that she may/The sacred ceremonies there partake,/The
which do *endlesse matrimony* make." He imagines the wonder

---

ciò la stanza di otto versi è grandissima, *perchè il numero ottonario, come*
dicono gli aritmetici, è primo fra i numeri solidi, *e cubi, che hanno pienezza,*
e gravità . . . per questa cagione ancora è perfetto l'ottonario, siccome
quello, che si compone dal quaternario duplicato; *onde si forma una tessera*
saldissima, e dal binario quadriplicatio." (*Opere* XII, 190-191.), (My italics)
It is because it is composed of two fours, or four twos, according to Tasso,
that the octave acquires a "texture of the utmost solidity," since the number
eight, as the arithmeticians say, is the first of the solid or cubic numbers.

[18] A. Kent Hieatt, *Short Time's Endless Monument: The Symbolism of the*
Numbers in Edmund Spenser's "Epithalamion," 1960.

of "even th'Angels which *continually*,/About the sacred Altare doe *remaine*." He invokes the Genius "in whose gentle hand,/ The bridale bowre and geniall bed *remaine*"; and he calls on the "high heavens"

> And all ye powers which in the same *remayne*,
> More then we men can fayne,
> Poure out your blessing on us plentiously,
> And happy influence upon us raine,
> That we may raise a large posterity.

(My italics)

It is the children which stem from the marriage who will repeat the cycle, and become, like the poem itself, "for short time an endlesse moniment." And this sense of continuity is emphasized by the repetition of the word "remain" (backed up by many of the long *A* sounds recommended for Magnificence),[19] just as in Sidney's marriage ode from the *Arcadia*

[19] When considering what would have been the equivalents in English poetry for the Greek vowels A and ω, it seems that the transference was not as simple as it was for Italian poetry, via Latin. English grammarians were more likely to be confused as to the nature of the vernacular sounds if they tried to follow the analyses of Latin grammarians. For example, Ben Jonson's *English Grammar*, which derives from Ramus, Terentianus, and Scaliger, as well as Mulcaster and Smith, reproduces the classic statement that "O is produced with a round mouth," but loosely covers all phonetic complexities with the remark that it "is a letter of much change, and uncertaintie with us" (*Works*, VIII, 475). Similarly it limits the discussion of *A* to sounds roughly comparable to "the French *à*," as in *apple*, *small*, or *balm*, and gives only the most cursory treatment to what is called "the diphthong Ai or Ay" as in *maid*, *said*, *day* (pp. 471, 498). This means that Jonson has totally failed to take account of the sound relationship between the four Middle English vowels and diphthongs *ā*, *ę̄*, *ai*, and *au*, as represented by the words *game*, *great*, *pain*, and *change*, respectively. These words, though once distinct in sound, coalesced, and are all now pronounced with the modern English diphthong [ęi]. According to Helge Kökeritz (*Shakespeare's Pronunciation*, 1953, p. 173) this coalescence took place "long before Shakespeare's time, probably in the first half of the 15th century," and by the sixteenth century their common sound had been raised to approximately [ę:]. E. J. Dobson, in *English Pronunciation, 1500-1700*, 1957, takes a far more conservative view of the date at which such coalescence took place, but he takes his main body of evidence, not from poetry, but from the work

the sense of continuity is made audible in the refrain: "O Himen long their coupled joyes *maintaine*."

Presumably Ben Jonson remembered Spenser's *Epithalamion* when he came to write his own for Jerome Weston and Lady Frances Stuart,[20] since he too creates an ode of twenty-four stanzas, governed continually by the presence of the summer sun, until in the nineteenth stanza the sun is dismissed in order that night may fall. Then the remainder of the poem is given over to developing the concept of a mighty family tree, the size and stability of which will benefit the country as a whole:

> And never may there want one of the Stem,
>   To be a watchfull Servant for this State;
> But like an Arme of Eminence, 'mongst them,
>   Extend a reaching vertue, early and late:
>   Whilst the maine tree still found
>   Upright and sound,
>   By this Sun's Noone sted's made
> So great; his Body now alone projects the shade . . .

And the growth of the "maine tree" is mainly a stylistic achievement; it is by the extraordinarily slow, firm pace of the verse and the long vowels that he is "made/So great" that he projects not a shadow, but a "shade."

Jonson also wrote a formal Pindaric ode, in which he attributes a similar magnificence, by similar means, to the de-

---

of the sixteenth and seventeenth century orthoepists, whose business it was to preserve and teach a "correct" pronunciation. They were therefore often unwilling to admit the currency of new pronunciations. The main point about Kökeritz's evidence, as against that of the grammarians, is that it shows what English poets had available to them as wide and hence resonant vowels. They could choose from the comparatively small group of words represented by Jonson's "French à" (*all, fall, art, balm*), where resonance depends not so much on the vowel as on the consonant which follows it, or they could choose from the vast group of words represented by *game, great, pain* and *change*, all pronounced, if we are to accept Kökeritz's evidence, not as a diphthong, but as the wide vowel [ɛ:].

[20] Ben Jonson, *Epithalamion; or, a song: celebrating the nuptials of that Noble Gentleman, Mr. Hierome Weston . . . with the Lady Frances Stuart . . .* in *Works*, viii, 252-258.

ceased Henry Morison.[21] Morison is described, in both senses of the word, as a "vertuous Sonne" whose life cycle, though short in temporal terms, was of full scale:

> All Offices were done
> By him, so ample, full and round,
> In weight, in measure, number, sound,
> As though his age imperfect might appeare,
> His life was of Humanitie the Spheare.

Jonson is presenting the idea of a life as "ample, full and round,/In weight, in measure, number, sound" as the ode itself; but he has taken the planetary metaphor far beyond mere compliment or pun by introducing the second figure of Lucius Cary, who is still alive, and whose existence balances that of Morison's in the grand design as the strophe and antistrophe of the Pindaric ode balance each other; for "fate doth so alternate the designe,/Whilst that in heav'n, this light on earth must shine." The cyclical concept is thus not only made more complicated in itself, but is actually related to the formal structure of the ode, which thus becomes explicitly part of the harmony of Nature. This prosodic symbolism had, moreover, been anticipated some time earlier, for in 1555 Jacques Peletier incorporated into his *Art poétique* the statement that the Pindaric ode was a symbol of heavenly motion: ". . . (selon la valeur meme du mot qui sinifie conversion ou contournemant): La Strofe etoet a l'example e imitacion du droet tour ou mouvemant du Ciel etele: e l'Antistrofe qui sinifie retour ou reversion, etoet a l'imitacion du cours retrograde des Planetes."[22] And Scaliger in his *Poetices* (1561) expands this by taking it back to the singing and dancing of the Greek chorus, who when they moved to the left were imitating the *primum mobile*, and when they moved to the right were imitating the motion of the planets, singing meanwhile the strophe and antistrophe respectively; but when they sang the

---

[21] Ben Jonson, *To the immortall memorie, and friendship of that noble paire, Sir Lucius Cary, and Sir H. Morison*, in *Works*, VIII, 242-246.

[22] Jacques Peletier du Mans, *L'Art poétique* (1555), ed. André Boulanger, 1930, pp. 179-180. The accents of the original have been omitted.

epode they would stand still, in imitation of the stability of the earth ("stantes Terrae quietem repraesentabant," p. 16).

Jonson's ode to Cary and Morison is rare in that it is a formal Pindaric ode. Most of the lofty odes written in England in this period use instead a modified canzone stanza; and yet several, as we have seen (and there were not very many written), are primarily concerned with that relationship between permanence and flux, stability and motion which was thought to be symbolized by the true Pindaric ode. It is because of this continued emphasis on what is firm and stable (presented often in terms of natural cycles) combined with a style which corresponds to the descriptions of Magnificence by Italian critics, that makes some knowledge of the Idea of Magnificence seem a reasonable hypothesis. A poet could presumably have arrived at a similar understanding of the lofty ode by reading Pindar, the epithalamiums of Catullus, the canzones of Petrarch, the prescriptions of Cicero and Quintilian for the high style, and by using his intuition and imagination; but if he had done all those things he might equally well have read Hermogenes, or Minturno on Hermogenes, and found under the heading of Magnificence both a firm place for the kind of praise he intended, and firm recommendations for creating a style to match. Ben Jonson, whom we know to have read the Hermogenic recommendations for Clarity, probably remembered Hermogenes on Circumlocution, and the analogy Hermogenes makes between the strophe and antistrophe in the ode, and *epanalepsis*, or the figure of "slow return." And one wonders whether Spenser, who almost certainly would have discussed Hermogenes with Gabriel Harvey, thought about *epanalepsis* (or the "Eccho sound" as Puttenham also calls it) when he developed his magnificent refrain, "That al the woods may answere and their eccho ring."

The odes we have been considering all, in one way or another, reach the position which Petrarch reaches in the *Triumph of Eternity*, when he praises those who have found the ford in the alpine torrent of life, the understanding of stability which gives meaning to the experience of flux. Since

Minturno gives so much weight to the "Triumphs" of Petrarch as examples of positive Grandeur it is worth considering whether there are in fact any analogous poems in English. It is clear that there was nothing produced in the English Renaissance to equal the structure of the "Triumphs" as a whole.[23] They are a series of allegorical dream-visions, in which the concept which is triumphant in each single poem is defeated by the triumph of the succeeding concept, so that erotic Love is defeated by Chastity, chaste love is defeated by Death, Death is defeated by Fame, Fame ultimately disappears in Time, but Time itself is ultimately transcended by Eternity. There is, however, a poem of which we are not sure we know the title, which is a very close analogy to the last two "Triumphs," taken together. Spenser's *Mutability Cantos,* whether or not they are part of *The Faerie Queene,* present in allegorical form the temporary triumph of Mutability, followed by her defeat by Order, as represented by God's vice-regent Nature; and their opposition is restated by the poet in the last two stanzas as being the opposition between movement and rest, time and eternity. For Spenser, as for Petrarch, the spectacle of Mutability makes him anxious to cast away the "love of things,"

> Whose flowring pride, so fading and so fickle,
> Short *Time* shall soon cut down with his consuming sickle.

But then, like Petrarch, Spenser turns his mind to

> . . . that same time when no more Change shall be,
> But stedfast rest of all things firmely stayd
> Upon the pillours of Eternity.

[23] There is an incomplete translation attributed to Queen Elizabeth of the *Triumph of Eternity* in an important commonplace book edited by Ruth Hughey (*The Arundel Harington Manuscript of Tudor Poetry,* 1960, I, 360-362). If this translation was indeed by the Queen, and was written in the second year of her reign, as Hughey suggests, her choice is a touching commentary on the difficulties of her position. There was also a complete translation of the *Triumphs* by Henry Parker, Lord Morley, in 1554; see Hughey, II, 456-460.

And beyond these generalities of statement, which could be accidental, there is the rather remarkable coincidence that Mutability's case for domination is summed up in the following words:

> Then since within this wide great Universe
> *Nothing doth firme and permanent appeare,*
> But all things tost and turned by transverse:
> What then should let, but I aloft should reare
> My Trophee, *and from all, the triumph beare?*
>
> (My italics)

Can it, after all, be coincidence that this should echo so closely the opening of Petrarch's *Triumph of Eternity*, which begins with the poet remembering the triumph of Time, and saying therefore, "Da poi che sotto'l ciel cosa non vidi/Stabile, & ferma . . . ?"

It is also surely no coincidence that Spenser in the *Mutability Cantos*, especially at the end, achieves a greater "sternenesse of . . . stile," as he himself puts it, than at almost any point that one can think of in *The Faerie Queene*. There is no better way of demonstrating this than by comparing the style of Nature's judgment with the comparable section of Mutability's speech. Mutability begins the summation of her case in these words:

> Lo, mighty mother, now be iudge and say,
> Whether in all thy creatures more or lesse
> CHANGE doth not raign and beare the greatest sway:
> For, who sees not, that Time on all doth pray:
> But Times do change and move continually.
> So nothing here long standeth in one stay:
> Wherefore, this lower world who can deny
> But to be subiect still to Mutabilitie?
>
> (VII, 47)

Nature chooses to reply in the same terms, but with what a difference:

> I well consider all that ye have *sayd,*
> And find that all things stedfastnes doe *hate*

91

And *changed* be: yet being rightly *wayd*
They are not *changed* from their first *estate*;
But by their *change* their being doe *dilate*:
And turning to themselves at length *againe*,
Doe worke their owne perfection so by *fate*:
Then over them *Change* doth not rule and *raigne*;
But *they raigne* over *change*, and doe their *states*
  maintaine.

(VII, 58)

Conviction is carried by the greater control of syntax, the fact
that there are twice as many long *A* sounds (indicated by my
italics) in Nature's speech, making it possible for her to re-
verse the position of "change" and "raigne" with complete
finality, and the fact that the last word which the audience
hears in Mutability's stanza is her own name, whereas what
echoes out of Nature's stanza is the word "maintaine." The
terms of argument in both stanzas are the same, but being
"rightly wayd" with devices recommended for the Magnificent style, they produce the opposite conclusion from that
which Mutability intends. It is not that Mutability's speech
would fall outside the style of height or "sternenesse" or Magnificence, but rather that it is prevented from sounding as firm
as Nature's, which is the quintessence of natural stability.

In all this discussion, attention has been focused on the style
and subject matter of Magnificence, and the ways in which
it may have influenced the development of the English Renaissance ode. A glance back at the examples chosen will show
that in every case the lofty ode uses longer, more complex
stanzas, with longer lines, than would have been the case if
the subject matter had been less serious. Drayton's *Ode to
Cupid* which follows the *Ode to Apollo* shows up the weighty
structure of its predecessor by its own lightness and brevity;
Spenser's April eulogy to Elizabeth performs the same function for the elegy in "November"; Jonson's ode in honor of
Cary and Morison is preceded by an almost absurdly frolic
ode *In Celebration of Her Majesties Birth-Day, 1630*. And fre-

quently, in order to prevent these longer, more complex stanzas from falling apart, a greater syntactical complexity and suspension is used.

It might be argued that, instead of explaining this in terms of the recommendations for Splendor and Circumlocution, it could be more simply explained in terms of the ordinary decorum of line length, common to Italy, France, and England, by which lines of up to eight syllables were usually regarded as unsuitable for serious matters, whereas pentameter and upwards was regarded as potentially grave. Thus the shortest lines of all, which the Elizabethans as well as ourselves knew as Skeltonics, were anathematized by Puttenham as the lowest and cheapest: "Such were the rimes of Skelton . . . being in deede but a rude rayling rimer and all his doings ridiculous, he used both short distaunces and short measures pleasing onely the popular eare" (p. 84). On the other hand Puttenham calls pentameter a "very stately and Heroicall" measure and states that hexameter is "for grave and stately matters fitter than for any other ditty of pleasure" (p. 72). Similarly, in 1619 Alexander Gil remarks that drama and epic have settled down, for the most part, with iambic pentameter, but "nevertheless Spenser's epic, or heroic poem, has each ninth line a hexameter, for the sake of gravity, and a firm foundation."[24]

What is odd, however, about this decorum in England is the extremes to which it is taken. As Thomas Campion realized, it was not necessary to go beyond the pentameter to find a sufficiently "artificial" medium for serious verse,[25] and reverence for classical poetry was sufficiently displayed in hexam-

[24] Alexander Gil, *Logonomia Anglica* (1621), ed. R. C. Alston, 1968, p. 142: "Scenicum, & Epicum, uno fere carminis genere contenta sunt: illud est ut plurimùm pentametrum. Spenceri tamen Epicum, sive Heroicum, novum quemque versum habet hexametrum; ad gravitatem, & quandam stationis firmitudinem.

[25] Thomas Campion, *Observations in the Art of English Poesie* (1602), in *Elizabethan Critical Essays*, II, 335: "Our English monasillables enforce many breathings which no doubt greatly lengthen a verse, so that it is no wonder if for these reasons our English verses of five feete hold pace with the Latines of sixe."

eters, as in France, or hendecasyllables in Italy. But the English interest in still longer lines, fourteeners, poulter's measure, and even sixteeners, is of such a perverse kind that it does not seem to be explained by either of these motives. Nor is it to be accounted for by the precepts of Ciceronian rhetoric, for Cicero defines the best period as consisting of not more than four *membra* or clauses, which should be neither too short nor too long, and suggests that each clause should roughly correspond in length with a hexameter verse (*Orator.* LXVI, 221-222); and the *Rhetorica ad Herennium* includes among the vices of style the use of over-long clauses or periods, which harm both the ears of the audience and the speaker's lungs (IV. xii, 18). Even Demetrius, who does recommend the use of long clauses in elevated passages, remarks: "We must not make our clauses very long, for then the sentence lacks measure and is hard to follow. Even poetry rarely ventures upon a meter which is longer than the hexameter, for it is absurd for meter to lack measure so that we forget where the verse began before we get to the end of it."[26]

In other words, the ordinary decorum of "measure" (which distinguishes, for example, Drayton's ode to Apollo from his ode to Cupid) takes in England an exaggerated turn for which there has been, so far, no explanation. It is true that once poulter's measure and fourteeners had been discovered by Wyatt and his successors, the long measures proved relatively easy for inferior poets to handle, and it is also true that they were useful for line-by-line translations from the more condensed Latin, as in Phaer and Golding. But why should Puttenham, who personally finds fourteeners highly tedious, feel obliged to admit that "yet may the meetre be very grave and stately" (p. 83), and why should Gabriel Harvey take the trouble to annotate his copy of Gascoigne's *Certayne Notes* to the effect that poulter's measure is suitable not only for "Psalmes and Himpnes," but also for "sum heroical discourse, or statelie argument"?[27] We know that Harvey knew and lectured on Hermogenes. In the absence of other explanation, we can account for the exaggeration of "measure" in terms

[26] *A Greek Critic: Demetrius on Style*, tr. Grube, p. 61.
[27] *Elizabethan Critical Essays*, I, 362.

of the Idea of Splendor, and its long Members, "quanto più lunghi, tanto più splendidi." The assumption is that, toward the end of the sixteenth century, the influence of Hermogenes came to bear on the English measures already in existence, and gave a special status, under the heading of Splendor, to the very long ones, a status which registers itself both in critical comments and in their continued use.

Perhaps the best proof that these long measures were still regarded as serious by many poets (several decades after they are usually supposed to have gone out of fashion) is the fact that they appear in funeral elegies, a practice still recorded by Alexander Gil in 1619.[28] The greatest of the "great occasions" of mourning was, among poets anyway, the death of Sidney himself, and accordingly it is mourned in long measures by Constable, Sir Edward Dyer, and Richard Barnfield.[29] The first is in hexameters, the second in poulter's measure, and the third in fourteener couplets, with occasional internal rhyme:

> That England lost, that Learning lov'd, that every
>   mouth commended,
> That fame did prayse, that Prince did rayse, that
>   Countrey so defended,
> Here lyes the man: lyke to the Swan, who knowing
>   shee shall die,
> Doeth tune her voice unto the Spheares, and scornes
>   Mortalitie.

Probably Sidney would have enjoyed this completely inappropriate artifice, for although he himself used the long measures occasionally for serious purposes (*Astrophil and Stella* contains

[28] Alexander Gil, *Logonomia Anglica*, p. 145: "Heptametrum prioris aetatis metafrastis Faiero, Goldingo, aliisque in usu erat: recentioribus raro solum est, sed in materia tristiori cum hexametro nonnunquam miscetur, in elegos."

[29] Henry Constable, *To Sir Philip Sydneyes soule*, in *Poems*, ed. Joan Grundy, 1960, p. 169; Sir Edward Dyer, "Silence augmenteth grief, writing encreaseth rage," published in 1595 in the collection of pastoral elegies which is named for Spenser's *Astrophel*; Richard Barnfield, from *Lady Pecunia*, in *Poems*, ed. Montague Summers, 1936.

a serious and quite unsingable "song" in fourteeners), he also explicitly parodies both the long measures and the language of elaborate praise. The *Arcadia* contains the *contreblazon* of the wench Mopsa, attributed significantly enough to Alethes, the truthful man, which begins:

> *What length of verse can serve* brave Mopsa's good
>   to show,
> Whose vertues strange, and beuties such, as no man
>   them may know?

(My italics)

It is coincidence that Sidney should thus parody in advance the laborious praises heaped on him after his death; but it is perhaps not coincidence that he should choose to mock the long measures which are never less splendid than when the object of praise is unworthy of it, and that he should give his speaker a Greek name which reminds us of ἀλήθεια or the Idea of Verity.

There is a clash between theory and the requirements of the vernacular here too, and perhaps the Elizabethans never realized how less than splendid the long measures sounded, even when their subject was genuinely praiseworthy. But, having noted this, this chapter ends with a poem which somehow manages to resolve this conflict, the poem for which the chapter is named. Yeats chose to write "High Talk" in lines of fifteen syllables, subsuming in one wild prosodic metaphor both the difficulties and triumphs of those who still attempt high talk:

> Processions that lack high stilts have nothing that
>   catches the eye.
> What if my great granddad had a pair that were
>   twenty foot high,
> *And mine were but fifteen foot,* no modern stalks
>   upon higher.

(My italics)

The advantage of ending a chapter with Yeats's "processions" is that, unlike Auden's "great occasions," they are not entirely a thing of the past.

CHAPTER 4

"Savage Indignation": *Elizabethan Satire*

> Swift beating on his breast in sibylline frenzy blind . . .
> *Saeva Indignatio* and the labourer's hire.
> (William Butler Yeats, *Blood and the Moon*)*

AGAIN and again the poetry of Yeats, itself highly decorous, provides points of instruction or focus in discussions of earlier poetry, because Yeats always ascends to the creative tower by an "ancestral stair." For Yeats, Jonathan Swift was both an inspiration and an emblem, partly because of his Irishness, but mostly because of his anger; and in the lines quoted above Yeats identifies Swift as the type of Juvenalian satirist whose work is prophetically inspired, and whose inspiration is rage. The reason for quoting these lines here is that this chapter will explore the Juvenalian tradition of satire in the Renaissance, and will claim a direct causal link between the *style* of Juvenalian satire in England and the Ideas of Reproof defined by Hermogenes—Asperity, Vehemence, and Vigor, which are the negative side of the Idea of Grandeur.

Instead of using the method of other chapters (to describe the Ideas first and then find poetry that seems to fit them), it is best here to turn first to Elizabethan satire, and suggest why it seems to require more explanation than it has yet been given.[1] A useful place to start is with the invocation which

---

* From *Collected Poems*, William Butler Yeats. Reprinted by permission of Macmillan Co.

[1] The major discussions of Elizabethan satire are those of Hallet Smith, in *Elizabethan Poetry* (1952), pp. 194-256; John Peter, *Complaint and Satire in Early English Literature* (1956); Alvin Kernan, *The Cankered Muse: Satire of the English Renaissance* (1959); and A. F. Caputi, *John Marston, Satirist* (1961). None of these critics feels fully able to account for the sudden change, both in tone and style, which takes place in satire in the last decade of the sixteenth century. The reasons given, whether sociological (urbanization creates new social evils), literary (a stronger and more systematic interest in Juvenal), or psychological (the influence of Marston's obsessive personality) are both partial and tentative. In this chapter I hope to present a fourth—a

begins the ninth satire of John Marston's *Scourge of Villanie*, an invocation in which Marston personifies the concept of Reproof as the Satirist's Muse, and speaks in terms of an inspiration close to "sibylline frenzy":

> Grim-fac'd *Reproofe*, sparkle with threatning eye
> Bend thy sower browes in my tart poesie.
> Avant yee curres, houle in some cloudie mist,
> Quake to behold a sharp-fang'd Satyrist.
> O how on tiptoes proudly mounts my Muse,
> Stalking a loftier gate then Satyres use.
> Me thinkes some sacred rage warmes all my vaines,
> Making my spright mount up to higher straines . . .[2]

What is clear from this passage, beyond his conviction of inspiration, is that Marston is not sure whether the decorum of satire permits the kind of style he wishes to use. The reason for his uncertainty is that the three traditions which lie behind Renaissance thinking on satire are not only somewhat confused in themselves, but contradictory when brought together.

These traditions are: first, that satire takes its character from the personality of the rough and hairy satyrs of early Greek drama—a notion which was based on false etymology; second, that one could learn to write satire by imitating the classical satirists—a notion which ignores the vast difference between Horace and Juvenal; and third, that satire is a low genre, conventionally written in the *genus humile*, the third of Cicero's Three Styles. This third tradition has been accepted as axiomatic by some modern critics, though it is the least well documented, and although most Elizabethan satirists pay little more than lip service to it. It is clear that these three

---

rhetorical reason for the change both in tone and style, which is intended to reinforce, rather than replace these other hypotheses.

[2] Marston, *The Scourge of Villanie*, ix, in *Poems*, ed. A. Davenport, 1961, p. 158. In the same satire, Marston attacks one Mutius, probably Joseph Hall, for his less than serious satire: "How il me thought such wanton Jigging skips/Beseem'd his graver speech . . ." (p. 159). It should be noted, however, that in the eleventh satire of the *Scourge*, Marston dismisses "Grim Reproofe," the muse of high satire, and invokes instead a more comic inspiration.

traditions cannot be combined successfully; if a poet felt able to blend the rustic crudity of satyr speech with the highly civilized savage indignation of Juvenal, he would be the less able to make them lie down conceptually with the third style, characteristically described by Puttenham as a "low, myld, and simple maner of utterance, creeping rather than clyming."[3] It is obvious that Marston, who identifies himself at times with both Juvenal and the satyrs, is carefully dissociating himself, in the invocation to Reproof, from the third or Low style, and claiming to operate in the first, or High style. It is significant also that for the second satire of the *Scourge* Marston chooses Juvenal's motto, "It is difficult to refrain from writing satire" [Difficile est Satiram non scribere] since this motto stands for (and considerably understates) the uncontrollable aspect of the Juvenalian approach, in which the wickedness of the times puts the poet into a divine frenzy of recrimination, similar to the inspiration which elevates the epic poet. This aspect of Juvenal's influence was recognized by English poets from Skelton onwards, and Skelton actually includes the same motto in *Why Come Ye Not to Court?*:

> I am forcibly constrained
> At Juvenal's request
> To write of this geste
>
> . . .
>
> *Quia difficile est*
> *Satiram non scribere*![4]

Nothing could be further from this frenetic approach to satire than the urbanity of Horace, whose work naturally coincides with the notion that satire belongs in the third style, and from whose work, very probably, this "rule" developed. It is by no means easy to discover by whom, and at what stage, satire was placed in the *genus humile*. Rosemond Tuve accepts this placing, presumably on the basis of Francesco

---

[3] George Puttenham, *Arte of English Poesie*, ed. G. Willcock and A. Walker, 1936, p. 152.
[4] John Skelton, *Complete Poems*, ed. Philip Henderson, 1959, p. 343.

Elizabethan Satire

Sansovino's *Discorso in materia della satira* (1560),[5] and Wesley Trimpi cites the *De Satyra Horatiana* of Heinsius and the definition of satire by Minturno in the *De Poeta* (1559), both of which advocate a plain and relatively simple approach according to the Horatian ideal.[6] But Minturno, in the later *Arte Poetica* (1564), distinguishes between the cautious darting reproof of Horace and the wide-open, harsher approach of Juvenal, who spreads "a full sail of anger."[7] And even Heinsius, in propagating the Horatian ideal as fully as he can, has continually to admit that neither Juvenal nor Persius lived up to it, both of them being more audaciously grandiloquent than his theory will admit.

Most of the Elizabethan satirists make passing reference to the Horatian ideal, or a "low" concept of satire, and then proceed with the contemporary fashion for its opposite. It might perhaps be argued that in Marston the satirist's sense of elevation at his vision of evil is only temporary, a permissible breaking of generic decorum under stronger pressures, and thus parallel to the momentary elevation in pastoral of the shepherd who may soar at a vision of beauty.[8] But such an argument could not apply to the satires of Everard Guilpin, which were published together with his epigrams under the title of *Skialetheia* (1598). Guilpin carefully distinguishes the low and comic epigram from the high and serious satire; the epigram is a "quick Couranto of [his] merry Muse," while the satire "hath a nobler vaine." The satire is analogous, in its ability to punish, to Hell, whereas the epigram is merely

[5] Rosemond Tuve, *Elizabethan and Metaphysical Imagery*, 1947, p. 241.

[6] Wesley Trimpi, *Ben Jonson's Poems: A Study of the Plain Style*, 1962, pp. 12-19, 79-83.

[7] Minturno, *Arte Poetica*, p. 272: "De' quali Giovenale con tanto più spiegate vele per lo mare dello sdegno si lascia andare."

[8] See, for example, Spencer's *Colin Clouts Come Home Againe*, ll. 616-621:

> Colin (said *Cuddy* then) thou hast forgot
> Thy selfe, me seemes, too much, to mount so hie:
> Such loftie flight, base shepheard seemeth not,
> From flocks and fields, to Angels and to skie.
> True (answered he) but her great excellence,
> Lifts me above the measure of my might . . .

Bridewell, the corrective of less mortal but more human errors. Satire is the "Tamberlaine of vice"; and Guilpin's style does indeed make it clear that this concept is translatable into style, at least at times:

> Oh that mens thoughts should so degenerate,
> Being free borne, t'admit a slavish state:
> They disclaime Natures manumission,
> Making themselves bond to opinion:
> Whose gally-slaves they are, tost on the sea
> Of vulgar humors, which doth rage and play,
> According as the various breath of change
> Calmes or perturbs her smooth brow. Is't not strang[e]
> That heav'n bred soules, discended from above
> Should brooke such base subiection? . . .[9]

One of the reasons given by Wesley Trimpi for the "low" tradition of satire is that its origins were close to those of Greek comedy. The alternative association is, of course, with Greek tragedy, and the satyr plays which were known to have accompanied them. The definition of a distinctly tragic genre of satire was made explicitly by John Dryden in *The Original and Progress of Satire* in 1692.[10] But Renaissance satirists occasionally go out of their way to emphasize a nonhumorous

[9] Everard Guilpin, *Skialetheia or A Shadowe of Truth* (1598), Shakespeare Association Facsimiles, No. 2, 1931, D7v-8r.

[10] Dryden, *A Discourse Concerning the Original and Progress of Satire*, in *Poetical Works*, ed. Joseph Warton, 1811, IV, 260: "What disreputation is it to Horace, that Juvenal excels in the tragic satire as Horace does in the comical." Dryden also takes direct issue with one of Trimpi's major sources, and quotes the definition of satire in the *De Satyra Horatiana* of Heinsius, in order to defy it (pp. 265-266):

> I cannot but observe, that this obscure and perplexed definition, or rather description, of satire, is wholly accommodated to the Horatian way; and excluding the works of Juvenal and Persius, as foreign from that kind of poem. . . . But how come lowness of style, and the familiarity of words, to be so much the propriety of satire, that without them a poet can be no more a satirist, then without risibility he can be a man? Is the fault of Horace to be made the virtue and standing rule of this poem? Is the *grande sophos* of Persius, and the sublimity of Juvenal, to be circumscribed with the meanness of words and vulgarity of expression?

approach. So Donne rejects laughter at the beginning of his fifth Satire:

> Thou shalt not laugh in this leafe, Muse, nor they
> Whom any pitty warmes; He which did lay
> Rules to make Courtiers, (hee being understood
> May make good Courtiers, but who Courtiers good?)
> Frees from the sting of jests all who in extreme
> Are wreched or wicked: of these two a theame
> Charity and liberty give me. What is hee
> Who Officers rage, and Suiters misery
> Can write, and jest?[11]

In prose satire, too, there is Thomas Nashe, and his mocking self-definition in *Nashes Lenten Stuffe* (1599):

> Let me speake to you about my huge woords which I use in this booke, and then you are your own men to do what you list. Know it is my true vaine to be *tragicus Orator*, and of all stiles I most affect & strive to imitate Aretines, not caring for this demure soft *mediocre genus*, that is like water and wine mixt together; but give me pure wine of it self, & that begets good bloud, and heates the brain throowly.[12]

Even when the associations of satire are comic it is possible to have elevation both of style and attitude, if we are to judge from Ben Jonson, who subtitled *Every Man Out of his Humour* (1599) a "Comicall Satyre," but brings on as his Prologue the character of Asper. Asper stands for the Juvenalian inability to hold silence and for the inflated approach to diction and metaphor, both of which show up clearly in this speech:

> Who is so patient of this impious world,
> That he can checke his spirit, or reine his tongue?
> Or who hath such a dead unfeeling sense,
> That heavens horrid thunders cannot wake?
> To see the earth, crackt with the weight of sinne,

[11] John Donne, *Poems*, ed. H.J.C. Grierson, 1963, I, 168.
[12] Nashe, *Nashes Lenten Stuffe* in *Works*, ed. R. B. McKerrow, 1958, III, 152.

Hell gaping under us, and o're our heads
Blacke rav'nous ruine, with her saile-stretch wings,
Ready to sinke us downe, and cover us.
Who can behold such prodigies as these
And have his lips seal'd up? not I; my language
Was never ground into such oyly colours,
To flatter vice and daube iniquitie:
But (with an armed, and resolved hand)
Ile strip the ragged follies of the time,
Naked, as at their birth . . .[13]

One is left wondering which satirists did exemplify the
tradition that satire was a humble genre, written in a style
which was simple and unmetaphoric, if permissibly pointed.
It seems that the only obviously "lowly" satires, apart from
those of Joseph Hall, are closely connected with pastoral, such
as Spenser's, or those of Thomas Lodge, whose *Fig for Momus*
(1595) mixes together satires, eclogues, and epistles, until it
is virtually impossible, without the titles, to tell which are
which. The satires of Hall are in a different category. Hall
frequently refers to the genre as "lowly," and admits that his
own is a "quiet stile." But, as Caputi points out, Hall attributes the simplicity of his own style at least partly to failure,
and would have done differently had he not been hampered
by the vernacular in his attempt to imitate Juvenal:

My Muse would follow them that have foregone,
But cannot with an English pineon.[14]

The unfortunate fellow had the fate so often reserved for
pioneers, that of being slated for incompetence by those who
later profited from his experiments, and perhaps Hall deserved
this more than some, for his satires show obvious signs of his
not having worked things out in advance. He wants his satires
to be simultaneously lowly, and hairy, and Juvenalian; and as
a result is continually having to admit failure. Marston ob-

[13] Jonson, *Every Man Out of his Humour*, in *Works*, ed. C. H. Hereford
and P. Simpson, III, 428.

[14] A. F. Caputi, *John Marston, Satirist*, p. 44. The lines from Hall come
from the Prologue to *Virgidemiarum*, III, Satire 1.

jects strongly to Hall's "tricksie lerned nicking straine," which he describes by the Latin motto, *Non laedere, sed ludere, non lanea, sed linea, non ictus, sed nictus potius* [Not harmful, but playful, not homespun, but fine spun, not striking, but nicking rather].[15] And Milton, who thought himself at one time provoked by Hall, interrupts the debate on church reform by a violent attack on anyone who could be foolish enough to put forward the idea of "toothless satires":

> Which for him who would be counted the first English Satyr, to abase himselfe to, who might have learned better among the Latin, and Italian Satyrists, and in our own tongue from the vision and Creed of Pierce plowman . . . manifested a presumptuous undertaking with weak, and unexamin'd shoulders. . . . *For a Satyr as it was borne out of a Tragedy, so ought to resemble his parentage, to strike high*, and adventure dangerously at the most eminent vices among the greatest persons, and not to creepe into every blinde Taphouse that fears a Constable more than a Satyr.[16]

Hall's problem is partly that he has failed to separate, even in intention, the two main streams of satire, the comic and Horatian from the tragic and Juvenalian (and it is possible that the separation was not clearly made until Dryden's *Original and Progress of Satire*). But it is also because he finds himself, by his own admission, unable to reproduce Juvenal's effects in the vernacular. Milton accuses him of ignoring the precedents available both at home and abroad, and Hall admits in his "Post-script to the Reader" that, apart from the satires of Ariosto, he "could never attaine the view of any for [his] direction."[17] But a far more valuable source for consultation on technique, as Milton must have been aware, were the continental critics, especially Minturno and Scaliger. In Scaliger and Minturno, as also in lesser Italian critics, there are instructions for developing a Juvenalian style; that is, a style

[15] Marston, *Poems*, p. 159.

[16] John Milton, *Works*, III, 329. (My italics)

[17] Joseph Hall, "A Post-script to the Reader," in *Poems*, ed. A. Davenport, 1949, p. 99.

which corresponds roughly to that of Juvenal or Persius in Latin, and exactly to that of the Juvenalian satires in English of Marston, Guilpin, and Donne. But the instructions as to how to create these effects are not to be found, as one might expect, under discussions of classical satire. They are to be found instead under the very different heading of the Neoplatonic Ideas of Hermogenes, and in particular the Ideas of Reproof.

The three Ideas of Reproof may be translated as Asperity, Vehemence, and Vigor, and all three are subcategories of the Idea of Grandeur. Asperity ($\tau\rho\alpha\chi\acute{\upsilon}\tau\eta s$) is to be used when reproving someone of superior rank, or at least someone to whom one cannot with impunity be rude. Thus, says Sturm, Asperity is appropriate for Ulysses when reproving Achilles, or for the populace when reproving the orator, but not for the orator who wishes to reprove the populace (p. 149). In that situation, or others where greater freedom of expression is required, the style called for is Vehemence ($\sigma\phi o\delta\rho\acute{o}\tau\eta s$). With Vehemence one reproves equals, inferiors, or known criminals and enemies of the state, and obvious examples from forensic oratory are Cicero's orations against Catiline (pp. 161-163). Vehemence consists mainly in exaggerating all the attitudes and characteristics of Asperity, and they are differentiated from the third style of Reproof, $\dot{\alpha}\kappa\mu\acute{\eta}$ or Vigor, by being curt in their approach, whereas Vigor is expansive.

The Sentence in both Asperity and Vehemence consists in the objects of the attack, and the Method is to be straightforward, especially in Vehemence. The appropriate diction is more easily recognizable than in other Ideas, consisting of words which are harsh either in sound or in meaning, or both. Parthenio gives a list of words and phrases which he regards as harsh, and which prove to have been taken from the sonnets in which Petrarch vents his anger at the division of the papacy, sonnets which are also used by Minturno as illustrative of these Ideas.[18] The third of these sonnets (*Rime* cxxxviii)

[18] Bernadino Parthenio, *Della Imitatione Poetica*, 1560, pp. 203-207. Antonio Minturno, *Arte Poetica*, 1563, pp. 431-432: "L'Aspra, e molesta . . . usasi, quando il Senato, ò pur il Rè, overo alcuna persona, la qual'haver sì debba in

is worth quoting as an illustration both of the style of address and the sound-structures appropriate to Asperity and Vehemence, the words and phrases in italics being those picked out by Parthenio as definitive of these Ideas:

Fontana di dolore, albergo d'ira,
Scola d'errori, e templo d'eresia,
Giá Roma, or Babilonia falsa e ria,
Per cui tanto si piange e si sospira;
O fucina d'inganni, o *pregion dira*,
Ove 'l ben more, e'l mal si *nutre* e *cria*,
Di vivi *inferno*, un *gran miracol fia*
Se Cristo teco al fine non s'adira.
Fondata in casta et umil povertate,
Contr'a' tuoi fondatori alzi le corna,
Putta sfacciata: e dove hai posto spene?
Ne gli adúlteri tuoi? Ne le mal nate
Richezze tante? Or Constantin non torna;
Ma tolga il mondo tristo che'l sostene.

[Fountain of sorrow, dwelling-place of wrath, school of errors and temple of heresy, once Rome, now Babylon false and wicked, through whom there has been so much weeping and sighing; O forge of fraudulence, o cruel prison, where the good perish, the bad flourish and cry aloud, Hell of the living, it will be a great marvel if Christ's wrath does not descend on you in the end. Founded on chaste and humble poverty, against your founders you lift up your horn, shameless strumpet: in what do you place your hope? In your adulteries? In so much ill-gotten wealth? Constantine will not now return; let the miserable world which sustained him also disappear.]

It is clear that Parthenio picked out words like "nutre" and "miracol" for their harshness of sound alone, whereas "Putta sfacciata" unites unpleasantness of sound and meaning. Sturm adds the precise comment that the consonants most desired in producing Asperity are those which are most difficult for

riverenza, apertamente, sì riprende con severità di sentenze . . . quali eran quei quattro Sonetti del Petrarca, che la santitâ del Signor nostro Papa Paolo Quarto par ragionevolmente haver voluto, che de Canzoniere si tolgano."

children to pronounce, *r*, *p*, *t*, or their Greek equivalents, and especially *r*, the snarling letter (*"canina litera"*).[19]

The Figures recommended by Hermogenes for Asperity are powerful apostrophes and rhetorical questions and irony, all of which are only too obvious in the sonnet by Petrarch just quoted; but in the Vehement style one may in addition use the Figure of *Indicatio*, that is, one may attack one's victim with pronouns (*hic, iste, ille*), which are denigrating by their rejection of personality as well as by their brevity. Their use is one of the devices which distinguish Vehemence from the more dignified approach of Asperity. In both styles the Members or phrases must be short, in Vehemence extremely so, to give the impression of uncontrollable indignation proceeding by outbursts. Scaliger recommends short questions like *Quis? Quid? Cur? Tu?* and phrases as jabbing as punches (*quasi pugiones*, p. 483). Hermogenes insists that one must avoid any impression of rhythm, smoothness, or pleasant sound, presumably because by the offense to their ears the audience is stirred up to reject both the criminal and the crime; the object is actually to "exasperate" them. Presumably the speaker should be able to disassociate himself from the unpleasantness, and make it clear that his own dignity and moral fiber are unimpaired by contact with pitch, and that if given an honorable subject matter, his speech would immediately again become harmonious and controlled.

The third style of Reproof, Vigor, differs, as we have said, by being expansive where the others are concise. In the style of Vigor, as Minturno puts it, one can attack more ornately and more copiously (pp. 432-433), since it uses the Sentence and Method of Asperity in combination with the long phrases and periods of its conceptual opposite, Splendor, the style of panegyric. Minturno cites, as an example of Vigor in action,

[19] There appears to be a traditional connection between "the dog's letter" and the satiric mind. In Barclay's *Ship of Fools* (ed. T. H. Jamieson, 1874, I, 182), we find the remark that "This man malycious whiche troubled is with wrath/Nought els soundeth but the hoorse letter R." John Aubrey in his *Lives* passes on Dryden's comment that Milton himself "pronounced the letter R very hard (*littera canina*). A certain sign of a satirical wit."

the sonnet in which Petrarch attacks and defeats Death for
its partial victory over Laura (*Rime*, cccxxvi):

> Or hai fatto l'estremo di tua possa,
> O crudel Morte; or hai'l regno d'Amore
> Impoverito; or di bellezza il fiore,
> E'l lume, hai spento, e chiuso in poca fossa;
> Or hai spogliata nostra vita, e scossa,
> D'ogni ornamento, e del sovran suo onore:
> Ma la fama e'l valor, che mai non more,
> Non è in tua forza: abbiti ignude l'ossa.

[Now you have done the utmost of your power, O cruel
Death; now you have robbed the kingdom of love; now you
have taken the flower of beauty, and put out its light, and
closed it in a narrow grave; now you have despoiled our life,
and shaken from it every ornament, and its sovereign honor:
but fame and valor that shall never die are not within your
power: you have but the bare bones.]

In this useful "example" Vigor is seen to be a relaxed form
of Reproof, based on the kind of conviction that allows a
more leisurely development of the list of crimes, in this case
the conviction that Death the robber is actually the loser. One
might follow Minturno's example and identify as Vigor the
style of Donne's very similar sonnet, "Death be not proud,
though some have called thee/Mighty and dreadfull," and
contrast it to the obviously Vehement sonnet which follows
it in his Divine Poems, "Spit in my face you Jewes, and pierce
my side,/Buffet, and scoffe, scourge, and crucifie mee"; or
one might take Sidney's attack on Desire in *Certain Sonnets*
and show how it modulates from a Vehement opening into
Asperity and ends in the expansive parallel reproaches of
Vigor:

> Thou blind man's marke, thou foole's selfe chosen snare,
> Fond fancie's scum, and dregs of scattred thought,
> Band of all evils, cradle of causelesse care,
> Thou web of will, whose end is never wrought;
> Desire, desire I have too dearely bought,

With price of mangled mind thy worthlesse ware,
Too long, too long asleepe thou hast me brought,
Who should my mind to higher things prepare.
But yet in vaine thou hast my ruine sought,
In vaine thou madest me to vaine things aspire,
In vaine thou kindlest all thy smokie fire;
For vertue hath this better lesson taught,
Within my selfe to seeke my onely hire:
Desiring nought but how to kill desire.[20]

Such "examples" of formal Reproof are easy to find, in English poetry as in Italian; but there is one literary phenomenon so startling in its likeness to these recommendations that one wonders how it could have been missed. The likeness is between the Ideas of Reproof, especially Vehemence, and that peculiar development of late sixteenth-century poetry in England, the so-called formal verse satire. The descriptions of the Ideas of Reproof match virtually word for word the descriptions of the style of Marston, Guilpin, and Donne. So Alvin Kernan remarks that "the most obvious quality of [Marston's] lines is their rugged, uneven progression which is achieved by the use of a number of devices: short phrases or words which break up the flow . . . difficult and harsh words . . . prosaic phrases . . . and a high proportion of monosyllabic words."[21] Similarly Caputi says of Marston that "to produce harshness he used long compound nouns, abrupt phrases, catalogues of epithets, elisions, combinations of plosive consonants, and extreme dislocations in the metrical pattern."[22] The style they describe is found in its extreme form in Marston's *Scourge of Villanie*, at the beginning of the first satire:

Marry God forfend, Marius swears he'le stab,
Phrigeo, feare not, thou art no lying drab.
What though dagger hack'd mouthes of his blade sweares
It slew as many as figures of yeares

20 Philip Sidney, *Poems*, ed. W. A. Ringler, Jr., p. 161.
21 Alvin Kerman, *The Cankered Muse*, p. 97.
22 A. F. Caputi, *John Marston, Satirist*, p. 44.

Aqua fortis eate in't, or as many more,
As methodist Musus, kild with Hellebore . . .

Moreover there are just as useful examples in Donne, as, for
example, at the opening of this fourth satire:

Well; I may now receive, and die; My sinne
Indeed is great, but I have beene in
A Purgatorie, such as fear'd hell is
A recreation to, and scarse map of this.
My minde, neither with prides itch, nor yet hath been
Poyson'd with love to see, or to bee seene,
I had not suit there, nor new suite to shew,
Yet went to Court; But as Glaze which did goe
To'a Masse in jest, catch'd, was faine to disburse
The hundred markes, which is the Statutes curse;
Before he scapt, So'it pleas'd my destinie
(Guilty of my sin of going,) to thinke me
As prone to all ill, and of good as forget-
full, as proud, as lustfull, and as much in debt,
As vaine, as witlesse, and as false as they
Which dwell at Court . . .

It is surely more than a coincidence that effects like these
(which suddenly appeared in England in the 1590's) should
follow instructions for writing under the Ideas of Reproof,
instructions which were current in Italy from about 1560 to
1590, and which were also available in Sturm's 1571 edition
of Hermogenes. Under the headings of Asperity, Vigor, and
especially of Vehemence, English poets could find descriptions of *high* styles of Reproof, already associated with the
elevation they admired in Juvenal and Persius, and, in addition, already partly assimilated to the problems of the vernacular languages. In fact, Sturm's commentary on Hermogenes
explicitly links the styles of Juvenal and Persius with the
Ideas of Asperity and Vehemence. Sturm points out that the
best examples of the diction of both Asperity and Vehemence
are to be found among the satiric poets, especially Persius.[23]

[23] Johannes Sturm, *Scholae . . . De Formis Orationum*, 1571, p. 163:

This is one indication of how Renaissance writers might have made the natural connection between satire and the Ideas of Reproof. One might see another in the fact that Ben Jonson gave the respectable satirist in *Every Man Out of his Humour* the name of Asper, the style of Asperity, and described him as being "an ingenious and free spirit, eager and constant in reproofe, without feare controuling the world's abuses."[24] Jonson, however, disapproved strongly of Vehemence, if we are to judge by his treatment of Marston in the *Poetaster*, and the way in which Marston, as Crispinus, is there punished for his bombast and his lack of "modesty."[25]

There is also evidence of the same connection between satire and the Ideas of Reproof in the controversial prose of

---

"Neque nos meliora vocabula possumus invenire, quàm apud Satyrico Poëtas: maximè verò apud Persium: qui . . . valde vehemens est."

[24] Jonson, *Works*, III, 423. Asper's opening words in the speech already quoted, "Who is so patient of this impious world," are a direct translation of Juvenal's first satire: "nam quis iniquae tam patiens urbis." This adds to the impression that he is Jonson's representative of the high and tragic satirist, as compared to the two other satirical figures in the same play, Macilente, the malcontent, and Carlo Buffone, whom Jonson describes as "a Publike, scurrilous, and prophane Jester." As Hallet Smith suggests (*Elizabethan Poetry*, pp. 254-256) this analysis of the satiric personality into three different types shows Jonson's awareness of the need for dignity and impersonality in satire; but it also shows, I think, Jonson's awareness of the difference between high and low satire.

[25] Jonson, *Works*, IV, 304-315. In this play, as compared to *Every Man Out of his Humour*, there is no formal approval given to the Juvenalian satirist, but only to the Horatian one, whose position is defined as anger controlled by *modesty* and free from personal malice, p. 301:

> Tis not the wholesome sharpe moralitie,
> Or modest anger of a satyricke spirit,
> That hurts, or wounds the bodie of a state;
> But the sinister application
> Of the malicious, ignorant and base
> Interpreter . . .

It is more than likely that Jonson has here used "modesty" as a rhetorical term, as Milton understood it and resented its use in the title of *A Modest Confutation*, and that he, like Milton, sees Modesty as being opposed to Vehemence.

Milton, but where Jonson attacks the overvehement style of Marston, Milton is concerned to defend himself against a similar charge. In the same pamphlet in which Milton attacks Hall for his low concept of satire, and defines his own lofty concept of the genre, he defends his own diction and tone in controversy by naming it "vehemence" and by giving various different justifications for its use. If, he says, it were merely a stylistic question "whether a vehement vein throwing out indignation, or scorn upon an object that merits it, were among the aptest *Ideas* of speech to be allow'd, it were my work, and that an easie one to make it cleare both by the rules of best rhetoricians, and the famousest examples of the Greek and Roman Orations."[26] Since the italicization of *Ideas* is Milton's own, and since he recommended the study of Hermogenes in *Of Education*, we can be reasonably sure of the derivation of his concept of Vehemence.[27] But since, he says, "the Religion of it is disputed, and not the art," he provides religious justifications also. Luther "writ so vehemently against the chief defenders of old untruths" because he was temperamentally incapable of moderation. And even God himself, "who is the author both of purity and eloquence," can occasionally be found using shocking language, "as fittest in that vehement character wherein he spake." Also, in the *Reason of Church Government*, Milton cites the additional precedent of Jeremiah and his inability to keep silence under the strain of prophetic zeal, an interesting parallel to the Juvenalian outburst. Jeremiah cried aloud, because he was "weary with forbearing, and could not stay." Which might, Milton says, "teach these times not suddenly to condemn all things that are sharply spoken, or vehe-

[26] Milton, *An Apology for Smectymnuus*, in *Works*, III, 312.

[27] T. Kranidas, in "Decorum and the Style of Milton's Anti-Prelatical Tracts," *SP*, LXII (1945), 176-187, suggests that Milton's concept of Vehemence comes from Demetrius and his "forcible" style. But D. L. Clark, in "John Milton and 'the fitted stile of lofty, mean, or lowly,' " *Seventeenth-Century News*, XI (1953), 5-9, draws the same conclusion that I do, that Milton's reference to Ideas is a specific reference to the Hermogenic theory of style. Compare also J. Milton French, "Milton as Satirist," *PMLA*, LI (1936), 414-429.

mently written."[28] In other words, Milton associated Vehemence with satire, and both with religious controversy.

This defense of Vehemence in a religious context is of further interest since there were writers who took the opposite side and maintained that religious causes had nothing to gain from a satirical tone. In the first place, there is the opinion of Francis Bacon, one of the authorities Milton is concerned to defend himself against in the *Apology*. Bacon, in *An Advertisement Touching the Controversies in the Church of England*, remarks that

> Indeed, bitter and earnest writing may not hastily be condemned; for men cannot contend coldly and without affection about things which they hold dear and precious. . . . But to leave all reverent and religious compassion towards evils, or indignation towards faults, and to turn religion into a comedy or satire . . . to intermix Scripture and scurrility sometime in one sentence; is a thing far from the devout reverence of a Christian, and scant beseeming the honest regard of a sober man.[29]

Similarly, Robert Burton defends himself uneasily against the charge that in the *Anatomy of Melancholy* he has been too satirical for a Divine.[30] Thomas Nashe, at the beginning of *Christ's Teares over Jerusalem* (1593) bids a "hundred unfortunate farwels to fantasticall Satirisme," and declares in-

---

[28] Milton, *Reason of Church Government*, in *Works*, III, 231. See also the *Pro Se Defensio*, in *Works*, IX, 109: "And if I have uttered naked words in your reproach, I should be at no loss to defend myself by the practice of gravest authors; who have always been of opinion, that words naked and plain, indignantly uttered, have a meaning far different from obscenity—that they express *the utmost vehemence of reproof*." (My italics) In this treatise also Milton claims that "modesty" and "vehemence" of speech are not incompatible if the motives of the speaker are pure: "If, indeed, this maxim of the orator be just and commendable, that modesty and severity are compatible in the same countenance, why, in like manner, should they not be compatible in the same mouth? The modesty of no modest person is impaired by a vehement and galling reprobation" (p. 183).

[29] Francis Bacon, in *Works*, ed. J. Spedding et al., I, 76-77.

[30] Robert Burton, *The Anatomy of Melancholy*, ed. F. Dell and P. J. Smith, 1927, p. 102.

stead for a new kind of "living vehemence," to come from rejecting rhetorical skill and becoming instead the "pure and simple Orator" of Christ.[31]

But the Divine who shows most uneasiness, in retrospect, over the language and attitudes of reproof is the one who may very well have been responsible for the development of satirical vehemence in the 1590's, and that is Donne, in his later role of Dean of St. Paul's. Donne, in his sermons, frequently remembers, it would seem, his earlier satirical enterprises, and seeks to deny their premises. In one sermon, preaching on the text "Take heed what you hear," he warns his congregation:

> Come not so neare evill speaking, as to delight to heare them, that delight to speake evill of Superiours. . . . We make *Satyrs*; and we looke that the world should call that *wit*; when God knowes, that that is in a great part, self-guiltinesse, and we doe but reprehend those things, which we our selves have done, we cry out upon the illnesse of the times, and we make the times ill.[32]

Similarly, he remarks in another sermon that reproof can go bad in the wrong hands, for "a malicious man will turne a Sermon to a Satyre, and a Panegyricke to a Libel" (v, 332); while on the other hand, he says, the gentle and constructive reproof administered by the Holy Ghost reverses the process, and "makes a Satyr, and Slander, and Libell against me, a Panegyrique, and an Elogy in my praise" (vi, 316).

These last two sermons are, moreover, among those in which Donne appears to be taking issue with one of the satirist's chief terms, our central word "reproof." This is the term personified by Marston at the beginning of the ninth satire of the *Scourge*, which is now, for convenience, repeated:

> Grim-fac'd *Reproofe*, sparkle with threatning eye
> Bend thy sower browes in my tart poesie.
> Avant yee curres, houle in some cloudie mist,

---

[31] Thomas Nashe, in *Works*, ed. R. B. McKerrow, ii, 12, 15-16.
[32] Donne, *Sermons*, ed. G. R. Potter and E. M. Simpson, vii, 408.

Quake to behold a sharp-fang'd Satyrist.
O how on tiptoes proudly mounts my Muse,
Stalking a loftier gate then Satyres use.
Me thinkes some sacred rage warmes all my vaines,
Making my spright mount up to higher straines . . .

In this invocation, Marston not only identifies his Reproof
with the elevation of high style, but he also dignifies it with
the words "sacred rage." Donne, in his sermons, had continually to grapple with the implications of sacred rage in
biblical terms, and he had, also, to grapple with the fact that
the three duties of the preacher had been defined as to reprove, to exhort, and to rebuke. Again and again he worries
about the abuse of these duties by authoritarian and inclem-
ent speakers. The Whitsunday sermon preached on the text
"And when he is come, he will reprove the world of sin,"
devotes much of its space to a redefinition of reproof according to St. Augustine:

> This word, that is here translated *To reprove, Arguere,*
> hath a double use and signification in the Scriptures. First
> to reprehend, to rebuke, to correct, with Authority, with
> Severity. . . . And secondly, to convince, to prove, to make
> a thing evident, by undeniable inferences, and necessary
> consequences; So, in the instructions of Gods Ministers, the
> first is *To reprove,* and then *To rebuke*; So that reproving is
> an act of a milder sense, then rebuking is. . . . That reprov-
> ing then, which is warrantable by the Holy Ghost, is not a
> sharp increpation, a bitter proceeding, proceeding onely out
> of power, and authority, but by inlightning, and informing,
> and convincing the understanding. . . . A reproofe, is a
> proofe, a proofe by way of argument, against another man,
> who holds a contrary opinion . . . and after all this, the re-
> proofe must lie in argument, not in force, not in violence.
>
> (VI, 317-318)

This position is repeated frequently enough[33] to give some sub-

[33] See *Sermons* V, 332: "This word that is here to Rebuke, Jacach, is for
the most part, to Reprove, to Convince by way of argument." And again,
Sermons VII, 215: "Therefore this word, Reproof, admitting a double signifi-

stance to the suspicion that this is rather a hobbyhorse of Donne's. His anxiety is partly a pragmatic one, for, in the context of religious controversy, a satirical vehemence is likely to do more harm than good. So he remarks, using the metaphor of healing common to both satires and sermons, that "Physitians may catch the plague by going about to cure it. An over-vehement, and unseasonable reprehender of a sinne may contract that, or a greater sin himselfe. . . . There is a religious abstinence, in not answering our Adversaries, though their libels, and increpations, and contumelies tend to the dishonour of God" (IX, 284).

Surely this position is a deliberate answer to the Juvenalian pose of involuntary outbursts and "sacred rage." Where Milton cites Jeremiah ("I was weary with forbearing, and could not stay") as a precedent for "things that are sharply spoken, or vehemently written," Donne cites St. Ambrose's observation about David, that "Though it troubled him, hee could hold his peace, when his reply might exasperate others" (IX, 284). Milton, of course, was writing ten years later than Donne, and the connection, if there is one, must be in the nature of a counterrevolution, so to speak. That is, Donne is rebelling against the satirical tone he helped to develop, and against vehemence, unless from the mouth of an angry God himself; and Milton is rebelling against luke-warmness in controversy, and seeking to replace satire as one of its weapons, without which, he feels, it can no more bite than the toothless satires of Joseph Hall.

In such contexts, where theories of satire and reproof are being discussed and interchanged, the word "vehemence" appears with such frequency that one can say, with almost complete certainty, that it is a rhetorical term. This does not seem to be true of Asperity and Vigor. One might say that this is in-

---

cation, one by way of authority, as it is a rebuke, an increpation, the other as it is a convincing by argument, by way of instruction, and information . . . according to S. Augustines later interpretation of these words; (for in one place of his workes, he takes this word, Reproofe, in the harder sense, for rebuke, but in another, in the milder) we have and must pursue the second signification of the word . . ."

evitable, because the orator, poet, or preacher is always going to have more matter for reproof in those equal or beneath him, while kings and generals are less often or less obviously in the wrong. A more likely explanation is that Vehemence, being the most exaggerated form of Reproof, is easier to recognize, easier to describe, easier to attack. There is one notable exception to this, however, which deserves comment, since it has already found its way into modern criticism in a somewhat misleading form. The word *asprezza* appears and reappears in the criticism of Torquato Tasso so often that it was quite properly recognized by F. T. Prince as a rhetorical term of much importance for Tasso's theory of epic. Unfortunately, this recognition was somewhat incomplete. Prince goes to the fifth book of the *Del Poema Eroico*, and fastens upon Tasso's statement that "beyond all other things which cause magnificence in Tuscan poetry is the sound, or, so to speak, the clamour, of the double consonants, which strike the ear in the last place of the verse."[34] In the course of Prince's argument, this recommendation, along with that for hiatus, becomes identified with the term *asprezza*, and this term then becomes the secret, not only of Tasso's epic style, but, following Tasso, of Milton's also. In fact, these recommendations for creating an audible strength or harshness in verse are only part of a long list of recommendations for creating "il parlar grande, e magnifico," Tasso's version of the high style. What Prince has not realized is that Tasso's view of the high style is arrived at eclectically by combining the prescriptions of Cicero, Demetrius, and Hermogenes; and that *asprezza*, rather than being an all-embracing term, derives from the Asperity of Hermogenes, and is only a subcategory of the Idea of Grandeur. Thus the recommendation for dense or harsh consonantal texture (producing Asperity) is preceded by that for

[34] F. T. Prince, *The Italian Element in Milton's Verse*, 1962, p. 54. In an earlier passage (pp. 38-40) Prince gives a wider definition of *asprezza*, which he translates as roughness or difficulty, but fails to connect it with Hermogenes, although the rhetorician's name actually appears a paragraph earlier, when Prince quotes Orazio Ariosto's definition of Tasso's epic style as being according to the Idea of Magnificence.

the long *A* and *O* (producing Magnificence) and long members and periods (producing Splendor); and the whole discussion of the grand style is shortly followed by a discussion of the Idea of Beauty, and its relationship to the grand style and the heroic poem.[35] It follows that what is true of Tasso would be equally true of Milton, who pauses in the *Apology for Smectymnuus* to attack those who are ignorant of "the *ideas*, and various kinds of stile" (*Works*, III, 347), and would certainly not make the mistake of using the devices of Asperity where the subject matter did not warrant it.

It seems, then, that our understanding of English Renaissance satire, both in verse and prose, can be considerably improved by reference to the Hermogenic Ideas of Reproof. Asperity, Vehemence, and Vigor help to explain both the violence and the deliberate elevation of the satires, as well as the terms in which the theoretical arguments are conducted, the arguments about what kind of satire is best and most effective, and whether a satirical tone has any place in sermons or religious propaganda. The importance of the rhetorical background of these terms, especially of Vehemence, cannot be overestimated, especially when knowledge of it also swings into focus two other terms which recur in the theory of satire, and which also derive from the Seven Ideas. A theory of satire based on Hermogenes is not complete without reference to Modesty, that part of the Idea of Ethos which most ingratiates the speaker with his audience, and to Verity, the Idea which convinces the audience that the orator or poet is speaking the truth. Modesty enters the debate on satire, for example, in Jonson's definition of the proper "Satyricke spirit" in the *Poetaster* as "the wholesome sharpe moralitie,/Or modest anger" of the Horatian writer (*Works*, IV, 301); in the statement of Heinsius that Horace excells in the combination of Modesty with Verity;[36] and in Milton's attempts, in the *Pro Se Defensio*,

---

[35] Tasso, *Del Poema Eroico* in *Opere*, XII, 144, 145, 169.

[36] Heinsius, *De Satyra Horatiana*, p. 161: "Jam cum nulla sit dicendi idea, quae lenius occultiusque lectorem sibi vindicat quam Aequitas, si Veritas accedat; Juvenalis ut plerunque his destituitur, ita ubique has divinitus adhibuit hic noster." [Now although there is no Idea of Speech which more gently

to claim that "the modesty of no modest person is impaired by a vehement and galling reprobation" (*Works*, IX, 183). Verity enters the debate, not in opposition to Vehemence, but closely allied with it (as indeed the two styles are closely related) whenever a satirist prides himself on telling the naked truth. So Barnaby Rich, in a discussion of the "reprehensions" of satire, remarks that they are unpopular because "smoothing *Flatterie* is more dearly esteemed, then reprehending *Veritie*," and like the satirists themselves, defines Verity in terms of the vocabulary of nakedness: "A naked tale doth most truly set foorth a naked trueth, and veritie then shines most brightly, when she is in least bravery."[37] The connection between "a naked trueth" and a truthful vehemence is clear enough, and clearly indicated, for example, in Milton's statement about his controversial style: "words naked and plain, indignantly uttered . . . express the utmost vehemence of reproof" (*Works*, IX, 109). And the most obvious connection between satirical vehemence and ἀλήθεια, the Idea of Verity, appears in the title of Everard Guilpin's satires, *Skialetheia or A Shadowe of Truth*.

I would not for one moment claim, of course, that the essential nature of this debate between zeal and moderation, naked anger or modest control, was much changed by the arrival of Hermogenic Ideas, or the knowledge that terms once comparatively vague had now acquired a specific rhetorical content. The debate itself did not change, but the style of satire did, and that is the concern of this chapter. It remains to link this debate with another closely related opposition. If the statement of Barnaby Rich that "veritie then shines most brightly, when she is in least bravery" implies an opposition between a naked and a modest anger, it also implies the ancient opposition between truth and adornment, or, in Hermogenic terms, between the Ideas of Truth and Beauty. It so happens that the period

and secretly claims the reader for its own than Modesty, if Verity is added to it; as Juvenal is usually lacking in these, so our author admirably summons them everywhere.]

[37] Barnaby Rich, *Faultes Faults And Nothing Else But Faultes* (1606), Scholars' Facsimiles, 1965, B2r, K4r.

of formal verse satire in the 1590's closes with a poem which is both a satire on the other satires which precede it and a theoretical discussion of the nature of satire, though conducted lightly enough, to be sure; and in it the opposition between Truth and Beauty is made abundantly clear. John Weever's *Faunus and Melliflora* (1600) combines a mythological "history" of satire with erotic pastoral romance which culminates in the marriage of Faunus and Melliflora, one of Diana's nymphs, and the birth of their son. But since the nymph has offended by marrying, the child turns out to be the first satyr, whose descendants eventually accompany Brutus to Britain. The romance ends with an explanation of the nature of satiric poetry:

> This boone Diana then did aske of Iove,
> (More to be venged on the Queene of Love)
> That Faunus late transformed sonnes Satyres
> (So cald because they *sat*isfide her *ires*)
> Should evermore be utter enemies,
> To lovers pastimes, sportfull veneries.
> Jove granted her this lawful iust demand,
> As we may see within our Faerie land:
> The Satyres ierking sharp fang'd poesie,
> Lashing and biting Venus luxurie.[38]

(My italics)

Weever then proceeds to give examples of "the Satyres enmitie/Which Brutus left behind in Italie" by translating the first satire of Horace, the first satire of Persius, and a few lines of the first satire of Juvenal. There follows a poem on the revenge of Venus, which consists partly in bringing about the Stationer's Injunction against satires in 1599! Satisfied with the sacrifice of the offending satires in the state bonfires, Venus leaves England, and the poet is therefore able to write a concluding "Prophesie of this present year, 1600," in which he promises all satirists a general reform of morals, so that their work may cease.

---

[38] John Weever, *Faunus and Melliflora* (1600), Liverpool Reprints, No. 2, 1948, pp. 42-43.

Apart from its engaging irony, this mythical history of satire is valuable for its clear opposition of erotic and satiric poetry and their respective styles: the erotic, symbolized by the name of the heroine, Melliflora, "whose pen is flower and honnie sweete"; and the satiric, which flows instead with vinegar and gall. The opposition here is analogous to that between the Hermogenic Ideas of Beauty and Verity, as the next chapter on the Elizabethan sonnet will show. And in some respects Weever's poem is a more fitting conclusion to the period of vehement satires than the Stationer's bonfires. It restores to the satirist that ingredient of good humor and detachment without which, however well we may understand his literary and rhetorical models, he is likely to appear "full of sound and fury," as the archetypal ham.

CHAPTER 5

"True Nakedness": *Elizabethan Sonnets*

> I made my song a coat
> Covered with embroideries
> Out of old mythologies
> From heel to throat;
> But the fools caught it,
> Wore it in the world's eyes
> As though they'd wrought it.
> Song, let them take it,
> For there's more enterprise
> In walking naked.
>
> (William Butler Yeats, *A Coat*)*

WALKING NAKED" poetically, except in a relative sense, is impossible, and Yeats would probably have agreed that the statement of *A Coat* is as much a literary stance as any other. He might also, with some qualifications, have agreed with Puttenham's chapter "Of ornament Poeticall," in which the Elizabethan view of "embroideries" is most fully displayed. Puttenham believes that writers of every age, profession, and purpose must avail themselves of ornament to some extent, that even the Archbishop of Canterbury ought to speak "cunningly and eloquently, which can not be without the use of figures," and that poetry cannot "shew it selfe either gallant or gorgious, if any lymme be left naked and bare and not clad in his kindly clothes and coulours, such as may convey them somwhat out of sight."[1]

Nevertheless, one must be able to speak relatively, and though rhetorical cunning may be the basis of both, there is an immediate difference of appearance between a style which is lavish with "the flowers, as it were, and colours" of language, as Puttenham puts it, and one which *professes* bareness. These two extremes of style are represented in the Ideas of Hermog-

---

* From *Collected Poems*, William Butler Yeats. Reprinted by permission of Macmillan Co.

[1] George Puttenham, *Arte of English Poesie* (1589), ed. G. D. Willcock and A. Walker, 1936, p. 137.

enes by, on the one hand, Beauty and its lesser form Sweetness, and on the other by Verity. The opposition between them is made clear by Minturno's statement that the truthful writer "uses harsher rhythms, lest sweet ones should present the appearance of studiously acquired charm—something which must be avoided by him who wishes to show that he speaks the truth."[2] It is also pointed out by Hermogenes that devices of sound such as *antistrophe, isocolon,* or *homeoteleuton,* which make attractive patterns in the ears of the audience, are particularly valuable to an orator who does not want his statements examined too closely, and that such ornaments were particularly sought after by Isocrates, "because he was more interested in Beauty, and Diligence, than in probability, and Verity."[3]

The Idea of Beauty

For Hermogenes, Beauty (κάλλος) is both a general sense of harmony and proportion in a work and a distinct style which can be defined by means of the Eight Parts of analysis. It is by looking at the details of this definition that we shall best appreciate in what sense the Hermogenic opposition between Beauty and Verity is precise, more precise than it could ever be in the hands of those who merely protested the duplicities of art.

In the first place, Hermogenes refers the reader, for a full description of the beautiful Sentence or subject matter, to another category, that of Sweetness. The reason why he does so is presumably because Sweetness is a subcategory of Ethos, and under that larger heading the delectable matters he proposes are more closely controlled by the ethical motivation of all eloquence. The appropriate subject matter, then, for both Beauty and Sweetness is anything which is by its own nature delightful, "especially all fables, such as the birth of Venus or the feasts

[2] Antonio Minturno, *Arte Poetica,* 1563, p. 441: [The truthful writer] userà numeri più duri, accioche con i soavi non paia havere la piacevolezza studiosamente cercato: il che deè fuggire, che disidera mostrare, che dice il vero."

[3] Hermogenes, *Opera,* ed. H. Rabe, 1913, p. 301.

of the gods." Near-fables like the story of the Trojan war are included. All subjects which give delight to the senses are Sweet and Beautiful, and "it may generally be said that all matters of love are sweet."[4]

The Diction of Beauty is to be chosen for the neatness, sweetness, and briefness of its words, which would be a bland enough prescription were it not for the significant comment by Sturm that Beauty "requires a relaxed mind" ("animum sedatum") and it is for this reason that it avoids a difficult or otherwise strenuous vocabulary (p. 248).

In accordance with this aim of soothing and charming, rather than rousing or involving, all the audible parts of Beauty contribute toward a smooth, sweet flow of sound.[5] The Members or phrases should be of moderate length and continuous, not broken up by hiatus or any other form of harshness; vowels should be short rather than sonorous, and consonants light, with emphasis on *l, m, n*. Rhythm (if one is speaking about oratorical prose) should be as close as possible to verse without actually becoming metrical. The cadences, in marked distinction to those of the high style of Magnificence, should not be firm and stable, but light, and "as it were hanging and suspended." It is this last recommendation which, presumably, Minturno is interpreting in a strictly metrical context when he remarks that beautiful verse is not end-stopped (p. 436). And Lullius offers a characteristically personal example of a beautiful phrase: "Quid enim pulchrius hac, Antonii Lulli Balearis?" (p. 456).

Equally important in distinguishing Beauty, however, is its pattern of Figures, or rhetorical ornament. The list of figures recommended by Hermogenes contains three of the five "Gorgianic" schemes of Isocrates, *antithesis, parison,* and *polyptoton,* as well as four figures of simple and obvious repetition, *epanaphora, antistrophe, epanastrophe,* and *climax.* The list also includes the figure *hyperbaton* (classified by Puttenham in the *Arte of English Poesie* as "auricular" rather than witty) and the rather odd figure of making affirmations

[4] *Opera,* pp. 330-334.
[5] *Opera,* pp. 306-311.

out of two negatives.[6] Clearly the emphasis throughout is on rhetorical schemes rather than tropes, and on figures which are either purely "auricular," or figures of "copious amplification, or enlargement of language [which] doe also conteine a certaine sweet and melodious manner of speech, in which respect, they may, after a sort, be said *auricular*: because the eare is no lesse ravished with their currant tune, than the mind

[6] *Opera*, pp. 299-301. These figures perhaps need some explanation, with the exception of *antithesis*, which is the most easily recognizable, and obviously "artificial" if used as a principle of style, as in euphuism. *Parison* or *isocolon*, which Puttenham calls the "Figure of even" because "it goeth by clauses of egall quantitie," registers a formal pattern on the ear by providing clauses or phrases of equal length. *Polyptoton* is a subcategory of *paronomasia*, one of the Gorgianic devices, which is a form of wordplay in which words are audibly connected by some similarity in sound. In *polyptoton* the connection is made between repetitions of a single proper noun with different grammatical inflections. *Epanaphora* (*anaphora* or *repetitio*) uses the same word to begin a succession of phrases (or lines in a poem). *Antistrophe* or *conversio* repeats not the first word in successive phrases or lines of verse, but the last. *Epanastrophe* (*complexio* or *symploche*) is a combination of the last two figures. As Puttenham says (pp. 199-200), "Take me the two former figures and put them into one, and it is that . . . when one and the selfe word doth begin and end many verses in sute & so wrappes up both the former figures in one . . ." *Climax*, otherwise called *epicope, ascensus, gradatio*, or *catena*, is nicknamed by Puttenham (pp. 207-208) "the marching figure [or] the clyming figure, for Clymax is as much to say as a ladder," and he quotes an epigram by Jean de Meun:

> Peace makes plentie, plentie makes pride,
> Pride breeds quarrell, and quarrell brings warre:
> Warre brings spoile, and spoile povertie
> Povertie pacience, and pacience peace:
> So peace brings warre, and warre brings peace.

Hyperbaton merely means inversion of the expected word order. Puttenham uses this as a general name for all "auricular" figures "working by disorder," such as *parenthesis* or *hysteron proteron*; but the author of the *Rhetorica ad Herennium* (Loeb edition, p. 339) sees the function of *hyperbaton* in rhythmical terms: "In these periods we ought to arrange the words in such a way as to approximate a poetic rhythm." This is obviously relevant to the aims of Beauty as a style and an Idea. Finally, the figure of making affirmations out of two negatives, for which there does not appear to be a name, is surely self-explanatory. But to anticipate a later argument, it might be pointed out that Sonnet LXIII of Sidney's *Astrophil and Stella* is a dramatic and witty elaboration of this figure.

is with their sententiousness" (Puttenham, pp. 196-197). It is, incidentally, this emphasis on audible, rather than witty Figures, which mainly distinguishes the Idea of Beauty from the style of Elegance as described by Demetrius, a style which includes the concept of jest and witty point, and which accepts tropes like parody, allegory, and irony.[7]

The total impression of the Idea of Beauty, then, is one of a highly polished and ornate surface, of artifice which is acceptable because it is a sign of respect for the beauty of Nature, according to Sturm.[8] It is admirably described by wresting only slightly out of context the compliment to Penelope in Sir John Davies' *Orchestra*, where it becomes the dance of things:

> . . . your sweet beauty, daintily transfus'd
> With due proportion throughout every part,
> What is it but a dance where Love hath us'd
> His finer cunning, and more curious art?
> Where all the elements themselves impart,
> And turne, and wind, and mingle with such measure,
> That th'eye that sees it surfeits with the pleasure?[9]

The Idea of Verity

In complete opposition, the style of Verity (ἀλήθεια) must avoid any sign of "curious art," any sign of polish, any smooth-

---

[7] G.M.A. Grube, tr., *A Greek Critic: Demetrius on Style*, pp. 91-102. Indeed, as Grube points out in his introduction to the treatise (p. 31), Demetrius has made a serious mistake in including under the heading of Elegance "all witticisms, whether gracious or crude," and in many cases "the ideas he deals with have nothing in common with each other except a certain cleverness in the handling of words."

[8] Johannes Sturm, *Scholae . . . De Formis Orationum*, p. 244: "Hanc formam Graeci κάλλος nominant: quia pulchritudo ista debet esse conjuncta cum honestate: non debet esse cerussa, aut fuco meretricio ac cersita: sed a natura accepta, studio & diligentia conservata, virtutibus autem ornata: & hinc, propter diligentiam in conservando, ἐπιμελεια, vocatur." [The Greeks call this Form κάλλος, because beauty ought to be conjoined with honesty: it ought not to be a painted or meretricious beauty, but rather taken from nature, and preserved with care and diligence; and hence, on account of this diligent preservation, it is also called ἐπιμελεια.]

[9] John Davies, *Complete Poems*, ed. A. B. Grosart, I, 201.

ness or sweetness in its verse or prose. The Sentence of Verity may consist of all the emotions of the human heart, presented in such a way that they affect and involve the audience, and thus invoke a response which is as uncritical as that called for by Beauty; but here the intellect is subordinate not to the aesthetic but to the sympathetic sense, not to the eye and the ear but to the heart and the bowels, or to whatever organs happen to be the seat of the passions in one's particular era. Hermogenes makes the point that emotions tend to separate into two major categories; hard emotions like anger and scorn requiring one kind of "truthful" expression, and soft emotions like pity and grief requiring another. Thus, to appear truthfully angry, he recommends words which are brisk, sharp, and impetuous, as in Vehemence, whereas the Diction for the piteous appeal should be humble, low, and pure (*Opera*, p. 359). As far as the sound of Verity is concerned, Minturno interprets the cross-references to Vehemence in a way most suggestive of poetic developments; what is required, he says, is speech so audibly troubled that the audience actually experiences the perturbation of the speaker (p. 441), through the disturbance of their rhythmical expectations. Minturno also remarks that the sudden or violent beginning of a poem is truthful; and that the truthful writer should not forget to profess his candor, as did Petrarch in the early lines of the *Triumph of Fame*:

> Et io, di quali schuole
> Verra'l maestro, che discriva appieno
> Quel, ch'io vo dir in semplici parole?

> [And I, from what school (of rhetoric)
> Shall come the master, who could fully tell
> What I shall only say in simple words?]
>
> (ll. 14-16)

Finally, where the Idea of Beauty proclaims itself as an adorned style by using rhetorical figures unmistakable as church bells, the Idea of Verity proclaims its nakedness while using such figures as *apostrophe, erotema, diaporesis, aposiope-*

127

sis, or *epidiorthosis*, by which the speaker exclaims, questions, doubts, hesitates, and corrects himself. That these are "schemes of affection," as Henry Peacham classifies them, should not blind us to the fact that they are *schemes*, with all the strategic content that that word now carries.[10]

Here, then, are two Ideas conceptually and stylistically in opposition, and by that opposition claiming a place in a venerable tradition of ethical and aesthetic debate, between Art and Artifice, Art and Nature, Beauty and Truth, eloquence and wisdom, the words and the thing itself. What we have to do here is to demonstrate that these two Ideas influence Renaissance poetry in England in the form in which Hermogenes put them; that is, Platonic abstractions prevented from melting into one another, as abstractions tend to do, by the fact that they have issue in specific and opposed rhetorical activities, but united ultimately by an ideal of persuasion of

---

[10] *Apostrophe* or *exclamatio* is described in the *Rhetorica ad Herennium* (p. 283) as "the figure which expresses grief or indignation by means of an address to some man or city or place or object." It corresponds to Puttenham's figure of "Ecphonisis or the Outcry," which "utters our minde by all such words as do shew any extreme passion" (p. 212). *Erotema* or *rogatio* is simply rhetorical questioning, which expects no answer. *Diaporesis* or *dubitatio* is the figure by which the speaker seems to hesitate over a choice of words, or cast doubt upon his own authority. *Aposiopesis* (otherwise known as *apocope, praecisio, obticentia, interruptio, reticentia,* or *occultatio*), is a different kind of hesitation, that which actually leaves a sentence unfinished. Puttenham oddly lists this as an "auricular" figure, but indicates its emotive value by listing psychological reasons for its use—to show fear, shame, anger, "or by way of manace or to show a moderation of wrath" (pp. 166-167). *Epidiorthosis* (otherwise known as *epanorthosis, metanoia,* or *correctio*) occurs, as Puttenham says, when "we speake and be sorry for it, as if we had not wel spoken, so that we seeme to call in our word againe, and to put in another fitter for the purpose" (p. 215). There is, as E. K. informs us, "a pretty Epanorthosis" in the January eclogue of Spenser's *Shepheardes Calender*, when Colin exclaims "I love thilke lasse, (alas why doe I love?)." The classification of figures according to their *purpose*, which is the aim of Hermogenes in the περὶ ἰδεῶν, is not much in evidence in rhetorics which derive from the *Rhetorica ad Herennium*. It is, however, attempted by Henry Peacham in the *Garden of Eloquence* (1577), where these and other "schemes of affection" are distinguished from schemes intended to amplify or complicate, rather than dramatize, a speech.

which they are each a part. In this form, I contend, Beauty and
Verity function in the sonnets of Sidney and Shakespeare,
and in the lyrics of George Herbert, which is a contention large
enough for any single chapter to handle; but it is probable
that their influence extends a good deal further into lyric
poetry of the same period.

Truth vs. Beauty: The Poetic Stance

We know that Minturno chose, as his only illustration of
Beauty, the first thirty lines of Petrarch's *Triumph of Cupid*,
and it is clear that the most available Sentence for the use of
the Idea of Beauty would be the operation of Amor. If Spenser
or Daniel had been thinking of the Idea of Beauty, it could
scarcely have escaped them that there was a splendid decorum
in writing within it poems which took as their subject matter
the beauty of a woman, and where the aim was to "ravish"
at least the ear of the hearer. To Minturno, nothing would
have been more appropriate to Beauty than the undemanding
epanaphora of Spenser's *Amoretti* LXXXI, a placid and ascend-
ing blazon:

> Fayre is my love, when her fayre golden heares,
> with the loose wynd ye waving chance to marke:
> fayre when the rose in her red cheekes appeares,
> or in her eyes the fyre of love does sparke.
> Fayre when her brest lyke a rich laden barke,
> with pretious merchandise she forth doth lay:
> fayre when that cloud of pryde, which oft doth dark
> her goodly light with smiles she drives away.
> But fayrest she, when so she doth display,
> the gate with pearles and rubyes richly dight:
> throgh which her words so wise do make their way
> to beare the message of her gentle spright . . .

Sidney too, in one of his moods, produces almost flawless examples of the kind, including one sonnet in which the negative image of sickness is transformed into the positive image
of beauty by the pure magic of verbal repetition:

Stella is sicke, and in that sicke bed lies
Sweetnesse, that breathes and pants as oft as she:
And grace, sicke too, such fine conclusions tries,
That sickeness brags it selfe best graced to be.
Beauty is sicke, but sicke in so faire guise,
That in that palenesse beautie's white we see;
And joy, which is inseparate from those eyes,
Stella now learnes (strange case) to weepe in thee.
                    (*Astrophil and Stella,* ci)

However, as far as Sidney is concerned, this style is clearly
something which can be picked up and put down at will,
depending on the particular stance chosen by the lover. In
the fifth song of *Astrophil and Stella* he announces that since
Stella has ceased to behave sweetly, he will accordingly forgo
sweet writing, and in Sonnet lv he makes a similar avowal:

Muses, I oft invoked your holy ayde,
With choisest flowers my speech to engarland so;
That it, despisde in true but naked shew,
Might winne some grace in your sweet skill arraid.
. . .
But now I meane no more your helpe to trie,
Nor other sugring of my speech to prove,
But on her name incessantly to crie:
For let me but name her whom I do love,
So sweete sounds straight mine eare and heart do hit,
That I well find no eloquence like it.

Here is the very opposition described by Minturno. The
"choisest flowers" and "sugring" of speech appropriate to the
Idea of Beauty or the middle style are weighed against the
"true but naked shew," and, for the moment, found wanting
in the only respect which really counts—they have failed to
sweeten Stella's responses. At the end of the sonnet, therefore,
smoothness of rhythm is discarded for the irregular vibrations
produced by Stella's name, the metrical perturbations which
are a sign of Verity as an Idea.

It has, of course, been observed before that Sidney prepared the way for *Astrophil and Stella* by complaining in the *Defence of Poesie* about the artificiality of contemporary love poetry. The very passage in the *Defence* which is so often quoted is worth repeating here, because it might easily have been written with the Idea of Verity in mind:

> But truly many of such writings as come under the banner of unresistible love, if I were a mistress would never persuade me that they were in love; so coldly they apply fiery speeches, as men that had rather read lovers' writings . . . *than that in truth they feel those passions*; which easily (as I think) may be betrayed by that same forcibleness of *energia* (as the Greeks call it), of the writer.*

Now Energia is a word which could easily provoke many more pages of commentary than are appropriate here; a minimum of definition is required, however, for this term (which Sidney rather airily assumes to be the secret of a recognizably sincere poetry) shows considerable fluctuation in meaning. In the criticism of Tasso, for example, it is that quality by which the poet makes that which he is describing "as it were both seen *and heard*"; and in order to achieve it the poet must imitate "le voci de' fiumi, delle selve, de' venti, del foco, e del mare ed oltreciò de'metalli, e delle pietre, e delle fiere, degli uccelli, delle piume, ed in universale di tutti gl'instrumenti, e di tutti gli animali."[11] This amounts to an elaborate and serious theory of onomatopoeia or figurative sound as the basis of vividness in description. But Sidney's own understanding of the term, as Neil Rudenstine suggests,[12] is likely to have been

* Here, and elsewhere in this chapter, the italicizing of "truth," and phrases which depend on it, is my own.

11 Torquato Tasso, *Del Poema Eroico*, in *Opere* XII, 182-183. Tasso discusses as a lesser form of this art what he calls "i nomi finti, come, rombo, rimbombo, susurro, mormorio, sibilo . . ." and which correspond to simple onomatopoeia.

12 Neil Rudenstine, "Sidney and Energia" in *Elizabethan Poetry: Modern Essays in Criticism*, ed. P. J. Alpers, 1967, pp. 224-226. See also Richard Sherry, *A Treatise of Schemes and Tropes* (1550), p. 68, for a list of several types of devices of Energia, one of which is *Pathopeia*, "that is expressing of vehement affeccions and perturbacions, of the whych ther be two sortes.

directly influenced by that of Scaliger, who concentrates rather on the Energia of certain figures like apostrophe and prosopopeia, and their effectiveness in creating the impression of dramatic action in the *Aeneid*. In the context of amorous rather than heroic poetry, Scaliger's definition of Energia is readily modified to suit the needs of another decorum, and the exclamations, sharp questions, apostrophes, the "direction of speech to inanimate objects" which were seen as vitalizing the narrative action of the *Aeneid* now serve to vitalize and make "truthful" the emotional action of *Astrophil and Stella*. One could also say, I suppose, that the sonnet sequence fulfills Tasso's requirement that Energia should make the subject "both seen and heard," for what makes Astrophil's emotion evident is the sound of his human voice. As Rudenstine says, "we know his voice, witness his tale, and accept the Energia of his verse as the sign of his passion."

There is, however, another definition of Energia which Sidney might have known, and which is very much to the point in our discussion of the opposition between the beautiful and the truthful styles. In Puttenham's *Arte of English Poesie* (1589) there is a distinction made between two kinds of "ornament": one, which is called Enargia (notice the middle vowel) has as its function "to satisfie & delight th'eare onely by a goodly outward shew set upon the matter with wordes, and speaches smothly and tunably running"; the other, which is our term Energia, operates "by certaine intendments or sence of such wordes and speaches inwardly working a stirre to the mynde."[13] At one level this distinction can be seen as

---

The fyrste is called *Donysis*, or intencion, and some call it imaginacion, wherby feare, anger, madnes, hatred, envye, and lyke other perturbations of mynde is shewed and described, as in Ciceros invectives. Another forme is *Oictros*, or commiseracion, wherby teares be pyked out, or pyty is moved, or forgyvenes, as in Ciceros peroracions, and complaintes in Poets." This distinction between two kinds of pathetic energy, the hard one of anger and the soft one of grief, corresponds exactly to the two kinds of Verity as described by Hermogenes; and it is no little satisfaction to see that Sherry associates the softer form of *Pathopeia* with the subject of this chapter, that is, "complaintes in Poets," as expressed in the form of beseeching sonnets.

[13] Puttenham, *Arte of English Poesie*, pp. 142-143. *Enargeia* and *energeia*

little more than the conventional one between schemes and tropes, figures of words and figures of thought. But at another level it corresponds with fine exactness to the opposition between Beauty and Truth in the scheme of Hermogenic Ideas, Beauty being designed "to satisfie & delight th'eare onely . . . with wordes, and speaches smothly and tunably running," to create, as Sturm says, "animum sedatum," the relaxed mind; and Truth or Verity having the opposite function, "inwardly working a stirre to the mynde" and involving the audience in the passions of the speaker. It is also worth noticing that both Enargia and Energia are seen by Puttenham as *ornaments* designed to cover the nakedness of mere matter, and equally requiring the rhetorical education of the writer.

Clearly, if Sidney knew this or a similar distinction by the time he wrote the *Defence of Poesie,* he could not have written the passage on Energia as the source of sincerity without thinking back to the fifth song in *Astrophil and Stella,* where the lover contrasts two of his styles of persuasion, the "sugring of [his] speech" and his "true but naked shew." If Energia corresponds to his "true but naked" eloquence, then the other style, the one which turns Stella's sickness into sweetness, corresponds to Puttenham's Enargia. But since both are equally ornamental, and the "true but naked shew" depends as much upon rhetorical cunning as that sweetness which it replaces, Sidney would have seen no contradiction in terms in the way in which the opening sonnets of *Astrophil and Stella* discard the artifices of previous sonneteers by flagrantly artificial devices; nor would he have seen any theoretical clash between the opening line of his first sonnet, "*Loving in truth,* and faine in verse my love to shew," and its resolution by means of a pun:

> Thus great with child to speake, and helplesse in my throwes,
> Biting my *trewand pen,* beating my selfe for spite,
> "Fool," said my Muse to me, "looke in thy heart and write."

---

are two unrelated Greek words in origin, meaning clarity or brightness in the first case, and action or energy in the second.

The pen of the poet is a truant until it learns to look inward to the truth of personal experience rather than imitating "inventions fine" in the works of others; but the poet's independence, like his naked style, is a literary fiction, a poetic stance. It belongs to the Idea of Verity.

This first sonnet from *Astrophil and Stella* also serves to introduce my contention that the opposition between Beauty and Verity is present also, and even more importantly, in the styles and statements of Shakespeare's sonnets. It would have been virtually impossible for Shakespeare to write his own sonnet sequence without some reference to Sidney's. In fact, there seems to be one such reference in the crucial and central Sonnet CI, where Shakespeare explores the relationship between Truth and Beauty in love poetry, and there makes use of the same play on the word "truant":

> *O truant Muse* what shalbe thy amends,
> For thy neglect of truth in beauty di'd?
> Both truth and beauty on my love depends:
> So dost thou too, and therein dignifi'd:
> Make answere Muse, wilt thou not haply saie,
> Truth needs no collour with his collour fixt,
> Beautie no pensell, beauties truth to lay:
> But best is best, if never intermixt
> Because he needs no praise, wilt thou be dumb?
> Excuse not silence so, for't lies in thee,
> To make him much out-live a gilded tombe:
> And to be praisd of ages yet to be . . .

One level of this inward debate is concerned with style, and raises the question of whether the gilding of a subject already beautiful does not in some way falsify the subject. The Muse takes the position that ornamentation is falsification, and thus in effect accepts the opposition between the Ideas of Beauty and Truth. The poet here disagrees, using an argument parallel to Sturm's defense of the Idea of Beauty, that its function is essentially preservative, and that verbal gilding will prevent decay.

Nevertheless, in earlier poems in the sequence Shakespeare had taken the Muse's position, discarding rhetorical beauty for the blunt sincerity he claims as his own special achievement:

> So is it not with me as with that Muse,
> Stird by a painted beauty to his verse,
> Who heaven it selfe for ornament doth use,
>
> . . .
>
> *O let me true in love but truly write*
> And then beleeve me, my love is as faire,
> As any mothers childe. . . .

(xxi)

He contrasts the "strained touches [of] Rhethorick" which others use with his own verse, in which, he tells his friend, "Thou *truly* faire, wert *truly* simpathizde,/In *true plaine* words, by thy *true-telling* friend" (lxxxii). He too uses the metaphor of nakedness for unpolished style, begging that his friend's tolerance may clothe his "tattered loving" (xxvi). And, like Sidney, he gives metrical illustration of his "toung'tide Muse," whose very awkwardness compels more attention than the "polish'd form of well'refined pen": "Then others, for the breath of words respect,/Me for my dombe thoughts, speaking in effect" (lxxxv).

In other words, both Sidney and Shakespeare repeatedly express, within a highly artificial framework, either a desire to reject artifice in favor of sincerity (Sidney), or the inability to acquire stylistic polish (Shakespeare) which happily coincides with a belief that nakedness is more truthful. In Sidney's sequence, most of the relevant sonnets come at the beginning, and thus might be expected to define the tone of the whole. Shakespeare's sonnets about style are more scattered, though as numerous, and two of those already quoted fall in the group of ten sonnets *about* writing, about his talents as a poet and his fear of a rival poet, which form the mathematical center of the sequence. In addition, both poets play ostentatiously with the word "true" when trying to define the honest style.

135

It seems more than probable that both poets had learned directly or indirectly of the Idea of Verity as a style, had perceived its relevance to the formal courtship of the sonnet, and made its presence known in their own sequences not only by the appropriate devices, but also by hammering on the word "true." Neither would use it consistently, of course, for styles should be mixed; both know and make use of its opposition to the Idea of Beauty: and the slight difference in their attitudes, Sidney being young and arrogant in his rejection of artifice, Shakespeare being humble and "tongue-tied," suggests that Sidney's attitude is Verity alone, while Shakespeare's is that of Verity mixed with Modesty.

Truth vs. Beauty: The Intellectual Paradox

The first value of this explanation is that it accounts for the obviously rhetorical way in which both poets dismiss rhetorical formulas and flair, and allows us to accept the most "sugared" sonnets, as well as the most blunt and violent, as part of the same intention, which is to woo the hearer. But beyond this it becomes apparent, in both sequences, that Beauty and Truth have an interpretative value, and that knowledge of their opposition helps to define the quality of Platonism in both poets' minds. The opposition between Beauty and Truth is central, thematically and structurally, in both sequences; and at the same time both poets are intrigued by the way in which the Ideas can be made interchangeable.

The way is that of wit. In the fifth sonnet of *Astrophil and Stella* Sidney opposes the statements of Virtue to the irresistible facts of human beauty and love:

It is most true, that eyes are form'd to serve
The inward light: and that the heavenly part
Ought to be king, from whose rules who do swerve,
Rebels to Nature, strive for their owne smart.
It is most true, what we call Cupid's dart,
An image is, which for our selves we carve;
And, fooles, adore in temple of our hart,
Till that good God make Church and Churchman starve.

True, that true Beautie Vertue is indeed,
Whereof this Beautie can be but a shade,
Which elements with mortall mixture breed:
True, that on earth we are but pilgrims made,
And should in soule up to our countrey move:
True, and yet true that I must Stella love.

The interchange is made twice: virtue is truth, but so also, at the end, is the human beauty which enforces love; and virtue itself is defined as the "true Beautie," which, as the Platonic ideal, overshadows its human image. And there is a third ingenuity in the fact that the *anaphora* characteristic of the style of Beauty is here used to bring out the contrast between the two different kinds of truth. Astrophil, who admits elsewhere to the charge of reading Plato with merely intellectual assent,[14] never really progresses beyond this statement of opposing truths, leaving the philosophical question as unconsummated as his affair. The reconciliation promised by the phrase "True, that true Beautie Vertue is indeed" is not stated with any emotional conviction within the boundaries of the sequence, whatever we may think of the relevance of "Leave me o Love, which reachest but to dust." Within the sequence, the opposition between Truth and Beauty is a condensed version of that between Platonic idealism and passionate realism, the costly but noble state of tension in which Astrophil loves.

In Shakespeare's sequence the interchangeability of the Ideas becomes more important still, because the nature of beauty itself is under closer examination. If we go back to Sonnet CI, already discussed as an argument about style, it is clear that it can simultaneously be read as a philosophical

---

[14] In *Astrophil and Stella*, XXI, the lover is involved in defending himself against the accusations of a friend that all his reading of Plato is invalidated unless he applies its lessons about rational control:

> Your words my friend (right healthfull caustiks) blame
> My young mind marde, whom Love doth windlas so,
> That mine owne writings like bad servants show
> My wits, quicke in vaine thoughts, in vertue lame:
> That Plato I read for nought, but if he tame
> Such coltish gyres . . .

debate with his Muse. When the poet accuses the Muse of the "neglect of truth in beauty di'd," he means that he has unaccountably neglected to praise the virtues of his friend, which by happy coincidence are contained in a visibly beautiful boy; the truth of the personality consists in its moral integrity. But the Muse is working with a different kind of equation—the friend's beauty needs "no pensell, beauties truth to lay"—an equation in which truth is defined as natural human beauty, unadorned. On two counts, then, Beauty is true and Truth is beautiful, a fusion anticipated in a number of earlier sonnets.

So Sonnet LIV opens with the poet's exclamation: "O, how much more doth beautie beautious seeme,/By that sweet ornament which truth doth give!" and develops a comparison between the "truth" of a beautiful person and the essence of the true rose, which, in contrast to lovely but scentless brier roses, can be preserved in the form of perfume. This "truth" is partly naturalness, as we learn from sonnets LXVII and LXVIII, and partly moral integrity, as developed in sonnets LXIX and LXX. In the first pair, the boy is seen as the single survivor of a golden age, when physical beauty showed itself "Without all ornament, itself and *true*." But the next two sonnets give warning that if the mind does not match the fair exterior, however natural, the result will not be perfume, but the "rank smell of weeds."

In this way the 126 sonnets written to his friend are structured by opposed beauties and truths, and attempts to reconcile them. In the sonnets to his mistress the relationship between Ideas becomes more complicated still, because they are written under the icon of blind Cupid, in the knowledge that she is not beautiful in the eyes of the world, but only in his infatuated sight:

> O me! what eyes hath love put in my head,
> Which have no correspondence with *true* sight,
> Or if they have, where is my judgment fled,
> That censures falsely what they see aright?
> If that be faire whereon my false eyes dote,

What meanes the world to say it is not so?
If it be not, then love doth well denote,
Loves eye is not so *true* as all mens: no, . .

(CXLVIII)

They are also written in the knowledge that, whatever her exterior, the mind of his mistress is definitely neither beautiful nor true.

Finally, even the theme most generally recognized as characterizing the sequence—the preservation of beauty by procreation or poetic creation—is expressed in terms of these two Ideas. The first group of sonnets require the beloved to perpetuate himself in children, and the fourteenth sonnet brings the group to a climax with a prophecy read in the "constant stars" of the friend's eyes:

> . . . *truth and beautie* shal together thrive
> If from thy selfe, to store thou wouldst convert;
> Or else of thee this I prognosticate,
> Thy end is *Truthes and Beauties* doome and date.

If the friend will not cooperate, however, then it is up to the poet and his "truant Muse" to preserve his beauty in verse, an act which corresponds to the function of Beauty in the commentary of Sturm. And so the various meanings of Truth and Beauty flow together in the crucial hundred and first sonnet, to be reconciled under the weight of this necessity:

> Make answere Muse, wilt thou not haply saie,
> Truth needs no collour with his collour fixt,
> Beautie no pensell, beauties truth to lay:
> But best is best, if never intermixt . . .

The Muse may equivocate, balancing the two abstractions against each other. But the poet must finally push such equivocation aside and speak, regardless of whether the result is Beauty or Truth, or something "intermixt":

> Excuse not silence so, for't lies in thee,
> To make him much outlive a gilded tombe:
> And to be praisd of ages yet to be . . .

139

It is not going too far to say that the whole sequence is in one way or another about truth: the truth of love, or the fidelity of the three personae to each other; the truth of beauty, or its objective correlative either in the eyes of the world or in moral stamina; and the truth of art, or its ability to decline artifice, and its ability to preserve.

Truth vs. Beauty: The Opposition of Styles

All this means that we have here some real basis for avoiding the intentional fallacy, and for stating that, when the recommended techniques for creating Beauty and Verity appear in the sonnets of Sidney and Shakespeare, they are not there by coincidence. This means that we can (with considerably more justification than Minturno ever had) identify the Idea of Beauty as operating in Shakespeare's Sonnet xcviii:

> Nor did I wonder at the Lillies white,
> Nor praise the deepe vermillion in the Rose,
> They weare but sweet, but figures of delight:
> Drawne after you, you patterne of all those . . .

Here poet and reader alike are satisfied with smoothness of rhythm and "figures of delight." And equally we can identify Verity operating in the harsh apostrophes, the rhetorical questions, and the much rougher rhythms of Sonnet cxxxvii, where the love "of comfort" has given place to the love "of despair," and the "figures of delight" have consequently given place to the more energetic and disturbing "schemes of affection":

> Thou blinde foole love, what doost thou to mine eyes,
> That they behold and see not what they see:
> They know what beautie is, see where it lyes,
> Yet what the best is, take the worst to be.
>
> . . .
>
> Why should my heart thinke that a severall plot,
> Which my heart knowes the wide worlds common
>   place?

Or mine eyes seeing this, say this is not
To put *faire truth* upon so foule a face,
In things *right true* my heart and eyes have erred,
And to this false plague are they now transferred.

Shakespeare also frequently uses those figures of the Idea of
Verity which question, doubt, and anticipate blame, and which
are particularly appropriate in the context of infidelity, not
just as ornaments, but as dramatic moments or experiences in
the development of the sequence. Thus what would have been
in a rhetorical handbook merely a *figure* of self-accusation
becomes, in Shakespeare's Sonnet cx, the *experience* of self-
accusation, the total apology of the poet for himself:

Alas 'tis true, I have gone here and there,
And made my selfe a motley to the view,
Gor'd mine own thoughts, sold cheap what is most deare,
Made old offences of affections new.
Most true it is, that I have lookt on truth
Asconce and strangely. . . .

Sonnet cxv is another fine example of the dramatization of a
rhetorical figure, in this case the figure of *epidiorthosis*, by
which, as Puttenham says, "we speake and be sorry for it, as
if we had not wel spoken, so that we seeme to call in our
word againe." The sonnet opens with the poet's statement
"Those lines that I before have writ doe lie," and then proceeds to analyze the role of judgment in experience, and the
question of when, if ever, statements of commitment and
emotional value judgments can be made with certainty. There
is in fact a whole group of sonnets which all take their im-
petus and structure from the figures of doubt, hesitation, and
self-blame.[15]

[15] Sonnets: c ("Where art thou Muse that thou forgetst so long"); ci
("Oh truant Muse what shal be thy amends"); cii ("My love is strengthned
though more weake in seeming"); ciii ("Alack what poverty my Muse brings
forth"); cix ("O never say that I was false of heart"); cx ("Alas 'tis true, I
have gone here and there"); cxi ("O for my sake doe you with fortune
chide"); cxv ("Those lines that I before have writ do lie"); cxvii ("Accuse
me thus, that I have scanted all"). In some of these self-blame is expressed
indirectly by rebuking his Muse.

In Sidney's sequence the appearance of the style of Beauty is not only more frequent, it is also better documented by the poet himself. I have already drawn attention to Sonnet LV, where Astrophil resolves to put aside the "sugring" of his speech because it does not seem to be an effective method of wooing. Shortly after this one of the few events in the sequence occurs, and the lover's patience is rewarded with a kiss. Astrophil celebrates this event in a group of sonnets (LXXVI-LXXXII) which put into practice many of the specific recommendations for creating the style of Beauty. The one noticeable exception to this group is Sonnet LXXVIII, which is concerned not with celebrating the kiss, but with the emotion of Jealousy, "A monster, other's harme, selfe-miserie,/Beautie's plague," and even this sonnet makes emphatic use of *epanaphora* and *parison*. The overwhelming impression of this group of sonnets is that Sidney is making poetry out of the words "beauty" and "sweetness" themselves, with appropriate wordplay and repetition. Thus Sonnet LXXIX begins, "Sweet kisse, thy sweets I faine would sweetly endite,/Which even of sweetnesse sweetest sweetner art," and Sonnet LXXXII begins,

> Nymph of the gard'n, where all beauties be:
> Beauties which do in excellencie passe
> His who till death lookt in a watrie glasse,
> Or hers whom naked the Trojan boy did see.
> Sweet gard'n Nymph, which keepes the Cherrie tree,
> Whose fruit doth farre th'Esperian tast surpasse:
> Most sweet-faire, most faire-sweet, do not alas,
> From comming neare those Cherries banish me . . .

This is by no means the only place where the style of Beauty is predominant, but it is one of the most obvious; and it is followed, as I have already indicated, by the Fifth Song in which Astrophil once again announces a change of key, and that the "change in lookes" in Stella, perhaps provoked by the lover's boldness in stealing the kiss, requires once again a change of style in him. Other moments in the sequence are sonnets C and CI, where the luxurious description of Stella's unhappiness serves as a perfect definition of the style of Beauty as employed in lovers' complaints:

> O teares, no teares, but raine from beautie's skies,
> Making those Lillies and those Roses grow,
> Which ay most faire, now more then most faire show,
> While gracefull pitty beauty beautifies.
>
> . . .
>
> *O plaints conserv'd in such a sugred phraise,*
> *That eloquence it selfe envies your praise,*
> While sobd out words a perfect Musike give . . .

And when all this is so demonstrably appropriate to the Idea of Beauty, it is surely not by coincidence that Sonnet XLIV is constructed out of the figure of *climax*, and that Sonnet LXIII is a high-spirited dramatization of the figure of making affirmations out of two negatives:

> O Grammer rules o now your vertues show;
> So children stil read you with awfull eyes,
> As my young Dove may in your precepts wise
> Her graunt to me, by her owne vertue know.
> For late with heart most high, with eyes most low,
> I crav'd the thing which ever she denies:
> She lightning Love, displaying Venus' skies,
> *Least once should not be heard, twise said, No, No.*
> Sing then my Muse, now Io Pean sing,
> Heav'ns envy not at my high triumphing:
> But Grammer's force with sweet successe confirme,
> For Grammer sayes (o this deare Stella weighe),
> For Grammer sayes (to Grammer who sayes nay)
> *That in one speech two Negatives affirme.*
>
> (My italics)

Sidney, too, like Shakespeare, makes dramatic use of what we have called the "schemes of affection" which are characteristic of the Idea of Verity. In the earlier part of the sequence his questions, doubts, and moments of self-accusation are made in the context of his friend's disapproval and his own uncertainty. Thus Sonnet xxi admits the justice of his friend's reproach: "Your words my friend (right healthfull caustiks) blame/My young mind marde," and Sonnet xxxiv is constructed out of the emotional experience of *diaporesis*, the action of doubting being expressed in Astrophil's internal debate, and summed up by his statement, "Thus write I while I doubt to write." But in the later part of the sequence the schemes of Verity are caused by the alienation of Stella, as in lxxxvi,

> Alas, whence came this change of lookes? If I
> Have chang'd desert, let mine owne conscience be
> A still felt plague to selfe condemning me,

or in the hyper-rhetorical Sonnet xciii in which Astrophil actually invokes the personification of Truth in his defense:

> O Fate, o fault, o curse, child of my blisse,
> What sobs can give words grace my griefe to show?
> What inke is black inough to paint my wo?
> Through me, wretch me, even Stella vexed is.
> *Yet truth (if Caitif's breath might call thee) this*
> *Witness with me,* that my foule stumbling so,
> From carelesnesse did in no maner grow,
> But wit confus'd with too much care did misse . . .

But perhaps the most ingenious presentation of the style of Verity is in Sonnet vi, in which Astrophil spends the first eleven lines mocking the stylistic poses of other love poets, and then, in the last three lines, Beauty, Sweetness, and the middle style are discarded among the other poses for an avowal of artless sincerity, complete with rhythmically "trembling voice":

> To some a sweetest plaint, a sweetest stile affords,
> While teares powre out his inke, and sighs breathe out
>   his words:
> His paper, pale dispaire, and paine his pen doth move,
> Í căn spéake whăt Í féele, ănd féele ăs múch ăs théy,
> Bŭt thínke thăt ắll thĕ Máp ŏf mў státe Í dĭspláy,

When trembling voice brings forth that I do Stella
love.

Here, then, are deliberate attempts to embody in style these
two Platonic abstractions, and their even more Platonic opposition to each other. These devices of disturbed rhythm and
stated candor account largely for that illusion of the speaking
voice which sets Sidney and Shakespeare off from their fellow
sonneteers; and they are also most decorously integrated with
the dramatic and thematic content of the sequences as a whole.

Verity and the Sincerity Topos

If we wish to widen the context of Verity beyond these two
sequences it is easy to find examples of what appear to be statements of Verity, both in other sonneteers and in narrative
poetry which presents the discourse of lovers. Constable, for
example, opens a sonnet to the Countess of Shrewsburye with
the words "Playnlie I write because I will write true,"[16] and
in another contrasts the simplicity of his lyricism with the
high praise of other stylists:

> My teares are true, though others be divine,
> and sing of warres, and Troys new-rising frame,
> meeting Heroick feete in every line,
> that tread high measures on the Scene of Fame.
> And I though disaccustoming my Muse,
> to sing but low songs in an humble vaine,
> may one day raise my stile as others use,
> and turne *Elizon* to a higher straine.[17]

Daniel's fourth sonnet in *Delia* insists that his verses "Beare
not report of any slender fire,/Forging a griefe to winne a
fames reward," and later he echoes Sidney in his rejection of
devious imagery in favor of the true image of Delia herself:

> Let others sing of Knights and Palladines;
> In aged accents, and untimely words:
> Paint shadowes in imaginary lines,

---

[16] Henry Constable, *Poems*, ed. Joan Grundy, 1960, p. 145.
[17] Constable, *Poems*, p. 217.

Which well the reach of their high wits records;
But I must sing of thee, and those faire eies,
Autentique shall my verse in time to come . . .[18]

And even the author of *Zepheria* (1594) is, as usual, in weak
pursuit:

My Muse yet never journeyed to the Indes,
Thy Fair to purple in Slchermyan dye,
All on the weak spread of his eyes' wings
Sufficeth that thou mount, though not so high![19]

In narrative poetry there is the address of Cupid, who certainly ought to have known what he was doing, to Mirrha,
the unfortunate mother of Adonis, and one of the favorite
heroines of Ovidian poets:

By thee fair Maid a power farre above,
My heart is *the true index* of my tongue.
And by my naked words you may discover,
I am not traded like a common Lover.[20]

In Richard Lynche's *The Love of Dom Diego and Ginevra*
there is a description of a love letter and the process of its
composition which would have pleased Sidney:

Twas quickly read; (God knowes it was but short)
Griefe would not let the wryter tedious be,
Nor would it suffer him fit words to sort,
But pens it (chaos-like) confusedly.
Yet had it passion to have turn'd hard stones
To liquid moisture, if they heard his moanes.[21]

And finally, to confirm all this, there is a splendid parody in
a mock epyllion, or chaste maid's tragedy. The author of

---

[18] Samuel Daniel, *Complete Works*, ed. A. B. Grosart, 1963, I, 73.

[19] *Zepheria* (anon.), in *An English Garner*, ed. Edward Arber, 1904.

[20] William Barksted, *Mirrha, the Mother of Adonis: or, Lustes Prodegies* (1607), in *Seven Minor Epics of the English Renaissance*, ed. Paul W Miller, 1967, p. 116.

[21] Richard Lynche, *The Love of Dom Diego and Ginevra* (1596) in *Seven Minor Epics*, p. 79.

Willobie his Avisa or The True picture of a modest Maide and of a chast and constant wife (1594) proclaimed his fun in the title, for Avisa "Englished" is a *bird* the like of which was *never seen*. She successfully resists in turn the assaults on her chastity by a Cavaliero, a Frenchman, an English nobleman, and an elderly German merchant. And it is the merchant (Dydimus Harco, Anglo-Germanus) who produces a lumbering parody of the style and statements of Verity:

> I have to say, yet cannot speake,
> The thing that I would gladly say,
> My hart is strong, though tong be weake,
> Yet will I speake it, as I may.
> And if I speake not as I ought,
> Blame but the error of my thought.
>
> . . .
>
> I must be plaine, then give me leave.
> I cannot flatter nor deceive.[22]

The trouble with some of these examples, particularly those sonnets which reject artifice, is that we cannot be sure they present the Idea of Verity and not merely the *topos* of sincerity. Especially this is true of poets like Daniel who are known to have imitated the sonneteers of the Pléiade, who included sincerity, and hence anti-Petrarchanism, as an important part of their creed. R. J. Clements' study of the critical theory of the Pléiade demonstrated that similar statements of candor appear at the beginning of many sonnets:

> . . . as Petrarchanism became more questionable as a medium of expression, if a poet was to have a lady believe that his protestations were something more than mere flimflam, he had to take pains to assure her that he was not merely writing in the Petrarchistic vein. One finds all manner of these assurances in the Pléiade's amores. Belleau begins sonnets with, "Maistresse, croyez moy, je ne suis point menteur" and "je n'en mentiray point, quand ce baiser je pris."

[22] George Willobie, *Willobie his Avisa or The True picture of a modest Maide and of a chast and constant wife* (1594), ed. A. B. Grosart, 1880, p. 74.

When Desportes sits down to compose his first book of amoristic poetry to Diane, he strikes an anti-Petrarchistic note in the very first sonnet: "I'll not aggrandise with rich fictions your beauties, your disdain, my faith and my passion; it will suffice that my pen adhere to the truth."[23]

Clements himself points out that the doctrine of the Pléiade on sincerity has a long classical heritage, and himself defines the nature of this sincerity by using Hermogenes' term ἀλήθεια, and referring to "the seven characteristics of good poetry," by which he means the Ideas.[24] But whether or not the Pléiade's code of sincerity is partly descended from ἀλήθεια, it is not safe to assume that their remarks, or those of Daniel, or Constable, or Richard Lynche, are any longer consciously related to that Idea. What distinguishes these statements of candor from those of Sidney and Shakespeare is not merely that they are sporadic, but that they are not backed up by and integrated to a foundation of Platonic abstraction.

Verity and Religion: The Poetry of George Herbert

There appears to be only one other English poet whose work provides the same combination of internal evidence of Verity, and thematic justification for it. This is George Herbert, who had mentioned Hermogenes and his Characters in *A Priest to the Temple*, and there indicates the nature of his own sincerity. The most effective preacher, Herbert says, is "not witty, or learned, or eloquent, but Holy. A Character, that *Hermogenes* never dream'd of, and therefore he could give no precepts thereof."[25] Herbert's religious lyrics, however, reject artifice in exactly the same manner as do the sonnets of Sidney and Shakespeare, as part of a poetic stance of sincerity which he can take up or put down as necessary. But in this case the love relationship is with God, and it is

[23] R. J. Clements, *Critical Theory and Practice of the Pléiade*, 1924, pp. 28-29.

[24] Clements, p. 7.

[25] George Herbert, *A Priest to the Temple or, The Country Parson*, in *Works*, ed. F. E. Hutchinson, 1941, p. 233.

in terms of the Idea of Holiness that those of Verity and Beauty are reconciled.

Herbert, like Sidney and Shakespeare, frequently writes about writing, and in at least four poems explicitly contrasts a simple style with an ornate and inherently pleasing one. *Jordan I*, which rejects the modes of allegory, pastoral, and myth as Sidney had done, begins suggestively, "Who sayes that fictions onely and false hair/Become a verse? *Is there in truth no beautie?*" proceeds by means of rhetorical questions (an important device of Verity), and concludes with the poet's determination to "plainly say, *My God, My King.*" *Jordan II* does not reject other men's modes, but describes a process very like that of the first sonnet in *Astrophil and Stella*, in which the poet tosses and turns in an agony of invention, only to hear at the end an inward voice:

> How wide is all this long pretence!
> There is in love a sweetnesse readie penn'd:
> Copie out onely that, and save expense.

In *The Forerunners* the poet again bids farewell to literary artifice, this time in the belief that it is being taken from him perforce, by the dullness of old age. In so doing he makes it clear that, despite occasional protestations of plain speaking, he has also in the past made use of the "broider'd coat," the "lovely enchanting language, sugar-cane,/Hony of roses" which is now escaping him:

> Farewell sweet phrases, lovely metaphors.
> But will ye leave me thus? when ye before
> Of stews and brothels onely knew the doores,
> Then did I wash you with my tears, and more,
> Brought you to Church well drest and clad:
> My God must have my best, ev'n all I had.
> Lovely enchanting language, sugar-cane,
> Hony of roses, whither wilt thou flie?
> Hath some fond lover tic'd thee to thy bane?
> And wilt thou leave the Church, and love a stie?

> Fie, thou wilt soil thy broider'd coat,
> And hurt thy self, and him that sings the note.

Approaching inability to handle the beautiful style is, moreover, a general loss, because he is one of the few who know its proper use, and the proper definition of "true beautie":

> *True beautie* dwells on high: ours is a flame
> But borrow'd thence to light us thither.
> Beautie and beauteous words should go together.

Finally he resigns himself again to a plain-speaking which is almost inarticulateness, and which can only say from the heart, "Thou art still my God." We are back, in other words, with the opposition between abstract Truth and Beauty, and the attempt to reconcile them through the concept of a "true beautie" which, for Herbert, is specifically religious.

But the most striking example of apparent Verity in action occurs in Herbert's *A true Hymne,* in which he produces a religious parody of a "tongue-tied" pose like Shakespeare's (or the already parodied Dydimus Harco), and asks that the debit of his art be made up by the credit of his strength of feeling:

> My joy, my life, my crown!
> My heart was meaning all the day,
> Somewhat it fain would say:
> And still it runneth mutt'ring up and down
> With onely this, *My joy, my life, my crown.*
>
> Yet slight not these few words:
> *If truly said,* they may take part
> Among the best in art.
> The finenesse which a hymne or psalme affords,
> Is, when the soul unto the lines accords. . . .

It is worth noting that Henry Vaughan, as part of his infinite debt to Herbert, comments on this spiritual decorum in the preface to *Silex Scintillans*: *"It is true indeed,* that to give up our thoughts to pious Themes and Contemplations . . . is a great step towards perfection . . . but he that desires to excel in this kinde of Hagiography, or holy writing, must strive (by all means) for perfection and true holyness ... and then he will be able to write (with Hierotheus and holy Herbert) *A true Hymn.*"[26]

These four poems make it clear that Herbert consciously used opposing styles, one of which expresses the basics of his belief in monosyllables, and another which employs "lovely enchanting language" but which makes exactly the same statements, only "perhaps with more embellishment," as he puts it in *The Forerunners.* The two styles can make the same statements, and the language of Beauty can at any time be substituted for the language of Verity, because, unlike Sidney and Shakespeare, Herbert is always writing about "true Beautie."[27] The only qualification to this freedom of choice is that given in *The Forerunners,* when old age forces inarticulateness upon him. Otherwise he can at will apply the style of Beauty to the calm assertions of "Vertue," and the style of Verity to the turbulent emotions and antipatterns of *The Collar* and *Deniall.*

[26] Henry Vaughan, *Works,* ed. L. C. Martin, 1914, ii, 391-392.

[27] Since writing this chapter I have read Arnold Stein's chapter on "The Art of Plainness" in *George Herbert's Lyrics,* 1968, and am reassured to find that Mr. Stein also finds an opposition in Herbert's lyrics between Truth and Beauty, and indeed uses as evidence the same four poems, *Jordan I, Jordan II, The Forerunners,* and *A true Hymne,* especially the last. He sees, as I do, the opposition as Platonic (p. 11), and he also sees the statement of *The Forerunners* as "Platonic solution ... rather than Platonic division" (p. 17). However, Mr. Stein's remarks are all contained within the context of his belief that Herbert is dedicated to what he calls the "plain style" which he identifies with the third of the Three Styles of Cicero, as modified by the Christian rhetorical tradition developed by Augustine. Mr. Stein is therefore not able to see, as I do, Herbert moving at will between the styles of Beauty and Truth, and indeed, despite the statement of *The Forerunners,* seems to deny that Herbert ever really "desires to embellish the plain" (p. 22). What is odd about his otherwise informed discussion is that he actually quotes Herbert's comment about Hermogenes in *A Priest to the Temple,* with the comment that "Herbert does encourage one to think that he is aware of both fulfilling and going beyond the rules of classical theory" (p. 32, n.24), but never apparently considers what such a reference to Hermogenes implied for Herbert's knowledge of rhetorical theory.

The last poem which belongs in this chapter is also a parody, though a much less serious one than Herbert's re-working of the Beauty/Truth antithesis for antiamorous purposes. In the original version of Sidney's *Arcadia* there is recorded a contre-blazon, or poem of mock praise, for the country wench Mopsa. It consists in the ironic rearrangement of the elements of a conventional blazon—where a true beauty would have a rosebud mouth and a wide brow, it is Mopsa's mouth that is "heavenly wide"—and it begins with an absurd version of the lover's apologetic stance: "What length of verse can serve brave Mopsa's good to show,/Whose vertues strange, and beuties such, as no man them may know?"[28] It is surely not by coincidence that in the *Old Arcadia* this mockery of conventional amorous verse is attributed to a character whose name, knowing Hermogenes, we would immediately recognize—Alethes, the truthful man.

[28] Philip Sidney, *Poems*, ed. William A. Ringler, Jr., 1962, p. 12.

CHAPTER 6

"Courage Means Running": The Idea of Speed

Fearful 'had the root of the matter,' bringing
Him things to fear, and he read well that ran;
Muchafraid went over the river singing

Though none knew what she sang. Usual for a man
Of Bunyan's courage to respect fear
. . .

We fail to hang on those firm times that met
And knew a fear because when simply here

It does not suggest its transformation. Yet
To escape emotion (a common hope) and attain
Cold truth is essentially to get

Out by a rival emotion fear. We gain
Truth, to put it sanely, by gift of pleasure
And courage, but, since pleasure knits with pain,

Both presume fear. To take fear as the measure
May be a measure of self-respect. Indeed
. . .

There is not much else that we dare to praise.

(William Empson, *Courage Means Running*)*

IT MAY at first sight seem a curious entry into a discussion of the rhetoric of Speed to come by way of Empson's paradox that courage means running, and frequently running away. And yet, like the other modern poets who act as springboards for these chapters, Empson is looking backwards, not only to the psychological insight of Bunyan, but more generally to "those firm times that met/And knew a fear." As Auden laments the decay of the "great occasions," and Yeats audaciously attempts to recreate "high talk," Empson reduces the whole question of heroism into an intriguing paradox, and attempts to relate some of the modern escapisms to the older, larger ones.

* From *Collected Poems* of William Empson. Reprinted by permission of Harcourt, Brace & World, Inc.

153

The Idea of Speed

The basic paradox of Empson's poem is stated in the first few lines, and underlined by surprise. One expects "he ran well that read," and is given "he read well that ran." The relation between running and intelligent reading is thus brought to the attention of the poem's audience as something central, not only to Bunyan's pilgrim world, where the pilgrim's sense of direction is always dependent upon knowledge of the Book, but also to Empson's own world, where a poet's sense of direction is often reinforced by what he reads of "those firm times." It is fairly clear, for example, that the title of Empson's poem, *Courage Means Running*, derives not only from Bunyan's *Pilgrim's Progress*, but also from his *Heavenly Footman*, which is a very expanded definition of the concept of running as "fleeing for one's life."[1] Also, in the *Heavenly Footman*, Bunyan goes to considerable trouble to point out that one can't run well without reading at least the signposts:

The First Direction

If thou wouldest so run as to obtain the kingdom of heaven, then be sure that thou get into the way that leadeth thither: for it is a vain thing to think that ever thou shalt have the prize, though thou runnest never so fast, unless thou art in the way that leads to it. Set the case that there should be a man in London that was to run to York for a wager; now, though he run never so swiftly, yet if he run full south, he might run himself quickly out of breath, and be never the nearer the prize, but rather the farther off. Just so is it here; it is not simply the runner, nor yet the hasty runner, that winneth the crown, unless he be in the way that leadeth thereto. I have observed, that little time which I have been a professor, that there is a great running to and from, some this way, and some that way, yet it is to be feared most of them are out of the way; and then, though they run as swift as the eagle can fly, they are benefited nothing at all.[2]

[1] John Bunyan, *The Heavenly Footman*, in *Works*, ed. Henry Stebbing, n.d., IV, 177-192.

[2] Bunyan, *Works*, IV, 181.

The Idea of Speed

Apart from the unintentional commentary on the academic community, this passage is doubly interesting. Not only does it further explain what Empson means by "running," but it is also a very fine natural example of the rhetoric of Speed. I say a natural example because, unlike the sixteenth and seventeenth-century writers quoted elsewhere in this book, Bunyan never went to a university, and as far as is known had no formal rhetorical training beyond what he might have acquired from his local grammar school. His reading in prison, however, was obviously not circumscribed by the bible, including, among other things, the sermons of Lancelot Andrewes, and somehow or other he developed a much more learned and flexible style than is apparent from reading only the *Pilgrim's Progress*. If a critic like Minturno had been available for comment upon the Bunyan canon, he might very well have made the same distinction between the *Pilgrim's Progress* and the *Holy War* as Orazio Ariosto made between his two national heroic poems, that the first was written according to the Idea of Clarity but the second according to the Idea of Magnificence;[3]

[3] Orazio Ariosto, *Risposte ad alcuni luoghi del dialogo dell'epica poesie del Signor Cammillo Pellegrino*, in Torquato Tasso, *Opere*, x, 1823, 244-246: ". . . l'uno, ch'è l'Ariosto, proposto di usar nel sua poema il carattere, over l'idea dello stile chiamata da Ermogene dilucidità, dove l'altro, cioè il Tasso, ha avuto in mira di servare l'idea, o forma dello stile magnifico." The difference in style between Bunyan's two allegories is appropriate to their symbolism, the *Pilgrim's Progress* being, obviously, a quest, the *Holy War* being, obviously, an allegory of spiritual battle and seige. In the *Pilgrim's Progress* (appropriate to conversations on the road and contemplation in places of rest), the style consists of questions and answers as well as short sentences linked by the conjunctions "and," "then," and "now," though the oratorical model is the King James bible and Protestant catechism rather than classical *sermones* and dialectic. In the *Holy War*, as appropriate to councils of war, exhortations of troops, and challenges to the enemy, the style is that of the formal oration, and constantly designated as such. For example:

> Then stood forth Captain Judgment, whose were the red colours, and for an escutcheon he had the burning fiery furnace; and he said, "O ye, the inhabitants of the town of Mansoul, that have lived so long in rebellion and acts of treason against the king Shaddai; know, that we come not to-day to this place, in this manner, with our message, of our own minds, or to revenge our own quarrel; it is the King my Master that hath sent

while the *Heavenly Footman*, as a whole and especially in the passage chosen, shows clearly certain characteristics of style which Minturno would have recognized as appropriate to the Idea of Speed, as described by Hermogenes and developed in Renaissance commentary, particularly his own. And yet as applied to Bunyan such a remark is obviously only valid insofar as it describes the *effect* of his style, since writing according to the Ideas of Hermogenes can scarcely have been his intention. To begin in this way, then, indicates that my own intentions in this chapter are more modest than elsewhere. I do not think it is possible to demonstrate that sixteenth and seventeenth century poets in England knew and practiced the Idea of Speed; it is possible to show that they used deliberately a variety of speedy effects, and that these effects are anticipated by the combined recommendations for the Hermogenic Idea of Speed.

There is one further comparison to be made between Bunyan's work and the development of the Idea of Speed in the Renaissance. Bunyan retains to an unusual degree the earlier Renaissance delight in everything figurative, the "lovely conformitie, or proportion, or conveniencie, betweene the sence and the sensible," as Puttenham puts it in the *Arte of English Poesie* (p. 262). As originally described by Hermogenes, there is nothing figurative about the Idea of Speed, which has no appropriate subject matter or Sentence of its own, and is merely that quality of style which gives vivacity and energy

---

us to reduce you to your obedience to him; the which if you refuse in a peaceable way to yield, we have commission to compel you thereto. And never think of yourselves, nor yet suffer the tyrant Diabolus to persuade you to think, that our King, by his power, is not able to bring you down, and to lay you under his feet; for he is the former of all things; and if he touches the mountains, they smoke."

The complex structure and rhythm found here indicate some knowledge of classical or neoclassical rhetoric. And Bunyan, perhaps in imitation of Milton's technique in *Paradise Lost*, immediately confirms this by designating the speech as formal oratory, and commenting upon its effect on the audience: "Now while Captain Judgment was making of this oration to the town of Mansoul, it was observed by some that Diabolus trembled" (*Works*, III, 22).

to an oration which might otherwise become languid. In the Renaissance commentaries of Minturno, Parthenio, and Sturm, however, it is clear that the delight in making analogies "betweene the sence and the sensible" becomes more important than the accurate transmission of what Hermogenes intended. And it is this impulse which provides a guide for ourselves in moving from the commentaries to the poetry, since, not very surprisingly, it is in poems about speedy action of various kinds that the devices of Speed appear most convincingly.

According to Hermogenes, the Idea of Speed is achieved by the use of a Diction composed of short words, and by the use of short Members or phrases, which, however, are not prevented from following smoothly one upon the other by harsh consonants or hiatus. He particularly recommends trochaic rhythms and commends the tetrameter verses of Archilocus as particularly speedy, a remark which would not have gone unnoticed by anyone interested in applying Speed to poetics. He gives a list of figures which can be used in a concise form, such as *asyndeton, merismus, epanaphora,* or *antistrophe,* but which if used in an expanded form would destroy the speedy effect;[4] a lengthy *merismus,* for example, would suggest the Idea of Circumlocution, while a leisurely *epanaphora* would indicate that of Beauty.

As soon as the commentators begin to translate these recommendations, and to try and find examples of them in Latin or Italian poetry, it is clear that a shift of emphasis has occurred. In the first place, the original advice about diction is complicated by the transfers between languages of very different morphemic structures. Where Hermogenes recommends a Diction made up of short words, Minturno differs, at least on the surface, believing that in Italian polysyllables can slip by quickly because they lessen the number of primary stresses in a line;[5] but since he also specifies polysyllables which are

[4] *Opera,* ed. H. Rabe, 1913, pp. 312-320.

[5] Minturno, *Arte Poetica,* 1564, p. 437: "Usiamo le voci correnti, & i versi di pochi accenti." Naturally polysyllables produce fewer stressed syllables

without open vowels or harsh clashes of sound ("senza l'apritura delle parole, e l'aspro concorso, e scontro delle syllabe"), he is therefore basically in agreement with Hermogenes, and also with his own countryman Parthenio, who specifies short words, but those which are "correnti,"[6] or what Puttenham, in the *Arte of English Poesie*, would have called "slipper syllables."

Then, when Minturno is describing the Idea of Speed, he cites as examples a number of lines which have merely an audibly speedy movement, but he also cites the central and figurative line from Petrarch's *Triumph of Time*, "per la mirabil sua velocitate," with the remark that these lines are truly *expressive* of the velocity of those things which the poet wishes to figure forth (p. 437). The passage from which this line comes is an attempt to describe the terrible fear that the Triumph of Time is total and irrevocable, and Time is personified as the angry sun, who declares his intention to "double his winged speed" because, fixed in his unchanging cycle, he envies the freedom of mankind. The poet dreams he sees this threatened acceleration, and meditating upon it, announces the vanity of things:

> Poi che questo ebbe detto, disdegnando
> riprese il corso, più veloce assai
> che falcon d'alto a sua preda volando:
>   più, dico, né pensier porai già mai
> seguir suo volo, non che lingua o stile,
> tal che con gran paura il rimirai.
>   Allor tenn'io il viver nostro a vile
> *per la mirabil sua velocitate*
> vie più ch'innanzi noi tenea gentile,
>   e parvemi terribil vanitate

---

than a series of monosyllables, as is clear from Minturno's examples from Petrarch:

> L'antichissimo fabro Siciliano . . .
> L'oderifero, e lucido Oriente . . .
> Arbor vittoriosa, triomphale . . .

[6] Bernadino Parthenio, *Della Imitatione Poetica*, 1560, pp. 224-226.

fermare in cose il cor che'l Tempo preme,
che, mentre più le stringi, son passate.

(ll. 31-43)

[Thus did he speak; and then disdainfully began again,
more swift than falcon swooping on his prey; more swift,
I say, than thought could ever follow, even with language
or style, so that I gazed at him with great fear. Then I held
this life of ours cheap on account of its incredible speed,
more than I had before held it dear, and it seemed to be
a terrible vanity to set one's heart on the things which Time
crushes, which, while you clutch them, have passed by.]

Petrarch, in the process of describing the flight of the sun,
asserts that one cannot hope to match its speed, even with
language or style ("non che lingua o stile"); and yet it is
precisely this that the Idea of Speed attempts to do when it
is used figuratively, something which, according to Minturno,
Petrarch has achieved here. Moreover, the *Triumph of Time*
stands as an example, almost, one would think, a prerequisite,
for any English admirer of Petrarch to investigate if he himself
wished to explore in language and style the concept of transience.

Only slightly less suggestive to English poets would have
been the figurative examples of Speed given by Parthenio and
Scaliger from Latin poetry. Parthenio commends for its expression of "una singulare, & notabile celerità," the line from
Virgil's *Georgics* III, 284: "Sed fugit interea, fugit irreparabile
tempus," a line which is the nearest possible equivalent in
Latin to the line chosen by Minturno from the *Triumph of
Time*. And both Parthenio and Scaliger imply that Speed
can be figurative, not only of the passage of time, but also of
violently hasty action, as in battle. As an example of the short
phrasing characteristic of Speed, Parthenio cites the *Aeneid*
(VII, 577-578), "Turnus adest, medioque in crimini caedis, &
ignis/Terrorem ingeminat. Teucros in regna vocari" (p. 226);
and as an example of the use of *asyndeton* to create Speed,

159

The Idea of Speed

Scaliger cites one of the most famous lines from the *Aeneid* (IV, 595), "Ferte citi flammas, date tela, impellite remos."[7] By so doing, Scaliger and Parthenio are creating a link between the Hermogenic Idea of Speed and the elaborate tradition of onomatopoeia begun by Horace and developed by Vida, in which the rhythms of Virgilian lines are shown to symbolize falling oxen, galloping chariots, and the speedy military movements of energetic young men. These associations are expanded in a curious way by the commentary of Sturm, according to whom one of Speed's most effective figures, *syndrome*, or the use of two brief contradictory sentences, takes its name metaphorically from the clash of armies ("à concurrentibus hostibus, quorum uterque obviam procedit alteri, munitis suis armis" p. 270). Sturm also observes that the opposite of Speed is stylistic Laziness (αργος), which takes its name metaphorically from idle men, who, like Tityrus in Virgil's first Eclogue, are characteristically lounging in the shade (p. 269). It appears that in Sturm's mind stylistic Laziness is connected with pastoral, and Speed with battle and heroic exercise. It is also worth remembering that in the *Hebdomades* of Fabio Paolini, when the Seven Ideas are shown to be analogous to the seven planets, it is with the planet Mars that the Idea of Speed is aligned.[8]

The question now is: What had English poets discovered by this time about the pace of English verse, and how had they learned to modulate it? We know that, through the medium of their experiments with so-called classical verses, poets like Sidney and Spenser learned at least in theory to vary the pace of their verse by manipulating stress and syllabic length. That the emphasis in such experiments was on tempo rather than weight is indicated by the ironic remarks of Joseph Hall in *Virgidemiarum*, mocking:

> The nimble Dactils striving to out-doe
> The drawling Spondees pacing it below.

[7] Julius Caesar Scaliger, *Poetices Libri Septem*, 1561, p. 186.
[8] Fabio Paolini, *Hebdomades*, 1589, p. 37.

The Idea of Speed

The lingring Spondees, labouring to delay,
The breath-lesse Dactils with a sudden stay.[9]

Unfortunately the statements of the classicists are almost invariably confused by a belief, or pretended belief, in "orthographie," by which one altered the "length" of a word by artificially manipulating the spelling. Also, English obviously presents a problem not shared by either Latin or Italian, in that dactylic or *sdruccioli* effects are relatively difficult to achieve, and nimbleness or breathlessness has to be produced by other means.

It is worth looking closely at George Puttenham's attempts to deal with this problem in the *Arte of English Poesie*. Puttenham starts from the position that English, being primarily a monosyllabic language, cannot hope to reproduce classical rhythms, or what he calls "the running of their feete"; and he cannot resist pausing to elaborate the metaphor in terms of an actual race. Nothing, he says,

> can better shew the qualitie [of their feet] then these runners at common games, who setting forth from the first goale, one giveth the start speedely & perhaps before he come half way to th'other goale, decayeth his pace, as a man weary & fainting: another is slow at the start, but by amending his pace keepes even with his fellow or perchance gets before him: another one while gets ground, another while loseth it again, either in the beginning, or middle of his race, and so proceedes unegally sometimes swift sometimes slow as his breath or forces serve him: another sort there be that plod on, & will never change their pace, whether they win or lose the game . . .
>
> (pp. 68-69)

However, a few pages later, Puttenham decides that English can after all entertain most of the classical feet; and though his discussion is unbelievably confused, wavering between natural and artificial scansion, he nevertheless gropes his way

[9] Joseph Hall, *Virgidemiarum*, I. vi., in *Poems*, ed. A. Davenport, 1949, p. 17.

161

toward a rational understanding of what makes a syllable long or short, slow or fast. He objects, for example, to the artificial lengthening of the first syllable of "Penelope," because all the syllables of that name are "egally smoth and currant upon the toung" (p. 118); and he sets out quite neatly the qualities of vowels and consonants which will produce speed or retardation. Thus:

> a sound is drawn at length either by the infirmitie of the toung, because the word or sillable is of such letters as hangs long in the palate or lippes ere he will come forth, or because he is accented and tuned hier and sharper then another . . . contrariwise the shortning of a sillable is, when his sounde or accent happens to be heavy and flat, that is to fall away speedily, and as it were inaudible, or when he is made of such letters as be by nature slipper & voluble and smoothly passe from the mouth. *And the vowel is always more easily delivered then the consonant: and of consonants, the liquide more then the mute, & a single consonant more then a double, and one more then twayne coupled together.*
>
> (pp. 121-122; my italics)

Puttenham also remarks, a little earlier, that the consonants which are most "flowing and slipper upon the toung" are *N, R, T, D, L* (p. 115). All this shows that, through trying to apply classical scansion to English verse, a poet or critic could discover viable methods of producing speedy lines without the trisyllabic rhythms of Latin or Italian.

Secondly, Puttenham observes that the figures of *brachylogia* and *asyndeton*, which both call for short lists of things or events, separated by commas, are to be used "when either we be earnest, *or would seeme to make hast*" (p. 213; my italics). The words "seeme to" are significant, because although these figures had been associated with conciseness or brevity in the *Rhetorica ad Herennium*,[10] and although they would have been theoretically recognized as "speedy" by all readers of that fundamental textbook, short catalogues of words in Eng-

---

[10] *Rhetorica ad Herennium*, tr. H. Caplan, 1964, pp. 330-331, 403-405.

lish have in fact a retarding effect, because they increase the number of stressed syllables in a line. There is a clash between what the ear actually hears, and what the rhetorically trained mind thinks it ought to hear. On the other hand, a series of very short phrases can quite easily give the audible impression of breathlessness. As a result, *brachylogia* and *asyndeton* are most successful when used by poets in scenes of battle, where speed is only one element of the intended image, and perhaps subordinate to violence and confusion. So Daniel describes how "manifold Confusion" in the *Civil Wars* "Shoutes, cries, claps hands, thrusts, strives and presses neere" (II. 61. 1); Donne uses the "cutted comma," as Puttenham calls it, to considerable dramatic effect in Elegy XVI, in describing his wife's nightmare:

> . . . crying out, oh, oh
> Nurse, o my love is slaine, I saw him goe
> O'r the white Alpes alone; I saw him I,
> Assail'd, fight, taken, stabb'd, bleed, fall, and die . . .

Already an exaggerated device, it is used to an exaggerated degree in John Higgins' tragedy of Sir Nicholas Burdet in the *Mirror for Magistrates*, a "tragedy" which is an unintentional parody of the fighting ideal. And in Fairfax's translation of the *Jerusalem Delivered*, a poem almost totally devoted to warfare, the "cutted comma" appears so often that it gives the appearance of a stylistic tic.[11]

11 Fairfax tends to use *brachiologia* as a device for bringing a stanza to a close, and therefore largely destroys its speedy effect. See, for example, these stanzas from Canto I, viii-x:

> The sullen season now was come and gone,
> That forc'd them, late, cease from their noble war,
> When God Almighty from his lofty throne,
> Set in those parts of heaven that purest are,
> As far above the clear stars every one,
> As it is hence up to the highest star,
> Look'd down, and all at once this world behield,
> *Each land, each city, country, town and field.*
>
> All things he view'd, at last in Syria stay'd
> Upon the Christian lords, his gracious eye;

The Idea of Speed

The use of the "cutted comma" when we would "seeme to make hast," does, however, point to a less extreme and less formalized use of short phrases to create speedy effects. If we look back for a moment at the passage from Bunyan's *Heavenly Footman*, it is clear that Bunyan's rhetoric of Speed is largely dependent on short phrases, combined with a very light consonantal texture:

> Set the case that there should be a man in London that was to run to York for a wager; now, though he run never so swiftly, yet if he run full south, he might run himself quickly out of breath, and be never the nearer the prize, but rather the farther off. Just so is it here; it is not simply the runner, nor yet the hasty runner, that winneth the crown, unless he be in the way that leadeth thereto. I have observed, that little time which I have been a professor, that there is a great running to and from, some this way, and some that way, yet it is to be feared most of them are out of the way; and then, though they run as swift as the eagle can fly, they are benefited nothing at all.

It is also worth noticing how far Bunyan restricts himself to, or rather emphasizes, those consonants recommended by Puttenham as being "slipper," that is, *N, R, T, D, L,* except that he has added to them *F* and *TH,* as only appropriate to a context which involves being "out of breath." But the other

That wondrous look wherewith he oft survey'd
Men's secret thoughts that most concealed lie,
He cast on puissant Godfrey, that assay'd
To drive the Turks from Sion's bulwarks high,
And, full of zeal and faith, esteemed light
All worldly honor, empire, treasure, might.

In Baldwin next he spied another thought,
Whom spirits proud to vain ambition move:
Tancred he saw his life's joy set at naught,
So wo-begone was he with pains of love;
Boemond the conquer'd folk of Antioch brought
The gentle yoke of Christian rule to prove,
He taught them laws, statutes, and customs new,
Arts, crafts, obedience, and religions true.   (My italics)

most noticeable feature of Bunyan's style here has no precedent in Puttenham's remarks, though it was specifically mentioned by Hermogenes as one of the characteristics of the Idea of Speed. Hermogenes, more than other rhetoricians, insisted that the trochaic was the speediest rhythm going. And it is quite remarkable how many natural trochees Bunyan has managed to incorporate into this one passage. A natural trochee I define as a word of two syllables with a naturally trochaic stress pattern; but when one groups under this definition *London, wager, never, swiftly, quickly, never, nearer, rather, farther, simply, runner, hasty runner, winneth, leadeth, little, running, eagle, nothing*, it becomes apparent that their combined presence in this passage is not natural at all, but the result of very careful selection. It is also interesting to compare this list with Scaliger's remarks about figuratively speedy words, or words with stress patterns which are representative of their meaning, such as *statim, citus, celer, velox* (p. 207).

By analyzing Bunyan's rhetoric in this way, we can be certain that its "speed" is intentional, though without knowing whether it was learned or intuited. And if we find the same techniques being used in other equally appropriate contexts, it becomes reasonable to assume a common rhetoric of Speed, which cannot be accounted for by intuition alone.

There is a little-known poem of Sidney's, connected with the *Arcadia* but not part of it,[12] in which he devotes approximately 200 out of 550 lines to a description of the pastoral barley-brake races. This is surely a context in which the rhetoric of Speed would be appropriate, and Sidney certainly uses it, in the same ways in which we saw it operating in Bunyan's

---

[12] Philip Sidney, *A Shepheard's tale* . . . , in *Poems*, ed. W. A. Ringler, Jr., 1962, pp. 242-256. This poem refers to characters who also appear in the *Arcadia*, but Ringler makes the following remarks about its relationship to that poem: "The Countess of Pembroke apparently found the uncompleted poem among her brother's papers and inserted it at what she considered an appropriate location in the 1593 edition. Sidney, even if he had completed it, probably would not have included it in the *Arcadia*, because it is too obviously a poem of the contemporary Elizabethan rather than of the ancient Arcadian countryside" (p. 494).

Heavenly Footman. During the race, Strephon, one of the runners,

> With love drawne on, so fast with pace unmeet
> Drew dainty *Nous*, that she not able so
> To runne, brake from his hands, and let him goe.
> He single thus, hop'd soone with hir to be,
> Who nothing earthly, but of fire and aire,
> Though with soft leggs, did run as fast as he.
> He thrise reacht, thrise deceiv'd, when hir to beare
> He hopes, with dainty turns she doth him flee.
> So on the downs we see, neere *Wilton* faire,
> A hast'ned Hare from greedy Grayhound goe,
> And past all hope his chapps to frustrate so . . .

Here we find the same short phrasing, the same light consonantal texture, and the same consonants (except that Sidney has exaggerated the onomatopeia of breathlessness in the simile about the greyhound); and we also find the same accumulation of natural trochees, *dainty, able, single, nothing earthly, dainty, Wilton, hast'ned, greedy.* The lovely, and funny, lines in which Nous is described as being "nothing earthly, but of fire and aire,/Though with soft leggs" are a perfect example of the art of finding the "slipper" syllables in a rather unslippery language. And the only real difference in technique between Sidney's poem and Bunyan's prose is that Sidney is able to make effective and perhaps figurative use of enjambment, or the run-on line.

Racing is rather a specialized subject, and Sidney's context is hard to match; but there are of course a whole range of poems which take as their subject not the speed of human beings, but that of Time. Few of these poems have the broad philosophical implications of Petrarch's *Triumph of Time,* and the majority are amorous poems of *carpe diem.* In the late sixteenth century it became fashionable to write poems of *carpe diem,* as part of the minimally classical interest in Ovid, Horace and Catullus; and it also became fashionable, apparently, to write them in the rhetoric of Speed, using the alternative approach to short "members" by which the metrical lines themselves are kept short. It may be coincidental that Hermogenes had commended the tetrameter verses of the poet Archilocus as being particularly speedy, because they were "composed of trochees, truly the running rhythm." Whatever the source, the figurative speed of lines which are tetrameter in length and trochaic in rhythm was obviously recognized by Elizabethan poets; and the speed such lines produce is not the breathless haste of Sidney's runners, but the metronomically regular speed of Time.

All this was obviously understood by Raleigh and Marvell when they came to write their rather similar poems of *carpe diem*. Raleigh, in that ironically titled poem, *To his Love when he had obtained Her*, uses both short lines and trochaic rhythm to image the speed of Time from which the lover argues:

> Now Serena be not coy;
> Since we freely may enjoy
> Sweete imbraces: such delights
> As will shorten tedious nightes.
> Thinke that beauty will not stay
> With you allwaies, but away . . .[13]

Marvell uses the same technique, only more successfully, when trying to impress his own "Coy Mistress"; and his justly famous image of "Times winged Charriot hurrying near" could well be placed beside Minturno's archetypal example of Petrarchan speed ("per la mirabil sua velocitate") and Parthenio's archetypal example of Virgilian speed ("Sed fugit interea, fugit irreparabile tempus"). Jonson, Sidney, and Greville use the same technique, Jonson conventionally enough in his adaptation of Catullus:

> Come my *Celia*, let us prove,
> While we may, the sports of love;
> Time will not be ours, for ever:
> He, at length, our good will sever . . .[14]

[13] Walter Raleigh, in *Poems*, ed. Agnes Latham, 1962, p. 20.
[14] Ben Jonson, *Works*, VIII, 102.

Sidney and Greville use it in poems which were apparently written in friendly competition with each other. Sidney's eighth song in *Astrophil and Stella* begins by carefully identifying time and place:

> In a grove most rich of shade,
> Where birds wanton musicke made,
> May then yong his pide weedes showing . . .[15]

And Astrophil then proceeds to argue from both time and place that this is the appropriate moment for seduction. The partner to this poem occurs in Greville's *Caelica*, in which Astrophil's place is taken by Philocell, who is equally "passion rent" (the same phrase occurs in both poems), and whose wooing, equally unsuccessful, takes place:

> In the time when herbs and flowers,
> Springing out of melting powers,
> Teach the earth that heat and rain
> Do make Cupid live again;
> Late when Sol, like great hearts, shows
> Largest as he lowest goes.[16]

Though Philocell does not argue directly from either the spring or the sunset, the implication is clear. There are four other similar poems in *England's Helicon* (1600) which in their opening lines indicate a temporal bias: Breton's "In the merry moneth of May,/In a morne by breake of day"; Richard Barnfield's "Nights were short, and dayes were long"; the anonymous "As it fell upon a day,/In the merry moneth of May"; and the one which may be by Shakespeare, "On a day, (alack the day,)/Love whose moneth was ever May." And though the first conclusion to be drawn from these similarities is that the lesser poets were merely imitating the greater, it is more than probable that those who set the fashion knew what they were doing, and were intelligently relating short springs and brief beauties to their common understanding of the rhetoric of Speed.

[15] Sidney, *Poems*, pp. 217-218.
[16] Fulke Greville, in *Poems and Dramas*, ed. G. Bullough, 1939, I, 121.

The Idea of Speed

If indeed this common understanding was in fact partly derived from the Hermogenic Idea of Speed, there is a certain irony in finding it in such a pastoral context as *England's Helicon*, which is a collection of poems deemed by the collector to be pastorals, whether or not they were written as such. The irony is that pastoral stands for the leisured life, where the seasons turn, it is true, but there is no sense of the clock, and where the inhabitants of Arcadia usually behave, as Sturm says, like Virgil's Tityrus resting in the shade, in a way typical of stylistic Laziness. On the other hand, if *Courage Means Running*, as the title of this chapter and Empson's poem imply, it can incorporate the courage born out of fear, and so include that branch of pastoral which is not relaxed in the face of Time, but urgent. And it can certainly incorporate that kind of running which Marvell defines at the end of *To his Coy Mistress*, and which, though based on the fear of Time, is related metaphorically to heroic action:

> Now let us sport us while we may;
> And now, like am'rous birds of prey,
> Rather at once our Time devour,
> Than languish in his slow-chapt pow'r.
> Let us roll all our Strength, and all
> Our sweetness, up into one Ball:
> And tear our Pleasures with rough strife,
> Thorough the Iron gates of Life.
> Thus, though we cannot make our Sun
> Stand still, *yet we will make him run*.
>
> (ll. 37-46; my italics)

Marvell's poem, in fact, provides a striking contrast to Petrarch's answer to the triumph of Time. When Petrarch dreams he sees the sun, envious of human freedom, increase its own speed, he counters it with the *Triumph of Eternity*, with a vision of the end of the sun, the end of Time, and the end of swiftness. Marvell chooses, for this poem at least, the defiance of eroticism instead of the patience of faith, chases the sun across the sky, and goes down in a blaze of images of self-destruction. Petrarch's answer to Time's challenge is

169

given, appropriately enough, in the rhetoric of Magnificence, that which is firm and stable; but Marvell's answer, being the very opposite of Petrarch's, is given in the rhetoric of Speed.

There is one other speedy technique, already briefly mentioned, which requires more comment, not because it has anything to do with the Hermogenic Idea of Speed as such, but because it has, like the Idea of Speed, figurative implications. This is the technique of enjambment or the run-on line, which, as a glance backwards will show, is a very important supporting device in the speedy poems of Sidney, Raleigh, and Marvell. The mere use of run-on lines in running poems might suggest a figurative use; and the Renaissance tendency to extend the "lovely conformitie . . . betweene the sence and the sensible" is confirmed in this respect by an Italian critic, Vicenzo Toralto, writing on the sonnet in 1589. Weinberg translates Toralto to the effect that: "our nature abhors corruption, and on the contrary loves and desires eternity. Thus when we read a sonnet in which every verse represents for us an end, that is, corruption, our intellect suffers; and on the contrary, when we read another which has its verses running on into one another, it takes pleasure, for from them it derives an indefinable promise of eternity."[17] The value of this statement is that it ties together the two concepts which we have found operating under the Idea of Speed, that of "running" and that of transience, and the fear it inspires. A less explicitly metaphysical statement of the same notion occurs in Samuel Daniel's *Defence of Ryme* (1607): "Besides, me thinks sometimes to beguile the eare with a running out and passing over the Ryme, as no bound to stay us in the line where the violence of the matter will breake thorow, is rather gracefull then otherwise: wherein I finde my *Homer-Lucan*, as if hee gloried to seeme to have no bounds, albeit he were confined within his measures, to be in my conceit most happie."[18]

[17] Bernard Weinberg, *A History of Literary Criticism in the Italian Renaissance*, 1961, I, 229.

[18] Samuel Daniel, *A Defence of Ryme* (1607) in *Complete Works*, ed. A. B. Grosart, 1963, IV, 64.

The Idea of Speed

It is surely in the spirit of these or similar statements that Marvell ends the poem *To his Coy Mistress* with these lines:

> Thus, though we cannot make our Sun →
> Stand still, *yet we will make him run.*
>
> (My italics)

He intends to tear his "Pleasures with rough strife,/Thorough the Iron gates of Life," and knows that there is "no bound to stay us in the line where the violence of the matter will breake thorow." Similarly Toralto's statement gives a new relevance to the technique of one of Donne's Holy Sonnets (VII):

> At the round earths imagin'd corners, blow →
> Your trumpets, Angells, and arise, arise →
> From death, you numberlesse infinities →
> Of soules, and to your scattred bodies goe.

Rosemond Tuve has said of these lines that "it is not possible to separate the images from the metrical patterns in which they inhere";[19] but it is somehow more satisfying to be able to say, with Toralto, that our intellect takes pleasure in them, "for from them it derives an indefinable promise of eternity."

It is important to distinguish this kind of figurative run-on line from another branch of the same technique, which appears implicitly in Donne's satires, and explicitly in Marston's, where the satirist breaks up the structure of the couplets he has chosen "as if hee gloried to seeme to have no bounds," but does so not out of aspiration, but out of contempt—contempt for himself, for his medium, and for all the boundless stupidity and ugliness he sees around him. Again and again Marston announces the freedom of the satirist to break all bounds; in an address to his own meter (*Ad Rithmum*), he warns his couplet rhymes that if they hinder him at all in what he has to say he will simply ignore them:

> ... if you hange an arse, like *Tubered,*
> When *Chremes* dragg'd him from his brothell bed,

---

[19] Rosemond Tuve, *Elizabethan and Metaphysical Imagery*, 1947, p. 199.

Then hence base ballad stuffe, my poetrie
Disclaimes you quite, for know my libertie
Scornes riming lawes . . .[20]

And in one passage where he is ranting about insincerity, the figurative use of the run-on line is made quite plain:

       . . . Mylo doth hate →
Murder, Clodius coockolds, Marius the gate →
Of squinting Janus shuts? *runne beyond bound* →
of Nil ultra, and hang me when on's found →
Will be himselfe . . .[21]
(My italics)

In such cases, the breaking of metrical bounds by the run-on line does not belong in the rhetoric of Speed, but rather, as we have seen, in the rhetoric of Vehemence, which Donne and Marston almost certainly derived from the Idea of Vehemence itself.

My last convincing example of the figurative run-on line comes from the poetry of Samuel Daniel himself, and from the debate poem *Musophilus*, which is Daniel's personal answer to the apparent triumph of Time. In *Musophilus* Daniel sees the answer to transience neither in religious faith, as did Petrarch, nor in eroticism, as did Marvell when addressing his coy mistress; he sees it rather as Spenser and E. K. did at the end of the *Shepheardes Calender*. All things may "perish and come to theyr last end, but workes of learned wits and monuments of Poetry abide for ever." And Daniel is concerned to defend the "workes of learned wits" against Philocosmus, the man of action, the lover of things of this world. Musophilus not only compares the fruitlessness of materialistic activity,

    Gath'ring, incroching, wresting, joyning to,
    Destroying, building, decking, furnishing,
    Repayring, altring, and so much adoe . . . (ll. 111-113),

to the monumental achievement of a fame like Chaucer's; he also upholds the essentially conservative nature of the schol-

---

[20] John Marston, *Poems*, ed. A. Davenport, 1961, pp. 128-129.
[21] Marston, *Poems*, pp. 103-104.

arly mind against all forms of "giddy innovation," especially those which would seek to make scholarship more practical. And his main reason for this stand is given in terms of a metaphor of running wild, and an obviously figurative run-on line:

> For never head-strong Reformation will →
> Rest, till to th'extreame opposite it runne,
> *And over-runne the meane* distrusted still,
> As being too neare of kinne, to that men shunne:
> For good, and bad, and all, must be one ill,
> When once there is another truth begunne . . .
>
> (ll. 731-736; my italics)

It will be apparent by now that the Hermogenic Idea of Speed is of less importance in understanding English poetry of the Renaissance than the Ideas of Grandeur, Beauty, or Verity. This is partly because its appropriate contexts are more limited, and partly because the rhetoric of Speed was to some extent developed by other means, such as the experiments with classical meters. This is not to say that it is not helpful, and it may, via Minturno's criticism, have directly influenced the development of some Elizabethan poems on the subject of Time and transience. But the Idea of Speed is also, perhaps, of more practical use as an analytical tool for poems of the twentieth century, when Ideas of Grandeur and Beauty may be hard to find, but Speed still kills. Some modern poets, of course, have learned their techniques directly from the Elizabethans. W. H. Auden's tetrameter songs on the passing of Time, some of which are markedly trochaic in rhythm, look back to Elizabethan songs of *carpe diem*. Marvell's treatment of "Time's winged chariot" would seem to have been a shaping influence on John Betjeman's *Before the Anaesthetic*:

> I, breathing for a moment, see
> Death wing himself away from me
> And think, as on this bed I lie,
> Is it extinction when I die?
> I move my limbs and use my sight:

The Idea of Speed

Not yet, thank God, not yet the Night.
Oh better far those echoing hells
Half-threaten'd in the pealing bells
Than that this "I" should cease to be—
Come quickly, Lord, come quick to me.[22]

But, as far as one can tell, it is not so much a particular model as a general understanding of the rhetoric of Speed, which shapes John Crowe Ransom's elegy for a child. *Bells for John Whiteside's Daughter* contrasts the remembered speed of the living child with the immobility in which she now lies "so primly propped," and does so by using all the devices which were part of the rhetoric of Speed in the Renaissance—the short lines, the light consonants, natural trochees, and run-on lines:

There was such speed in her little body,
And such lightness in her footfall,
It is no wonder that her brown study
Astonishes us all.

Her wars were bruited in our high window.
We looked among orchard trees and beyond,
Where she took arms against her shadow,
Or harried unto the pond

The lazy geese, like a snow cloud
Dripping their snow on the green grass,
Tricking and stopping, sleepy and proud,
Who cried in goose, Alas,

For the tireless heart within the little
Lady with rod that made them rise
From their noon apple-dreams, and scuttle
Goose-fashion under the skies!

But now go the bells, and we are ready;
In one house we are sternly stopped

[22] John Betjeman, *Before the Anaesthetic*, in *Collected Poems*, 1958, p. 36. Reprinted by permission of John Murray, Ltd.

To say we are vexed at her brown study,
Lying so primly propped.[23]

It is of course possible, without any rhetorical training, to understand intuitively the craft of a poem like this; but it is surely more satisfactory to be able to see it as part of a general understanding, an Idea of Speed both as style and subject matter, which exists the more fully when both the poet and his audience have specific knowledge of its elements. Otherwise the poet is likely to be left in the less than satisfactory situation of Empson's Muchafraid, who may have gone "over the river singing," but "none knew what she sang."

[23] John Crowe Ransom, *Bells for John Whiteside's Daughter*, in *Selected Poems*, 1947, p. 8. Reprinted by permission of Alfred A. Knopf, Inc.

CHAPTER 7

"The Grand Master-Piece to Observe": *Renaissance Epic*

> We were the last romantics—chose for theme
> Traditional sanctity and loveliness;
> Whatever's written in what poets name
> The book of the people; whatever most can bless
> The mind of man or elevate a rhyme;
> But all is changed, that high horse riderless,
> Though mounted in that saddle Homer rode
> Where the swan drifts upon a darkening flood.

> (William Butler Yeats,
> *Coole Park and Ballylee, 1931*)*

I₦ *ottava rima* almost obscured by its half rhymes, Yeats laments the decay of the heroic, and it is surely not by accident that this, like many of his poems written out of disillusionment with Irish politics and civil war, uses the "heroic" stanza of the late sixteenth century.[1] It was in *ottava rima* that Daniel and Drayton chose simultaneously to celebrate and lament the English civil wars of the past, and they inherited it from the Italian epic, and perhaps also from the Portuguese, as a "grave" stanza. Yeats's "high horse riderless"

* From *Collected Poems*, William Butler Yeats. Reprinted by permission of Macmillan Co.

[1] In the essay called "A General Introduction to My Work," *Essays and Introductions*, 1961, pp. 521-522, Yeats speaks of his use of traditional stanzas: "If I wrote of personal love or sorrow in free verse, or in any rhythm that left it unchanged, amid all its accidence, I would be full of self-contempt because of my egotism and indiscretion, and forsee the boredom of my reader. I must choose a traditional stanza, even what I alter must seem traditional . . . . Ancient salt is best packing." Although later in the same essay he states that he rejected the characteristic meters of the Renaissance as a medium for his expression of the Irish "Heroic Age," it seems clear that, when he returns to the unheroic present, Yeats uses the verse forms of the Renaissance as a form of metrical parody and satire, much as Eliot uses echoes from Spenser and Shakespeare in *The Wasteland*.

is thus an appropriate symbol for this chapter, because it not only illustrates his fine sense of decorum in the choice of poetic media, but also his characteristic ambivalence to the epic tradition. On the one hand he looks back for encouragement and consolation to the Homeric or the Irish heroic past, and on the other hand he accepts the lesson of bitter experience that the old heroic ideal is not adaptable to modern existence. Yeats would not protest, I think, to find himself used as an introduction here, since the subject of this chapter covers so many of his own preoccupations, and links the epic tradition both with decorum of style and with Neoplatonic Ideas.

More specifically, it is the purpose of this chapter to deal with the Seventh Idea, δεινότης, which may be translated as Gravity, Eloquence, or Decorum, and to apply it to the development of Renaissance epic. In the first place I will show that epic in this period tends to display a mixture of styles as modulations on a basic style, which is supposed to be grand; and secondly I will suggest that as the tradition developed, under the pressure of different nationalistic instincts, it showed a steady movement away from romanticism and toward a somber and critical or "grave" approach to heroism.

This final chapter thus has a double purpose and structure which, not entirely by coincidence, corresponds to the two meanings of δεινότης (or Gravity, as I shall call it) which were handed down to the Renaissance commentaries on Hermogenes, and appear there as a source of fruitful confusion. To avoid confusing ourselves, it is best to begin carefully, by quoting from Grube's lucid account of how the two meanings of δεινότης developed in classical criticism before Hermogenes. Deriving originally from Plato's *Phaedrus* (272a), δεινότης and its synonym δείνωσις are used by Demetrius to mean: "the forceful, passionately intense manner which he, alone among critics, isolates as a separate "style." . . . This same meaning of δείνωσις is found in Quintilian who gives a good definition of it as (6.2.24) *rebus indignis, asperis, invidiosis addens vim oratio*, that is, to intensify things shameful, cruel

177

or hateful, and he remarks that Demosthenes possessed the capacity to do this to a high degree."[2] From this meaning of the word, which essentially refers to a quality of style, or, in Demetrius, a fully developed style of the "terrible," Grube proceeds to account for the other meaning, which is partly contradictory: "The adjective δεινός, however, also means clever in our Classical texts, as in the phrase δεινός λέγειν, a phrase so common that both the adjective and the noun δεινότης (cleverness or skill) came to be applied to rhetorical cleverness without further qualification."

In other words, by the time of Hermogenes, the term can mean a quality of style (forcefulness), a distinguishable forceful style, or the ability to mingle all possible qualities and styles into a meaningful and effective whole. Rather than make a choice between these alternatives, Hermogenes apparently decided to compromise between them, and thus handed down to his commentators and translators problems of choice and interpretation which were resolved in a number of different ways.

Hermogenes begins his description of the Seventh Idea forcefully enough with the statement that, in his opinion, δεινότης means nothing other than the right use of all the previously described Ideas. He then proceeds to take issue with the tradition which interprets the term as meaning merely that which terrifies, and which takes the figure of Odysseus as the chief exemplar of the δεινός orator, because he is described in the third book of the *Iliad* as terrible in speech, "with words falling from his lips like flakes of winter snow."[3] Such a style, Hermogenes, says, was entirely appropriate when Odysseus was addressing Paris or the Trojans; but one also has to take into account Odysseus' own account (*Odyssey* VIII. 170-173) of the heaven-born orator, whose speech is both honey-sweet and reverential. Thus, says Hermogenes, the characterization of Odysseus as the δεινός orator depends on his ability, demonstrated throughout the epics of Homer, to modulate

[2] G.M.A. Grube, *A Greek Critic: Demetrius on Style*, 1961, pp. 136-137.
[3] *Opera*, ed. H. Rabe, 1913, p. 370.

from one style to another according to the appropriateness of the occasion.

So far this is all admirably straightforward; but then Hermogenes cannot resist the temptation to further define the ways in which the supreme orator is distinguished from those who do not possess δεινότης. The first step is to define such an orator as one who in every way sets himself apart from the vulgar crowd; and the second step is to comment on the recondite "sentence," diction, method, and rhythms which the supreme orator is most likely to use. The result is, in effect, the description of a seventh style which is very little different in its total effect from that of the Second Idea—Grandeur—with appropriate combinations and modulations between its six parts, both positive and negative. And it is the inclusion of some of the effects of Asperity, Vehemence, and Vigor which bring δεινότης full circle to mean, finally, a grave, forceful, and occasionally "terrible" style.

Our first indication that Renaissance commentators and translators were distracted by this double tradition appears in the names they give to the Seventh Idea. In Minturno, for example, it appears as *La Grave*, in Parthenio as *Gravita*, in Scaliger as *Gravitas*, in Delminio as *Gravitate* or *Severitate*, but in Sturm and Gaspar Laurentius it is called *Eloquentia*, and Sturm frequently substitutes for this the name of *Decorum* itself. The names, however, do not necessarily indicate which part of the tradition is involved. Minturno and Parthenio do, in fact, treat the Seventh Idea as a style, and only as a style, virtually indistinguishable from the Second Idea. Scaliger, on the other hand, while using the name of Gravity, nevertheless gives only a generalized account of it as "that prudence which organizes all the parts of an oration into a composite whole."[4]

However, if we turn from oratory to poetry, there is one kind of poetic endeavor which can resolve these differences quite naturally. A poet seeking instruction on how to write a "grave" poem of limited scope, such as a lofty ode or even

[4] Julius Caesar Scaliger, *Poetices Libri Septem* (1561), 1964, p. 177.

179

a verse "tragedy," might find all that he needed in the way of stylistic guidance under the heading of the Second Idea— Grandeur. But if he planned to embark on an epic, he would be so well aware of its necessary scope, and the test of maturity that it implied, that he would want to incorporate as many Ideas as possible into his work, according to the principle of "decorum" which is the basis of the Seventh Idea. Finally, to find under the heading of the Seventh Idea a series of stylistic recommendations which are virtually cross-references back to the Second Idea would be more helpful than confusing; for it would suggest to the poet that the desired mixture of styles should rest on the firm foundation of a recognizably grave or great style, and that the other Ideas should be seen as modulations to and from this basic style.

As an illustration of Renaissance criticism which connects Gravity, as I shall call it from now on, with the writing of epic, there is the *Risposte* of Orazio Ariosto to those critics who unfavorably compared his uncle's *Orlando Furioso* to Tasso's *Gerusalemme Liberata*. Orazio starts from the defensive position that the *Orlando Furioso* does not, unlike most heroic poems, and unlike Tasso's, have as its base a high style; and that it is, moreover, foolish to compare it with the *Gerusalemme* because the two poems were deliberately written under different Hermogenic Ideas, Ariosto having chosen to write *mainly* under the Idea of Clarity, and Tasso *mainly* under that of Magnificence. But then the *Risposte* makes an important qualification:

> Ma perch'io abbia detto che lo stile dell'Ariosto sia puittosto da porsi sotto la forma della dilucidità, che della magnificenza; non vorrei però ch'altri pensasse ch'egli fosse tale, che disconvenisse a materia eroica: perchè, oltre che ne'luoghi opportuni molto ben sa l'Ariosto vestir la magnificenza, e pigliar la grandezza, come per esempio in tutto l'abbattimento di Parigi; egli poi anco non è senza quegli ornamenti, i quali parte propri, e parte participatigli dalla idea della venustà. . . . Il qual miracoloso effetto nasce

dall'aver egli saputo al par d'ogni altro trovare, e trovata, usar quella maniera d'orazione, che si può dir carattere di tutti i caratteri, e idea de tutte le idee, tanto lodata da Aristotile, e da lui chiamata *decora*. [5]

[But because I have said that the style of Ariosto is on the whole to be placed under the form of Clarity, rather than Magnificence; I would not however wish others to think that he carried this style to the point at which it was inappropriate for heroic material: because, apart from the fact that in the right place Ariosto was well able to clothe Magnificence and paint Greatness, as for example in the whole seige of Paris, he was also not lacking in those ornaments which partly belong and partly participate in the Idea of Beauty. . . . This miraculous effect comes from his having known where to find each (style) and, having found them, known how to use that kind of oration, which one can call the Character of all Characters, and the Idea of all Ideas, so much praised by Aristotle, and named by him Decorum.]

In other words, Orazio Ariosto is here claiming epic stature for the *Orlando Furioso*, despite the fact that it does not have a basically "grave" style, and because in it Ariosto has achieved the Hermogenic ideal of δεινότης or decorum, the appropriate blending of Ideas into a harmonious whole. Orazio does not specifically name the Seventh Idea, but it is clear that in this context "the Character of all Characters, and the Idea of all Ideas" can mean nothing else, especially when it is identified with decorum; and it is also clear that for Orazio, at least within this polemical context, the decorous principle of Gravity is a more important requirement of epic than the attainment of a basically grave style. It is also worth noticing that Minturno, who seems to regard Gravity only as a style, nevertheless says firmly that it is "proprio dell Heroico Poeta" (p. 442). Presumably, had he too been writing after the publica-

---

[5] Orazio Ariosto, *Risposte . . . ad alcuni luoghi del dialogo dell'epica poesia del Signor Cammillo Pellegrino* (1585), in Torquato Tasso, *Opere*, x, 245.

tion of the *Gerusalemme Liberata*, he would have been able to illustrate the style he envisages as "proper to the Heroic Poet" from an Italian epic, rather than, as he is forced to do, from the canzones and "Triumphs" of Petrarch.

Apart from the logical connection thus made between the supreme test of the orator, as Hermogenes saw it, and the supreme test of the mature poet, as the Renaissance saw it, there was, of course, the connection made by Hermogenes himself between the Idea of Gravity and the epics of Homer. Not only does Hermogenes identify Odysseus as the type of the δεινός orator, infinitely flexible to the needs of the situation, but he also cites Homer as the supreme example of the poetic (as compared to the political or judicial) orator, and one who is himself expert in all aspects of Gravity or decorum.[6] From the very beginning, then, the Seventh Idea is associated with epic poetry. It seems only reasonable to assume that some of the poets who sat down to write an epic in their own language to rival those of Homer would have the Seventh Idea in mind.

Camoens: Os Lusiadas

Since it is the figure of Odysseus the voyager who, of all Homeric figures, is most closely associated with Gravity, it is appropriate to begin with the Renaissance hero who most resembled him, Vasco da Gama, and with the *Os Lusiadas* of Camoens, published in 1572. At the beginning of his first canto, Camoens states the relation of his hero to Odysseus and Aeneas:

> Of the wise Greek, no more the tale unfold,
> Or the Trojan, and great voyages they made,
>
> . . .
>
> Forget all the Muse sang in ancient days,
> For valor nobler yet is now to praise.[7]

[6] *Opera*, p. 390.

[7] Luis de Camoens, *The Lusiads*, tr. L. Bacon, 1950, p. 3. I have used this lively and accurate translation generally in preference to my own, or to the equally lively but unreliable seventeenth-century translation by Richard Fanshawe, which nevertheless provides useful evidence about Renaissance atti-

He also makes a specific request to his Muses, the nymphs of the river Tagus, to supply him with a grand style to fit his subject:

And you, my nymphs of Tagus, who created
Within me such a genius new and glowing,
If ever yet your stream was consecrated
In humble verses which were my bestowing,
Grant me a music great and elevated,
Give me the style magnificent and flowing,
For thus your springs, so Phoebus doth ordain,
Shall never envy Hippocrene again.

Give me sonorous fury vast and strong,
No country reed or any pan-pipe base,
But the loud trump, whose notes to war belong,
Which burn the breast and lighten in the face;
And equal to their actions make my song,
Who gave such aid to Mars, your glorious race . . .[8]

---

tudes to Camoens' epic. The original (*Os Lusiadas*, ed. J.D.M. Ford, 1946) reads:

> Cessem do sábio Grego e do Troiano
> As navegações grandes que fizeram;
> . . .
> Cesse tudo o que a musa antigua canta,
> Que outro valor mais alto se alevanta!

[8] Canto I, iv-v. In the Portuguese these stanzas are as impressive as the style they invoke:

> E vòs, Tágides minhas, pois criado
> Tendes em mi um novo engenho ardente,
> Se sempre em verso humilde celebrado
> Foi de mi vosso rio alegremente,
> Dai-me agora um som alto e sublimado,
> Um estilo grandíloco e corrente,
> Porque de vossas águas Phebo ordene
> Que não tenham enveja às de Hippocrene!
>
> Dai-me ũa fúria grande e sonorosa,
> E não de agreste avena ou frauta ruda,
> Mas de tuba canora e bellicosa,
> Que o peito acende e a côr ao gesto muda!
> Dai-me igual canto aos feitos da famosa
> Gente vossa . . .

This invocation, though on the face of it conventional, is more specific in its description of the required style than any other Renaissance epic, or indeed than Virgil himself. The style is to be not only "grandíloco" but also "corrente," which reminds us of the firm and even pace of Hermogenic Magnificence; and it is to show the progression from the pastoral pipe to the heroic trumpet ("não de agreste avena ou frauta ruda,/ Mas de tuba canora e bellicosa"), which reminds us of the opening of Spenser's *Faerie Queene*, and suggests that Spenser has combined the invocations of the *Aeneid* and the *Lusiads* in his own:

> Lo I the man, whose Muse whilome did maske,
> As time her taught, in lowly Shepheards weeds,
> Am now enforst a far unfitter taske,
> *For trumpets sterne to chaunge mine Oaten reeds . . .*
>
> (My italics)

The basic style of the *Lusiads*, then, is to be a great and sonorous one; that is the style of the narrator. But within this framework Camoens has placed the speeches of his characters, most of whom speak in a style quite different from his own, and quite different from each other. So in the fourth canto there are the contrasting speeches of Don Nuno Alvares, who urges the Portuguese into battle, and that of a venerable Lusitanian who tries to hold back Da Gama's expedition. Nuno is described as speaking "In words more forceful than delectable, . . ./Hand on sword, wrathful, with no grace of style," and he hurls at the Lusitanians a series of rhetorical questions and apostrophes, including the gun-shot repetitions of "What?" specifically recommended by Scaliger for the style of Vehemence.[9] The use of the Idea of Vehemence would be entirely appropriate here, in view of the fact that Nuno feels the Lusitanian soldiers to be beneath him both in rank and moral courage, and because his purpose, like that of the

---

[9] Canto IV, xiv-xix: In the Portuguese, Nuno is described as "reprovando . . . Com palavras mais duras que elegantes,/A mão na espada, irado e não facundo," and the first two stanzas of his speech begin with the single word "Como?"

Juvenalian satirist, is to lash his audience into a state of personal shame. A different decorum can be seen in the speech of the venerable but unidentified Lusitanian who seeks to hold back the expedition. Because he is old, and speaks out of the wisdom of experience, and also because he is addressing not the Lusitanians themselves, but the abstract concept of Honor by which they now move, his language is much more metaphorical than that of Nuno, and his exclamations are not personal explosions of anger but rhetorical gestures:

> Fell Tyrant of the soules! Life's swallowing Wave!
> Mother of Plunders, and black Rapes unchast!
> The secret minder, and the open Grave,
> Of Patrimonies, Kingdoms, Empires vast!
> They call thee noble, and they call thee Brave
> (Worthy to'have other names upon thee cast!):
> They call thee Fame, and Glory soveraign:
> Titles with which the foolish Rout is tane.[10]

If the speech of Don Nuno can be seen as an example of Vehemence, that of the old man is rather in the style of Asperity, and is indeed highly reminiscent of the major speech of Asper in *Every Man Out of his Humour*.

Different again in style and attitude is the speech of Da Gama, defending himself against charges of piracy and deception by the King of Malabar. Da Gama's language is simple and unmetaphorical, and instead of the repeated "What?" of Nuno's speech, Da Gama's is constructed on the

---

[10] Canto IV, xcvi. In this case I have used Richard Fanshawe's translation (*The Lusiad, or Portugals Historical Poem* [1655], ed. J.D.M. Ford, 1940), which gives a more accurate impression of the rhetorical structure of the stanza:

> Dura inquietação d'alma e da vida,
> Fonte de desemparos e adultérios,
> Sagaz consumidora conhecida
> De fazendas, de reinos e de impérios!
> Chamam-te illustre, chamam-te subida,
> Sendo dina de infames vitupérios;
> Chamam-te fama e glória soberana,
> Nomes com quem se o povo néscio engana!

repetition of "If" by which the king's objections are anticipated and answered one by one, and which leads to the final assertion of his own sincerity:

> "King, this is truth, for I would never say,
> For such uncertain good, such trifling gain,
> Instead of simple truth, as hope I may,
> A prologue long and falsified and vain.
>
> "And if, O King, you take my honor clear
> For what it is, faithful, and not two-faced,
> Then with all swiftness give me letters here,
> Of my return deferring not the taste.
> But if to you falsehood it still appear,
> Think well of reason that on proof is based.
> For one may see, if the clear mind attend,
> Truth is an easy thing to apprehend.[11]

The effect is that of the Idea of Verity, of one plain-dealing man addressing another in whose judgment he has perfect confidence; and it makes a fine contrast to the very different appeal of Lionardo to the nymph Ephyre, on the magical island which Venus has placed in the path of the Lusitanian fleet. Like all the rest of the nymphs of Tethys, Ephyre is only running away in order to draw on her pursuer, Lionardo; and his speech to her not only reflects the speed of his own pursuit, but actually associates the chase with the theme of *carpe diem* which, as we have seen, is often accompanied by the rhetoric of Speed:

> "Oh! flee me not! So may the little day
> Of this your beauty never take its flight
> For, only if your fleeting foot you stay,
> Shall you subdue my fate's outrageous might
>
> . . .
>
> My heart, once free, will you thus subjugate?
> Release it, and the swifter you will speed.[12]

---

[11] Canto VIII, lxv-lxxv. Camoens' word for "truth" or "sincerity" is "verdade," which appears five times in Da Gama's speech, suggesting the kind of thematic usage of the word which we have demonstrated in the sonnets of Sidney and Shakespeare.

[12] Canto IX, lxxvi-lxxxi: Ó não me fujas! Assi nunca o breve

Renaissance Epic

The difference in rhetoric could, and indeed should, have arisen quite naturally out of the differences in character and situation; but their combination within an epic poem both strengthens the contrast and suggests that the decorum Camoens is using is that of the Seventh Idea of Hermogenes, in which Vehemence, Asperity, Verity, and Speed would find their rightful place as modulations in a basically grand style. And this hypothesis is further strengthened by the response of Richard Fanshawe, who, when he produced his unreliable but lively translation of the poem in 1655, thought fit to draw attention to the deliberately rhetorical moments. So he points to the "dumb Rhet'rick" of Venus, who, wishing to move her father Jove to protect the Lusitanians, imitates one of the devices of Verity, by "making a fals Parenthesis. . . . As if her words obey'd not her commands" (II, 41). He also comments on the effect of Don Nuno's speech: "So Nunio animates, whom he did force;/Whose boyst'rous Rhet'rick such quick flame imparts" (IV, 21), and he makes even the King of Malabar rhetoric-conscious when he accuses Da Gama of evil intentions, because he brings no presents from his own monarch: "In Presents rich, in sumptuous Guifts and high,/Kings speak their loves: Their Rhet'rick's in their Hands" (VIII, 62).

Tasso: Gerusalemme Liberata

Apart from supplying footnotes, as it were, to the formal rhetoric of the Lusiads, Fanshawe's work is useful because it draws attention to the relationship between Camoens and Tasso, and the extent to which Tasso felt it incumbent upon him to rival not only the Greek and Roman epics, but the Portuguese also. In his prefatory address to the Earl of Strafford, Fanshawe remarks: "I Can not tell how your Lordship

---

Tempo fuja de tua fermosura!
Que só com refrear o passo leve
Vencerás da fortuna a fôrça dura.

. . .

Levas-me um coração que livre tinha?
Solta-m'o, e correrás mais levemente.

187

may take it, that, in so uncourted a language as that of Portugall, should be found extant a Poet to rival your beloved Tasso. How himself took it, I can; for he was heard to say (his great Jerusalem being then an Embrio) He Feared No Man But Camoens. Notwithstanding which, he bestow'd a Sonet in his praise." And Fanshawe goes on to say that, just as Tasso attributed the excellence of Guarini's *Pastor Fido* partly to the groundwork accomplished in his own *Aminta,* so Camoens would have been justified in attributing part of the success of the *Gerusalemme* to his own pioneering work in the *Lusiads*: "So, and for the same cause, might my Portingall have retorted upon Him with reference to his own Epick way: If He Had Not Seen My Lusiad, He Had Not Excell'd It."[13]

It is not possible to estimate how much imitation of Camoens there is in the *Gerusalemme Liberata* as far as style is concerned, though there are several convincing analogies. Tasso's invocation to his Muses does not emphasize style, but rather his own peculiar concept of heroic truth.[14] But Tasso's interest in style is demonstrated by the considerable variety of speeches, several of which seem to have a similar decorum to those in the *Lusiads*. For example, the role of Da Gama

13 Richard Fanshawe, tr., *The Lusiad,* p. 3.
14 Torquato Tasso, *Gerusalemme Liberata,* I, ii-iii:

> Musa tu, che di caduchi allori
> Non circondi la fronte in Elicona,
>
> . . .
>
> Tu rischiara il mio canto, e tu perdona
> Se intesso fregi al ver, s'adorno in parte
> D'altri diletti che de'tuoi le carte.
>
> Sai, che la corre il mondo ove più versi
> Di sue dolcezze il lusinghier Parnaso,
> E che'l vero condito in molli versi
> I più schivi allettando ha persuaso.

Here Tasso is so concerned to defend, under the old Horatian notion of sugaring the pill, the fabulous and amorous elements in his poem, that his remarks would be most misleading if taken as descriptive of his style. The emphasis on "diletti," "dolcezze," and "vero condito in molli versi" would be a more appropriate introduction to the style of Spenser's *Faerie Queene,* which, ironically enough, Spenser himself describes as "stern."

as the plain-speaking man of action against a background of
Eastern treachery is taken in the *Gerusalemme* by Goffredo
himself; in answer to the long and subtle speech of Soliman's
ambassador Aletes (known for his eloquence and for being
a "Gran fabbro di calunnie"), Geoffrey defines his own style:
"Risponderò, come da me si suole,/Liberi sensi in semplici
parole" (II, lxxxi). The role of Don Nuno as the man who
stirs up military spirit is roughly analogous to that of the
old man with the severe voice and the biting language ("il
mordace parlare") who appears to Soliman in his sleep and
reprimands him for his weakness in repulsing the Christians
(x, vi-xiv); presumably the Christian army, being on the
right side, are less in need of exhortation. And there is a
rather amusing reversal of roles in that part of Tasso's epic
which corresponds to the magical island of Venus in the
Lusiads, for in the Gardens of Armida, themselves a perfect
example of the Idea of Beauty, the Idea of Speed is similarly
exemplified in a chase, but here it is the man who is pursued.
Armida woos Rinaldo in the same context of *carpe diem* as
that used by Lionardo against the nymph Ephyre, except that
Tasso has expanded this into the influential (in two senses)
"rose-song" (XVI, xiv-xv); and when, despite this, he runs
away from her, she pursues him with all the short phrases
and breathlessness of the Idea of Speed presented in terms
of style:

> Forsennata gridava: O tu, che porte
> Teco parte di me, parte ne lassi,
> O prendi l'una, o rendi l'altri, o morte
> Dà insieme ad ambe: arresta, arresta i passi,
> Sol che ti sian le voci ultime porte;
> Non dico i baci: altra più degna avrassi
> Questi da te. Che temi, empio, se resti?
> Potrai negar, poichè fuggir potesti.[15]

[15] Tasso, *Gerusalemme Liberata*, XVI, xl. It is noticeable, also, that Edward
Fairfax in his translation of 1600 has made considerable effort to recreate in
English the short phrases, the run-on lines, and the general impression of
breathlessness given by the original:

> O thou that leav'st but half behind (quoth she)

We thus have, in Tasso's epic, signs of a deliberate and decorous mixture of styles which, on internal evidence, suggest knowledge of the Ideas of Hermogenes, and acceptance of the Seventh Idea as the principle of combination. But we also have the external evidence of Tasso's literary criticism, which shows that from a very early stage the Seven Ideas of Hermogenes were one of the shaping influences of his aesthetic theory, as well as his style. In the *Lezione . . . sopra il sonetto "Questa vita mortal" di Monsignor Della Casa*, which was published in 1582 but probably delivered as a lecture to the Academy at Ferrara before 1570,[16] Tasso equates the Second Idea of Grandeur with the grand styles of Cicero and Demetrius, a position which allows him to develop his own epic style on the basis of recommendations from all three. In the undated dialogue, *Il Ficino, overo de l'Arte*, which is supposed to be a discussion of aesthetics between Marsilio Ficino and Cristoforo Landino, Tasso declares that the process of artistic creation depends on the presence of Ideas in the mind of the artist, and states that Syrianus in his *Metaphysics*, Cicero in the *Orator*, and Hermogenes in the περὶ ἰδεῶν are all concerned with Ideas of speech, or the preconceptions of literary creation.[17] In *La Cavaletta, overo de la Poesia Toscana*, Tasso

---

Of my poor heart, and half with thee dost carry,
O take this part, or render that to me,
Else kill them both at once: ah! tarry, tarry,
Hear my last words; no parting kiss of thee
I crave, for some more fit with thee to marry
Keep them: unkind! what fear'st thou if thou stay?
Thou may'st deny as well as run away.

16 All authorities seem to agree that this lecture was written when Tasso was a young man lecturing at the Academy at Ferrara. For the passage in question, see *Opere*, xi, 45: ". . . quale sia la miglior di queste visioni, rimettendo per ora all'altrui guidicio, chiara cosa è che quella forma, che magnifica da Demetrio, grande da Ermogene, e sublime da Cicerone vien detta, è una medesima."

17 Tasso, in *Opere*, vii, 255: ". . . nell'anima de l'artifice, per opinione d'Aristotile ancora, sono le ragioni artificiali delle cose operate, come dichiara Siriano nel xii. de la Metafisica, e queste da noi sono chiamate idee, e così chiamò Marco Tullio quella del suo Oratore, ed Ermogene le forme del parlare . . ."

states that it is impossible to find, even in so limited a form as the sonnet, an Idea of style in its pure form, because the "forms" of speech are like natural forms, which are made up of different elements; and as "no element is entirely pure and simple, because fire mingles with air, and air with fire and water, and water with air and earth; so also each kind of speech is a mixture."[18] Finally, in 1594, a year before his death, Tasso published the *Discorsi del Poema Eroica*, in which he carries to completion both the aesthetic and the stylistic implications of the Seven Ideas. In the first book, as we have seen, he relates the theory of Ideas as artistic preconceptions or ideals of literary creation to his definition of the perfect heroic poem, and he also seeks to justify the presence of the Idea of Beauty in a heroic poem, despite the authority of Aristotle to the contrary.[19] In the second and

[18] Tasso, in *Opere*, VII, 276: ". . . niuno elemento è puro e semplice entieramente, perciochè il fuoco e mescolato con l'aria, e l'aria co'l fuoco e con l'acqua, e l'acqua con l'aria e con la terra; così ancora ciascuna maniera di parlare è mescolata."

[19] Tasso, in *Opere*, XII, 9, 15-17. For discussion of Tasso's use of the Idea concept in defining the heroic poem, see the last section of Chapter 1. The passage in which he challenges the authority of Aristotle, on the monopoly of Good in epic, sets up Hermogenes as an alternative guide:

Ma alcuni hanno voluto che il poeta non riguardi tanto alla bontà, quanto alle bellezze delle cose, fra' quali è il Navagerio, appresso il Fracastoro, laddove prova che il fine del poeta sia di riguardare nell'idea del Bello, quasi volendo contradire all'opinione, che mostrò Aristotele d'aver ne'libri morali, ne'quali dice che l'idea non giova cosa alcuna nell'operazione; ma qualunque fosse il giudizio d'Aristotele in quel luogho, dichiarato dal Greco espositore, a me non può dispiacere in alcun modo che il poeta rimiri nell' idea della bellezza: ma se più sono l'idee nelle quali suol dirizzar gli occhi l'oratore, come e piaciuto ad Ermogene, non so perchè il poeta debba considerare solamente quella della bellezza, e non l'altre sei similmente: ma peravventura parve al Navagerio che nella forma della bellezza fossero comprese tutte le altre, o che il Bello fosse in tutte, perciocchè nelle chiarezza, nella grandezza, nella velocità, nell'affetto, nella gravità, e nella verità è il Bello . . .

[But some have wished that the poet look not so much to the goodness, as to the beauty of things, among whom is Navagero, following Fracastorius, who proves that the poet's aim is to look for the Idea of Beauty, as if wishing to contradict the opinion which I show Aristotle to hold in the

third books he uses the Idea concept to justify the widest possible definition both of unity and truth in a heroic poem. In the fourth book he compares the Hermogenic scheme of styles with those of Cicero and Demetrius and decides in favor of Cicero's, a decision which is promptly reversed by his eclectic use of Hermogenes in his description of the heroic style;[20] and finally in the sixth book he returns to his defense of the Idea of Beauty, a gesture which reflects his uneasiness about the powerful and lovely influence of Armida over so much of the *Gerusalemme*.[21]

Tasso does not himself equate the Seventh Idea of Gravity with the principle of decorum, and seems, like Minturno, to treat it rather as a style, so that Gravity becomes almost synonymous with Grandeur in his criticism. But his theory of epic depends on the Idea concept at two levels and at two stages in the development of a poem: the Idea, principally of form and content, of the perfect heroic poem which preexists in

---

Ethics, in which he says that the Idea [of Beauty] is not useful. But whatever may be the judgment of Aristotle in this place, as given by the Greek expositor, I do not at all reject the concept that the poet should attend to the Idea of Beauty: but if there are more Ideas to which the orator should direct his eyes, as Hermogenes felt, then perhaps the poet should not consider only that of Beauty, but the other six also: But perhaps it seemed to Navagero that under the Form of Beauty could be contained all the others, or that Beauty exists in all, since in Clarity, in Grandeur, in Speed, in Ethos, in Gravity and in Truth there is Beauty . . .]

[20] Tasso, in *Opere*, xii, 132-134. Although Tasso decides in favor of the Ciceronian scheme on the grounds that it is simpler, he immediately proceeds to show that the Three Styles are broad categories which have to be subdivided, and he makes this subdivision in Hermogenic terms: "*La grave* forma è quella, che è piena di dignità, e l'aspra, l'affettuosa, e la veemente, *la mediocre*, la graziosa, la soave, la dolce, la piacevole, l'ornata, e la fiorita, *l'umile*, la chiara, ovver la facile, la semplice, l'acuta, la sottile, la motteggevole . . ." (p. 134; my italics).

[21] Tasso, in *Opere*, xii, 168-169. Here the defense of the Idea of Beauty is given in terms of "la maraviglia," or the sense of wonder, which Tasso considers to be one of the most important criteria of excellence in epic poetry; and he claims that though this sense of wonder may be created by presenting images of "cose brutte," terrible or awe-inspiring things, "la maraviglia delle cose belle è più durevole," the sense of wonder created by beautiful things is more long-lasting.

the artist's mind; and the Ideas of style which, though also preexistent in their own right, are also the mechanics by which the Idea of the epic can be actualized. Such an important application of the Idea concept to epic theory can scarcely have gone unnoticed by other aspiring epic writers; and one of the most important statements in the *Discorsi del Poema Eroico* must surely be the seemingly simple remark that "if the Ideas are many, and that of Magnificence, and that of Gravity, are different from that of Beauty, the epic poet directs the eyes to many Ideas."[22]

Daniel: The Civil Wars

One aspiring epic poet in England who could conceivably have seen all of Tasso's publications before completing his own major work is Samuel Daniel, who in 1595 published *The First Fowre Bookes of the Civile Warrs betweene the two houses of Lancaster and Yorke*, and continued to add more books until 1609. By 1603, at any rate, Daniel has read the *Gerusalemme Liberata*, since he comments admiringly upon it in the *Defence of Ryme*, and congratulates Tasso for not having been led astray by the fashion for "classical" verses. Moreover, it is almost certainly Tasso whom Daniel is imitating in his own choice of *ottava rima* for *The Civil Wars*. Certainly Daniel's concept of the heroic poem is closer to Tasso's than it is to Spenser's or Ariosto's; but Daniel has obviously moved that concept some steps further in the direction indicated by Tasso, away from the fabulous and delightful, and toward the truthful and grave. He even includes, in his Preface to the 1609 edition, an apology for the breach of historical accuracy which is involved in dramatic decorum, "that poeticall licence, of framing speaches to the persons of men according to their occasions"; and he almost apologizes for writing in verse, wherein, he says, despite prejudice to the contrary, "such as love this Harmony of words, may finde,

---

[22] Tasso, in *Opere*, xii, 169: "Ma se molte sono l'idee e quella della magnificenza, e della gravità sono differenti da quella della bellezza, a molte idee rivolge gli occhi il poeta eroico."

that a Subject, of the greatest gravitie, will be aptly exprest."[23]

Without jumping to any conclusions about the relationship in Daniel's mind between "greatest gravitie" and the concept of decorum, it is clear that in *The Civil Wars* Daniel has indeed used "that poeticall license, of framing speaches to the persons of men according to their occasions." Of women also, we might add, especially as Daniel apologizes in the 1609 Preface for a breach of historical decorum in his presentation of Queen Isabel, whose emotions he has made more mature than her historical age of fourteen would properly permit. One example of such emotions occurs when she sees from her window Richard brought captive into London, in such abject condition that she scarcely recognizes him:

> But stay: ist not my Lord himselfe I see?
> In truth, if 'twere not for his base aray,
> I verily should thinke that it were hee;
> And yet his basenes doth a grace bewray:
> Yet God forbid; let me deceived be,
> And be it not my Lord, although it may:
> Let my desire make vowes against desire;
> And let my sight approve my sight a lier.
>
> Let me not see him, but himselfe; a King:
> For so he left me; so he did remove.
> This is not he: this feeles some other thing;
> A passion of dislike, or else of love.
> O yes; 'tis he: that princely face doth bring
> The evidence of Majestie to proove:
> That face, I have conferr'd, which now I see,
> With that within my heart, and they agree.
>
> (II, 77-78)

One can see why Daniel should recognize this sophisticated response as being rather unsuitable for a fourteen-year-old. There is not only the extremely disconcerting wordplay in moments of tension (a characteristic also of Shakespeare's most extraordinary teenager, Juliet), but also the adult exploration

[23] Samuel Daniel, in *Complete Works*, ed. A. B. Grosart, 1963, II, 7.

of identity, and the political question of whether the selfhood
of a king is separable from his circumstances. But the final
sophistication comes not from inside Isabel, but is supplied
by the omniscient narrator, who comments on the dramatic
presentation of her speech:

> Teares, sighes and words, doubled together flowe;
> Confus'dly striving whether should do more,
> The true intelligence of griefe to showe.
>
> (II, 82)

In other words, what looks to the audience like an extremely
complex and deliberate piece of rhetoric is calmly asserted by
the poet to be instead the "true intelligence of griefe." Isabel's
speech is in fact a fine example of the Idea of Verity, the
broken, self-correcting, exclaiming style, which, while obviously using artificial patterns of speech, loudly proclaims its
lack of artifice. The short phrases not only indicate the fluctuation in Isabel's mind, but are the metrical sign, as Daniel says,
that her sighs "interpoint her words" (II, 83); and in addition
her speech is, like the "truthful" sonnets of Sidney and Shakespeare, a debate on the nature of Verity as an Idea, and the
relationship between appearance and reality:

> In truth, if 'twere not for his base aray,
> I verily should thinke that it were hee;
> . . .
>
> Yet God forbid; let me deceived be,
> And be it not my Lord, although it may:
> Let my desire make vowes against desire;
> And let my sight approve my sight a lier.

This speech of Isabel's is soon followed by the passionate
outburst of the bishop of Carlisle, who alone among the rebel
courtiers dared to attack the king's deposers. His speech,
which begins soberly enough, gradually increases in passion,
but where Isabel's is inward-directed and based on confusion,
Carlisle's is directed against Parliament and based on the certainty of righteous anger:

Have you not done inough? Blush, blush to thinke,
Lay on your harts those hands; those hands too rash;
Know that this staine that's made doth further sinke
Into your soules then all your blouds can wash;
Leave with the mischiefe done and doe not linke
Sin unto sin, for heaven and earth will dash
This ill accomplisht worke ere it be long;
For weake he builds that fences wrong with wrong . . .[24]

If Isabel's speech is an example of the Idea of Verity, then clearly Carlisle's speech is an example of Vehemence; and Daniel seems to confirm this by commenting on the effects of his speech, which were disastrous:

Stopt, there, was his too vehement speech with speed,
And he sent close to warde, from where he stood;
His zeale untimely, deem'd too much t'exceed
The measure of his wit, and did no good . . .

(III, 25)

Furthermore, the "too vehement speech" of Carlisle is obviously intended to be contrasted with that of Sir Thomas Blunt, who also opposed the government of Bolingbroke, but who is presented as a man of decorum, judgment, and foresight, whose language follows all the prescriptions for the Idea of Gravity as a style:

Judicious *Blunt* (whose learning, valor, wit,
Had taught true knowledge in the course of things;
Knew dangers as they were, and th'humerous fit
Of ware-lesse discontent, what end it brings)
Counsels their heat, with calme grave words, and fit,
(Words well fore-thought, that from experience springs)
And warnes a warier cariage in the thing;
Lest blind presumption worke their ruining.

(III, 37)

---

[24] This stanza appears in the 1597 edition of *The Civil Wars.* In 1609 the stanza was radically revised, perhaps to remove the rather clumsy use of repetition ("Blush, blush"; "those hands, those hands.")

This certainly sounds like the Idea of Gravity, especially as it is described in the commentary of Parthenio, as that style which uses "sentenze exquisite, & alte, prudentissime, & tali che non paiano esser venute in mente alla sprovista, ma bene considerate" (p. 244).

Finally, and on similar grounds, we can identify a good, clear example of the Idea of Speed, not this time within a speech but in a passage which describes the thought processes of King Edward IV, during his sudden infatuation with Lady Elizabeth Grey:

> The morning being comn (and glad he was
> That it was com'n) after so long a night
> He thought would have no morning (time did passe
> So slowe, and his desires ran on so light)
> A messenger with speed dispatched was,
> Of speciall trust, this Lady to invite
> To come t'his presence; though before the time
> That Ladies rise: who rarely rise betime.
>
> Yet soone she hastes: and yet that soone seem'd long,
> To him whose longing went so swift a pase . . .
> (VIII, 63-64)

There could scarcely be a better combination of the devices of Speed (the "slipper" syllables, the run-on lines, the natural trochees) with the concepts of speed (the messenger's going, the lady's coming, the racing of the king's desires).

Drayton: The Barons Warres

Daniel's *Civil Wars*, then, provide internal evidence of considerable strength that he was influenced by the Hermogenic rhetoric of Ideas in his concept of epic style, and that he deliberately combined as many of these Ideas as he could within the framework of a basically "grave" poem. He could have acquired his knowledge of the Ideas while he was at Oxford, and would probably have reinforced it to some extent by reading Italian criticism. In addition, Tasso's *Gerusalemme* was obviously an important model for his own epic.

And Daniel, in turn, was obviously of formative influence
when Michael Drayton began to revise his *Mortimeriados*
(1596) into a heroic poem in the manner of the *Gerusalemme*
and *The Civil Wars*. The product of this revision was *The
Barons Warres* of 1603, and Drayton's editors remark with
much truth that most of the revision seems to have been done
in imitation of *The Civil Wars*:

> . . . many of the changes made by Drayton in *The Barons
> Warres* might be summed up as an attempt to write a poem
> more like Daniel's. That is, a poem more historical, more
> critical, less romantic, less decorated. . . . [In *Mortimeriados*]
> Drayton deplores civil wars, pities the weakness and suffer-
> ings of Edward, revels in the love-story of Isabella and
> Mortimer, but makes little attempt to unify or articulate
> it. In *The Barons Warres* he does make this attempt, and
> the new opening stanzas, slow, orderly and dignified, pro-
> claim it.[25]

But the revision also provides an interesting parallel to that of
the transformation of *Gerusalemme Liberata* into the *Conquistata*, and we know that Drayton had read at least one version
of Tasso's poem by 1596, because his complaint, *Robert, Duke
of Normandy*, contains a reference to the *Gerusalemme*.

It is clear that in revising *Mortimeriados* into *The Barons
Warres* Drayton is aware that he is actually changing genres,
and moving from complaint, which is essentially a medieval
form, into the Renaissance genre of epic. The dedication to
Mortimeriados speaks of "these Tragedies" and opens with a

---

[25] Michael Drayton, in *Works*, ed. J. W. Hebel, 1931-1941, v, 63-64. The
editors of the last volume of the *Works*, which contains all the notes, were
K. Tillotson and B. Newdigate, and their analysis of Drayton's revisions provides useful support for my theory about the increasing antiheroic tendency
of Renaissance epic. They suggest that in his efforts to redress the balance
of history as against romantic heroism, Drayton has gone too far in the
other direction, and falsified history in order to demonstrate the evils of
civil war: Not only does he select his material with this in view, he announces and preaches it directly, and, especially in *The Barons Warres*, is at
pains to diagnose and comment on the situation. In these reflective, analytical
passages, there is a detachment, an intellectual effort, which is foreign to the
earlier poem; and it is here that Daniel's influence is most evident."

decorously doleful setting, reminiscent of Henryson's *Testament of Cresseid*:

> The lowring heaven had mask'd her in a clowde,
> Dropping sad teares upon the sullen earth,
> Bemoning in her melancholly shrowde,
> The angry starres which raign'd at Edward's birth . . .
>
> (ll. 1-4)

Mortimer himself is introduced thus:

> In all this heat his greatnes first began,
> The serious subject of my sadder vaine,
> Great Mortimer, the wonder of a man,
> Whose fortunes heere my Muse must entertaine,
> And from the grave his griefes must yet complaine . . .
>
> (ll. 43-47)

The Barons Warres, on the other hand, opens with full epic paraphernalia, including a rejection of "soft Layes and tender Loves" and a request for divine inspiration, while the stanza which introduces Mortimer has become this:

> In all that Heat, then gloriously began,
> The serious Subject of my solid Vaine,
> Brave MORTIMER, that some-what more then Man,
> Of the old HEROES great and God-like Straine,
> For whom, Invention doing all it can,
> His weight of Honour hardly shall sustaine,
> To beare his Name immortaliz'd, and hye,
> When he in Earth un-numbred yeeres shall lye . . .
>
> (I, 19)

In the process of revision, the "sadder vaine" has become "solid," the "tragic" rhyme royal has become the epic octave, the human and mortal has become the hero, half-man, half-god, and the complaint from the grave has become the sustained effort of epic invention.

This remains, of course, a statement of the poet's intention, and although the changes that Drayton makes do on the whole bear out this intention, *The Barons Warres* is still a compara-

tively slight poem when placed beside either *The Civil Wars*
or the *Gerusalemme*; in bulk and scope it bears the same relationship to them as *Paradise Regained* does to *Paradise Lost*.
And yet, even so, Drayton has managed to incorporate within
his basically "solid Vaine" changes and contrasts of style, or
comments upon style, which seem to reflect the Hermogenic
Ideas. The description of the Queen's bower in the sixth canto
is clearly Drayton's equivalent, in a nonfabulous context, of
the gardens of Armida, seen by Tasso as representing the
Idea of Beauty in his poem. The "extreme Passion" of King
Edward in the abdication scene corresponds to that of Daniel's
Isabel, and features the same combination of obvious artifice
with stated sincerity, "As ev'ry Sense playd the Tragedian,/
Truly to shew from whence his Sorrowes came" (v, 11). And
one of the most striking emblems of the change in the direction of epic is found in the revised version of this abdication
scene. In *Mortimeriados* all attention fastens on the king, and
his rather effeminate rhetoric, which is nevertheless intended
to invoke sympathy in the audience. In *The Barons Warres*,
however, Edward's appearance is preceded and balanced by
that of Adam Torlton, Bishop of Hereford, who is given the
same oratorical role as the "judicious Blunt" of Daniel's poem.
Where earlier in the poem (and throughout *Mortimeriados*)
Torlton is characterized as a man of extreme political and
rhetorical cunning, he now appears as:

> The best experienc'd in that great Affayre,
> A Man grave, subtill, stout, and eloquent,
> First, with faire speech th'Assembly doth prepare;
> Then, with a grace austere and eminent,
> Doth his Abuse effectually declare . . .   (v, 6)

Drayton does not reproduce, but rather reports Torlton's
speech; and then, as Daniel often does, sums up its effect on
the audience:

> The grave deliverie of whose vehement Speech,
> Grac'd with a dauntlesse, uncontracted Brow,
> Th'Assembly with Severitie did teach,

Each word of his Authentike to allow . . .

(v, 10)

It is hard to avoid the implication that Torlton is here being presented as the figure who speaks according to the Idea of Gravity (also translated as Severity and Eloquence by some of the Renaissance commentators), and whose presence in this scene represents the movement of the whole poem away from youthful emotionalism toward a more mature, experienced, and decorous vision of history. Like Odysseus, who was also known for his cunning, Torlton has become the "orator," both in the sense of being able to "intensify things shameful, cruel or hateful" (the sense in which Gravity can be a terrible style), as he relates the king's abuses of his position, and also in the sense of being the "best experienc'd" in this or any other situation. And when we consider how the titles of Drayton's earlier poems indicate a fascination with the Idea concept in at least some form,[26] it seems more than likely that these rhetorical effects and comments are not just the result of imitating Daniel, but a deliberate application to his own poem of Hermogenic Ideas.

Spenser: The Faerie Queene

The process of revision which can be seen here in the transformation of *Mortimeriados* into *The Barons Warres* reflects in a small way the development of the Renaissance epic as a genre—away from what is fabulous, exciting, or naively militaristic, toward a view of heroism that is tempered and controlled by experience and judgment. So the simple patriotism of Camoens, which depends for inspiration on the nymphs of the river Tagus, gives place to the more complex idealism of Tasso, who appeals to the Heavenly Muse, and whose subject is "l'armi pietose." The revisions which Tasso then made in order to transform the *Gerusalemme Liberata* into the *Conquistata*, though partly stylistic and artistic, were clearly designed to bring the poem still further in line with Church

---

[26] *Idea The Shepheards Garland,* 1593; *Ideas Mirrour,* 1594; *Endimion and Phoebe, Ideas Latmus,* 1595; and the revised sonnet sequence, *Idea,* 1619.

teaching and Aristotelian ethical criticism, for the overall effect is to increase the distinction between Christians and Saracens by idealizing the Christian heroes, by reducing the fabulous and amorous episodes, and by introducing obviously moral and religious passages, such as the vision of the Heavenly Jerusalem in Canto xx.[27] There still remains, however, Tasso's avowed principle of sweetening the Idea of the Good with as much as possible of the Idea of Beauty, and, as C. P. Brand has pointed out, the *Gerusalemme Conquistata* retains those passages describing the gardens of Armida which were both the most erotic and the most influential.[28]

When we come to Daniel, however, the movement toward Gravity is more systematic and more unified. The amorous is reduced to the historical infatuation of Edward IV for Lady Elizabeth Grey, and the slightly unhistorical, undecorous emotions of the young Queen Isabel, while the military action has been stripped of virtually all its idealism. Where Tasso invokes the Heavenly Muse, Daniel says, perhaps rather primly, "Come sacred Virtue; I no Muse, but thee,/Invoke . . ."; and where Tasso intends to celebrate "l'armi pietose," Daniel shows no trace of celebration in his own proposition:

I sing the civill Warres, Tumultuous Broyles,
And bloody factions of a mightie Land:
Whose people hautie, proud with forraine spoyles,
Upon themselves turn-backe their conquering hand;

[27] C. P. Brand, in *Torquato Tasso: A Study of the Poet and of His Contribution to English Literature*, 1965, feels that one should not overemphasize the moral or religious motivation for many of the changes, which may rather have been made for artistic reasons. At the same time he has to admit (pp. 126-127) that "the moral and religious intention certainly predominates in the new allegorical passages," and that the idealization of the Christians and blackening of the Saracens is not an artistic gain, but a flaw: "A superhuman confidence and calm replaces the poetical hesitancy of the *Liberata*." This may be a flaw if the assumption is that subtlety of characterization was Tasso's aim; but it would be the logical result of a revision designed to move the poem more firmly in the direction of the Idea of Magnificence, an Idea which requires firm affirmations and denials, and which does not admit any trace of hesitancy or doubt.

[28] Brand, p. 127.

Whil'st Kin their Kin, Brother the Brother soyles;
Like Ensignes all against like Ensignes band;
Bowes against Bowes, the Crowne against the Crowne;
Whil'st all pretending right, all right's throwne downe.

Drayton's proposition to *The Barons Warres* comes as close to this as it can without being a photographic reproduction; and both poets, we have seen, incorporate into the texture of their poems the dramatized figure of the "grave" orator whose experience and judgment is contrasted to the overemotional responses of other characters.

These poems of Camoens, Tasso, Daniel, and Drayton may seem at first sight rather a curious choice for an investigation of decorum in the Renaissance epic, since, with the exception of Tasso, none of them is usually regarded as being in the main stream of the epic's development (whatever that may be). However, having shown that there *is* a clear and conscious line of descent in these vernacular epics (another tradition to supplement the major Virgilian one), it should now be possible to go back in time and investigate the much more complex problem of rhetorical decorum in *The Faerie Queene*, where any tradition is harder to isolate within Spenser's infinite variety. The task is all the more necessary in view of Spenser's known connection with Gabriel Harvey, who called himself Pseudo-Hermogenes,[29] and who undoubtedly would have passed on to Spenser whatever he found in Hermogenes of value to a developing poet.

Spenser has conveniently indicated the position in his cosmology of Platonic Ideas in general. In the *Hymne of Heavenly Beautie* he creates a fine *climax* or *gradatio* (one of the figures recommended by Hermogenes for achieving the Idea of Beauty), in which each level of existence is described as more beautiful as it approaches nearer to God himself. Above earth, and the natural heavens of the planets:

Faire is the heaven, where happy soules have place,
In full enjoyment of felicitie,
Whence they doe still behold the glorious face

[29] See Chapter I, n. 32.

203

Of the divine eternall Majestie;
More faire is that, where those *Idees* on hie,
Enraunged be, which *Plato* so admyred,
And pure *Intelligences* from God inspyred.

(ll. 78-84)

And above these are ranged the nine heavens of the angelic
hierarchies, which are surpassed by God's own heaven again.
Between man and the angels, then, stand the Platonic Ideas;
and this is precisely the position of Faerie Land, with its capi-
tal City, Cleopolis, set as an ideal between all other cities and
the heavenly Jerusalem (1. x. 58). Within Faerie Land, Platonic
Ideas are in effect represented by the figures of allegory, who
are sometimes abstractions from the first moment they appear,
and sometimes achieve that status by progressive definition.
All this is obvious. What is less obvious, but more important,
is Spenser's Neoplatonic theory of the function of Arthur in
the poem. Arthur, Spenser states in the introductory Letter
to Raleigh, is to represent that total virtue which is "the perfection of all the rest and conteineth in it them all." This may
have something to do with Aristotle's *Ethics*, but it is also closely connected with the critical tradition enunciated by Tasso in
the *Del Poema Eroico*, that he "who wishes to form *the Idea
of a perfect Knight*" will not only prefer the historical and
Christian figures of Charlemagne and Arthur to legendary
and pagan ones,[30] but he will also, like Virgil, combine all
the heroic virtues into a single figure; and whereas Homer
divided these virtues up among his epic figures, Virgil "showed
a better sense of decorum in general, because he formed in
Aeneas piety, religion, continence, bravery, magnanimity, justice, and every other virtue belonging to *the* Knight."[31] Arthur

[30] Tasso, *Del Poema Eroico* (1594), in *Opere* xii, p. 45: "Oltre a ciò vuol
formare l'idea d'un perfetto Cavaliere, non so per qual cagione gli nieghi
questa lode di pietà, e di religione: laonde preporrei di gran lunga la persona
di Carlo e d'Artù, a quella di Teseo e di Giasone." Spenser could have read
an almost identical version of this statement in Tasso's earlier *Discorsi dell'Arte
Poetica* (1587). See *Opere*, xii, p. 203.

[31] Tasso, *Del Poema Eroico*, p. 106: "Ma Virgilio, se non m'inganno, vide
meglio il decoro generale, perchè formò in Enea la pietà, la religione, la

stands for the Neoplatonic Idea of knighthood in that he represents an amalgam of the pagan and Christian heroic virtues;
and he also performs the same function as that of the Seventh
Idea of Hermogenes, Gravity or Decorum, by which all the
other Ideas are combined into a persuasive and educational
whole.

However, as everyone knows, Arthur is not in fact allowed
to perform this function, as described in the Letter, but is
rather phased tactfully out in favor of Britomart, whose quest
for Artegall replaces Arthur's for the Faerie Queene, and by
Artegall himself, who is, at least in name, intended to be
Arthur's equal. And it is in Book v of *The Faerie Queene*
that we find the clearest evidence that Spenser knew about
the Seven Ideas of Hermogenes, and that the decorum of epic
writing required a mixture of those Ideas. Book v is in effect
an epic within an epic. It is introduced by a careful analogy
between heroes of the past, like Bacchus and Hercules, and
Artegall himself; and at the beginning of Canto II we are
reminded that the redress of wrongs has always been a test of
true heroism:

> Whilome those great Heroes got thereby
> Their greatest glory, for their rightfull deedes,
> And place deserved with the Gods on hy.

And it deals with those public themes and emblems of themes
which best distinguish the epic from other genres—good government, the mean between tyranny and unlawful rebellion,

---

continenza, la fortezza, la magnanimità, la giustizia, e ciascun' altra virtù
di Cavaliero . . ." In this case, the statement of the *Del Poema Eroico* represents a change from the *Dell'Arte Poetica*, where Tasso merely speaks of
the "sum of virtue" as being the perfection of each virtue separately, rather
than their aggregate, and makes Aeneas representative of only one virtue
instead of all:

> L'epico all'incontro vuole nelle persone il sommo delle virtù, le quali
> eroiche dalla virtù eroica sono nominate. Si ritrova in Enea l'eccellenza
> della pietà, della fortezza militare in Achille, della prudenza in Ulisse; e
> per venire ai nostri, della lealtà in Amadigi, della constanza in Bradamente;
> anzi pure in alcuni di questi il cumulo di tutte queste virtù.

> (*Opere*, XII, p. 207)

justice and mercy, the City and the commonweal. It is the nearest Spenser ever came to completing the other half of his attempt to rival Tasso, by illustrating the public virtues (*politice*) of Arthur, the perfect knight, "after that he came to be king." And it is therefore entirely appropriate that this book should show the clearest sense of epic decorum as Spenser might have derived it from the *Gerusalemme*.

Artegall has been instructed by Astraea in the methods of justice, and how "to weigh both right and wrong/In equall balance with due recompense." He has been equipped with an iron companion, Talus, who is described as being "Immovable, resistlesse, without end." And the two of them pursue a remarkably unwavering course (with the one embarrassing exception of Artegall's lapse into effeminacy) quite different in effect from the errors of Redcrosse, the odyssey of Guyon, the remarkable absenteeism of Calidore, or the "romance" wanderings of Books III and IV. Artegall's character is best exposed in the scene of Duessa's trial, where Arthur himself is moved to pity by the lawyers for the defense, but Artegall, having heard both sides carefully, remains in "constant firme intent." This emphasis on firmness recalls that first part of the Idea of Grandeur which Hermogenes called σεμνότης and Minturno translated as Magnificence, which registers itself upon the ear as "stabile e ferme" and deals, as one of its four primary subjects, with those qualities or virtues that make men seem equal with the Gods, such as Reason or Justice or Temperance. And this recollection becomes twice as interesting if one turns back to the appropriate section of the περὶ ἰδεῶν. For Hermogenes remarks that an example of a Magnificent subject would be the relationship between Law and Nature. One could, for example, have a Magnificent debate on the question of whether Law, as God-given, must remain constant, whereas Nature is unstable and unequal ("inaequabilis" in Sturm's translation).[32] What could be more

[32] Johannes Sturm, ed. and tr., *De Dicendi Generibus sive formis orationum Libri II*, 1571, p. 63:

Tertius ordo sententiarum in gravi dicendi genere est, de rebus, quae natura quidem divinae sunt & magnae: tamen plurimùm in hominibus spectantur.

in accordance with Hermogenes' suggestions here than Artegall's debate with the egalitarian giant, who also handles a
pair of scales, and "all things would reduce unto equality,"
because he does not understand that the natural world was
created in mysteriously balanced disproportion, and that what
appears to be the instability of Nature is actually cyclical
change regulated by divine law.

In fact, the conflict between Artegall and the giant is another version of that between Mutability and Nature herself,
which I have already identified as being in the spirit and
style of Magnificence. All the characteristics of that style are
present here also:

> Thou that presumst to weight the world anew,
> And all things to an equall to restore,
> In stead of right me seemes great wrong dost shew,
> And far above thy forces pitch to sore
> . . .
> For at the first they all created were
> In goodly measure, by their Makers might,
> And weighed out in ballaunces so nere,
> That not a dram was missing of their right,
> The earth was in the middle centre pight,
> In which it doth immoveable abide,
> Hemd in with waters like a wall in sight;
> And they with aire, that not a drop can slide:
> Al which the heavens *containe*, and in their courses
>   guide.
>
> Such heavenly justice doth among them *raine*,
> That every one doe know their certaine bound,
> In which they doe these many yeares *remaine*,
> And mongst them al no change hath yet beene found.

---

ut, si quis dicat de anima, quòd immortalis, aut de justitia, aut de tem-
perantia, aut si de caeteris virtutibus disseramus, aut de vita humana, *aut
quid lex, quidve natura, aut de similibus*. ut, Lex inventum est, & donum
Deorum, & quae sequuntur. Item *Lex verò publica est, & constituta
atque confirmata semper eadem omnibus: Natura verò instabilis est, &
inaequabilis* . . .   (My italics)

But if thou now shouldst weigh them new in pound,
We are not sure they would so long *remaine*:
All chaunge is perillous, and all chance unsound.
Therefore leave off to weigh them all againe,
Till we may be assur'd they shall their course *retaine*.
                                            (v. ii. 34-36)

And when the giant declares, as Mutability does, that the
evidence of his eyes shows him Nature far from firm and
stable, since the sea encroaches upon the land, and the earth
is "encreased" by the bodies of all its dead creatures, Artegall
replies first, as Nature does in the Mutability Cantos, that
cyclical change is, to the thoughtful, really evidence of permanence, but that the final refutation of the giant's position consists in the inscrutable ways of God: "All creatures must
obey the voice of the most hie./They live, they die, like as he
doth *ordaine*." As in the Cantos, the slow, steady pace of
these stanzas, the dense but not harsh consonantal texture,
the long, wide vowels, and especially the emphasis on the
words which I have italicized, "containe," "remaine," "retaine," and "ordaine," all work to create a style which is the
audible image of stability. As Artegall himself says, "the eare
must be the ballance" (v. ii. 47); and in this case the ear returns the verdict in favor of Artegall and his fusion of natural
process, divine law, and human justice into a single, stable,
world view.

   Having established this norm of a firm and measured style
to match his protagonist's virtue, Spenser is able to depart
radically from it when it suits the context. Compare, for example, his description of Artegall's encounter with the fleeing
Samient and her pursuers:

> So travelling, he chaunst far off to heed
> A Damsell, flying on a palfrey fast
> Before two Knights, that after her did *speed*
> With all their powre, and her full fiercely chast
> In hope to have her overhent at last
> . . .
> Soone after these he saw another Knight,

That after those two former rode apace

. . .

At length he saw the hindmost overtake
One of those two, and force him turne his face;

. . .

But th'other still pursu'd the fearefull Mayd;
Who still from him as fast away did flie,
Ne once for ought her *speedy* passage stayd . . .
(v. viii. 4-6; my italics)

The romance motif of the chased maiden, with the ironic implications inherent in the adjective, is one of Spenser's most
obvious debts to Ariosto, and the figure of flying Angelica.
But it also belongs in the more general context of Speed as an
important element in love or war, and in the tradition of
Strephon's pursuit of the shepherdess Nous, or Lionardo's
pursuit of the nymph Ephyre. And Spenser has apparently
taken pains to assemble the elements of Speed as a style—the
short words, the light consonants, the onomatopoeia of breathlessness (a remarkable accumulation of *f*'s and *h*'s), the natural trochees (damsell, flying, after, fiercely, former, other, fearefull, *speedy*) and the run-on lines, including the neatly figurative "overtake/One of those two.

Completely different again is the style in which Spenser
describes the two hags, Envy and Detraction, who are in league
with the Blatant Beast. Detraction, for example,

. . . was ugly, and her mouth distort,
Foming with poyson round about her gils,
In which her cursed tongue full sharpe and short
Appear'd like Aspis sting, that closely kils,
Or cruelly does wound, whom so she wils:
A distaffe in her other hand she had,
Upon the which she little spinnes, but spils . . .
(v. xii. 36)

One needs no rhetorical training to be able to detect the ugliness of sound here, produced by gaping diphthongs (to approx-

imate the effect of hiatus, which is difficult to produce in
English) and harsh combinations of consonants, especially
st and *sp*. But it could add considerably to our understanding
of Envy and Detraction to see them as examples of the style
and Idea of Vehemence, here perverted, as Spenser insists, to
attacking the good instead of the bad. So viewed, their importance extends beyond that of the historical allegory (the attack
on Lord Grey) to all those who misapply the tools of satire
by defaming what should be praised, and thereby create a
social, political, or literary injustice. The hags are, after all,
anticipated by the figure of Malfont, identified as a satirist by
the poet's statement that "the bold title of a Poet bad/He on
himselfe had ta'en, and rayling rimes had sprad." The hags
are followed by the Blatant Beast himself, who by the end
of Book vi has returned to rampage through Faerie Land—
coincidentally at the time when the craze for Vehement satire
was heightening in Elizabethan England.

One of the most curious signs of Hermogenic theory, however, appears in the trial of Duessa at Mercilla's court. When
the prisoner is brought in,

> Then up arose a person of deepe reach,
> And rare in-sight, hard matters to revele;
> That well could charme his tongue, and time his
> speach
> To all assayes . . .
>
> (v. ix. 39)

In this the lawyer Zeal belongs in the category of orators like
Daniel's "judicious Blunt" and Drayton's Adam Torlton,
who combine experience, flexibility of style for all occasions,
and the ability to "intensify things shameful, cruel or hateful."
For:

> Strongly did *Zele* her haynous fact enforce,
> And many other crimes of foul defame
> Against her brought, to banish all remorse,
> And aggravate the horror of her blame . . .
>
> (v. ix. 43)

But Spenser's version of the δεινός or "grave" orator is presented with some ambivalence, as a less than sympathetic figure. He may be technically on the right side, but he is arguing against such natural tear-jerkers as Pity, Grief, and Regard of Womanhead; and he is also likely to remind the audience of such unsavory rhetoricians as Despair or Archimago, who "well could file his tongue as smooth as glas" (I. i. 35). The fact is that in the nonpolitical books of *The Faerie Queene*, because of the importance of verbal temptations, suspicion of rhetorical skill becomes a dominant moral theme.

Indeed, one could argue that if the influence of the Seven Ideas is to be felt in the poem as a whole, it consists less in modulations of style (though these are important) than in modifications of the concept of a few Ideas with which Spenser was particularly concerned. So in his hands the Idea of Truth is not only Christianized, but required to be pure and simple in fact, and that aspect of the Idea of Verity which produces the *effect* of sincerity by artificial means is relegated to the enemy, in the person of Duessa/Fidessa. Similarly, the Idea of Beauty, as imaged in the person and surroundings of Acrasia, is qualified far more severely than it was in Tasso, since the aesthetic stasis of Spenser's false Venus is fixed in a posture of shame by the net of Guyon, and is contrasted to the well-earned rest of the true Venus in Book III, who keeps the living cycle turning. The Ideas appropriate to the satirist, too, are more noticeably represented in their abuse than in their right use; for example, note these Ideas as they appear in the figures of Envy and Detraction and the Blatant Beast, although there are passages, as for example in Arthur's attack on Night (III. iv. 55-59), where the techniques of dispraise are used honorably. Even the Idea of Simplicity, represented by the old shepherd Meliboe and the pastoral life of Book VI, is regretfully qualified by the poet, not only because Calidore is obviously neglecting his duties in staying there, but because its destruction by the Brigands shows the inadequacy of such a simple response to life when life must be lived in a fallen world.

This investigation into the decorum of *The Faerie Queene*,

though obviously superficial, may serve to open the way to more systematic studies; and this, hopefully, could also happen to Milton's *Paradise Lost*, which should certainly be expected to demonstrate "what the laws are of a true *Epic Poem . . .* what Decorum is, which is the grand master-piece to observe."[33] In Milton's epics, suspicion of rhetorical skill becomes even more firmly integrated with the meaning of the poems. In *Paradise Lost*, and also in *Paradise Regained*, the experienced and flexible orator is represented by Satan himself, and his relationship to the orators of Greece and Rome is never more clearly demonstrated than when he is about to seduce Eve. Moreover, when Satan tries to apply the same skills to the temptation of Christ in *Paradise Regained*, experience is found to be impotent in the face of innocence, and rhetoric is defeated by a new kind of decorum, the starkly simple but absolutely appropriate biblical quotation. But at the same time we can be quite sure that Milton's concept of decorum included the Seven Ideas, because in *Of Education* he recommends the study of Hermogenes as part of that process which is going to lead to the "grand master-piece to observe." It is also clear that he does pay great attention to modulations from the grand style; and when one considers the nature of these modulations—the lyrical husband-worship of Eve ("with perfet beauty adornd") in Book IV, the contrasting staccato quarrel of Satan and Gabriel which follows, the broken, self-accusing rhetoric of Adam's soliloquy in Book X as he explores the true nature of his fall—it looks as though the situations have been devised at least partly to show to advantage "the *ideas,* and various kinds of stile" which any good orator should know.[34]

With these qualifications, then, it can fairly be claimed that

[33] Milton, *Of Education* in *Works,* IV, 286. Needless to say, I do not accept the strange argument of Thomas Kranidas in *The Fierce Equation: A Study of Milton's Decorum,* 1965, p. 96, that "the word *masterpeece* itself is pejorative in other uses in Milton and in contemporary usages among the Puritans; it may perhaps be closer to the meaning of the modern word *gimmick* than to guiding principle."

[34] Milton, *Apology for Smectymnuus,* in *Works,* III, 347.

the development of Renaissance epic definitely owes something to Gravity, the Seventh Idea of Hermogenes, in both its senses —as a grave and occasionally terrible style which therefore requires a grave subject, and as the principle of combination and modulation between styles which is also called "Decorum." And whether the emphasis is on seriousness or flexibility, the quality of Gravity or Decorum is most likely to be possessed by a mature orator or poet, one who has learned by experience. George Puttenham has this to say on the subject in his *Arte of English Poesie*:

> verely it seemes to go all by discretion, not perchaunce of every one, but by a learned and experienced discretion, for otherwise seemes the *decorum* to a weake and ignorant judgement, then it doth to one of better knowledge and experience: which sheweth that it resteth in the discerning part of the minde, so as he who can make the best and most differences of things by reasonable and wittie distinction is to be the fittest judge or sentencer . . .
>
> (p. 263)

The talent which Puttenham describes is one that any author would be glad to assume, but it is absolutely essential to the student of Renaissance decorum, since the subject depends for its very existence on "reasonable and wittie distinction." At the same time the subject calls equally on the capacity of the student to draw things together, to make analogies as well as distinctions, because decorum of style is based on analogy. Puttenham expresses it in this way:

> This lovely conformitie, or proportion, or conveniencie betweene the sence and the sensible hath nature her selfe first most carefully observed in all her owne workes, then also by kinde graft it in the appetites of every creature working by intelligence to covet and desire: . . . and of man chiefly before any other creature as well in his speaches as in every other part of his behaviour.
>
> (p. 262)

213

Conclusion

THIS does not seem to be the kind of book for which a *useful* conclusion can be written—that kind of efficient summary of the argument which protects one from having to read the book itself. Therefore I have chosen rather to present, in conclusion, two of the most attractive examples of Renaissance patterning, in which Hermogenes finds his place. Both are attempts to explain why there should be Seven Ideas, not more, not less, and what their relationship is to other sevens.

The first of these occurs in Antonius Lullius' *De Oratione* (1558), when he is discussing the relationship of the Seven Ideas to the dialogues of Plato. Lullius decides first that if Hermogenes had been considering primarily the styles of the various speakers, he would have come up with more than Seven Ideas, but that he was influenced primarily by the *Symposium* and consequently by the number of speakers in it; "Therefore he was content with the number seven: because they were seven, who bore his symbols in the praise of Love" (p. 425). He then proceeds to rebuke Hermogenes for inexactness in the analogy, forgetting apparently that it is of his own making, because "there are only six characters who express each his own style, Socrates gathering them all into one as if in a bunch of flowers." The arbitrariness of this, however, is less important than what it shows about the desire to associate Hermogenes with Plato, and to show some mysterious rationality for the number that he chose. Lullius, it should be pointed out, divided the *De Oratione* into seven books, and he comments upon the source of this structure in expressing his admiration for the Seven Ideas. He also pauses in his seventh book to suggest a relationship between the Ideas and the seven planets, Jupiter, Saturn, Mars, Mercury, Venus, Sun, and Moon, which influence both character and artistic expression (pp. 497-498).

Lullius' alignment of the planets with the Seven Ideas is little more than a notion (and an eccentric expression of his interest in contemporary painting), but it may have influenced a far more serious attempt to develop the same concept some

214

Conclusion

thirty years later. In 1589 Fabio Paolini published the *Hebdomades*, an elaborate numerological work which devotes most of the first of its *seven* books to the Seven Ideas. Paolini was interested in astrology and in the magical aspects of Neoplatonism developed by Marsilio Ficino, and in the relation of both to oratory. He believed that the orator could acquire Orphic power over his audience by discovering and blending in his work the forms or ideas of things as conceived by the *anima mundi*. The main link between oratory and the *anima mundi* is via the number seven, because seven is the number of the planets which control human character and responses, and in Hermogenes, for whom he had great admiration, Paolini discovered the perfect oratorical scheme to fit his purposes. The Seven Ideas of style, with a little juggling, are matched with the seven planets, in nature and operation. Thus the Moon corresponds to Clarity; the Sun to Grandeur in all its six parts (Vehemence and Asperity are its arrows, Splendor its rays, etc.); Venus and Mercury together correspond to Beauty in its aspects both of pure beauty and of diligence; Mars, to Speed; Jupiter, to Ethos; and gloomy Saturn, to Verity, the sometimes bitter truth. Finally Gravity, since it consists in the right use of all the Ideas, corresponds to the star-bearing globe itself, which embraces all the others.[1]

Whatever one may think of the logic of this, it has a re-

[1] Fabio Paolini, *Hebdomades*, 1589, pp. 36-37:

Luna enim & pura dicitur Graecè καθαρὴ, & perspicua. Sol granditatem refert, & illius formas σεμνότητα propter munus divinationis, τραχύτητα, & σφοδρότητα, idest asperitatem, & vehementiam propter sagittas, undeapud Homerum, acerbam necem infert Grecorum exercitui, splendorem λαμπρότητα propter radios, περιβολὸη, idest circumductum propter continentem lationem, qua quotidie circunfertur, & peragrat coelestes regiones. Veneris, & Mercurii orbis, quoniam pari passu sequuntur Solem, referunt unicam formam, quae iccirco duplici nomine fuit ab Hermogene insignita, quorum alterum Veneri nempe κάλλος, idest pulchritudo, alterum Mercurio nempe ἐπιμέλεια, idest diligentia est accommodatum. Martis globus fero illo aspectu nobis γοργότητα, idest truculentiam repraesentat. Juppiter τὸ ἦθος, idest mores, sive affectus, cum dicatur quasi juvans pater. Saturnus τὴν ἀλήθεαν, idest veritatem. Stellifer verò globus, qui omnes amplectitur τὴν δεινότητα, idest gravitatem aptam, sive decorum, quae posita est in omnium apto usu formarum.

assuring magnanimity about it. "Curious Hermogenes" becomes for these writers Hermogenes the magician, who intuitively perceived the sources of motivation and the essence of psychological manipulation by the use of words. The Seven Ideas have become something far more interesting than just a rhetorical textbook, providing both a powerful stimulus to the imagination, and a flexible framework for the synthesizing intellect, as they work together in an attempt to make something shapely out of human experience. Obviously both Lullius and Paolini provide rather extreme examples of the Renaissance response to Hermogenes, but, being extremes, they provide the clearest possible illustration of how badly Hermogenes has been maligned by virtually all his modern assessors. For example, if one goes to the *Oxford Classical Dictionary* to learn something about Hermogenes, one will find under the heading of "Rhetoric, Greek" the following description of *Concerning Ideas*:

> ... a treatise notable for its obscure terminology, its endless classifications, distinctions, definitions, and rules, which added but little to the vital appreciation of style. ... Thus in the second and later centuries did Greek rhetoric revert to sterile scholastic standards and methods. It gave rise to a system which had disastrous effects on literature for centuries to come.[2]

It is this kind of surly dismissal of Hermogenes' rhetoric appearing in standard reference works, which must have dissuaded Renaissance scholars from investigating any further when they discovered his name mentioned by Tasso or Minturno or Milton or Herbert or Nashe. With any luck, this book will put an end to a long period of neglect and misunderstanding, and *Concerning Ideas* will be restored to its rightful place as a beneficent and not inconsiderable influence on the literary tradition.

[2] The author of this version of the anti-Hermogenes position is J.W.H. Atkins. I am grateful to Mrs. Bryant Putney, of Princeton University Press, for bringing it to my attention.

*Some Renaissance Editions and Translations
of Hermogenes, 1500-1650*

General Bibliography

Index

Some Renaissance Editions and Translations of Hermogenes, 1500-1650

1508   Aldus Pius Manutius, ed. *Rhetores in hoc Volumine habentur hi. Aphthonii Sophistae Progymnasmata. Hermogenis ars Rhetorica . . . Syriani. Sopatri. Marcellini Commentarii in Hermogenis Rhetorica.* 2 vols. Venice. (Vol. 1, pp. 19-160. Greek only)

1515   B. di Giunta, ed. *Rhetores in hoc Volumine . . . Hermogenis ars Rhetorica.* Florence: Philip Giunta. (Greek only)

1530-31 Ἑρμογένους τέχνη ῥητορική τελειοτατη, Paris: Christian Wechel. (Greek only)

1538   Antonio Bonfine, tr. *Hermogenis Tarsensis, Philosophi, ac Rhetoris acutissimi, de Arte rhetorica praecepta . . . Antonio Bonfine Asculani Interprete.* Lyons: Seb. Gryphius. (Latin only)

1544-45 *Hermogenis Ars Rhetorica absolutissima.* Paris: Jacob Bogardus. (Greek only. The British Museum copy, which is the only one I have seen, contains only the first two parts of the *Art of Rhetoric*, bound with a Latin translation of the *Concerning Status* by Jacob Tusanus.)

1550   Natalis Conte, tr. *Hermogenis Tarsensis Philosophi Ac Rhetoris Acutissimi de arte rhetorica praecepta. Apthonii (sic) item sophistae praeexercitamenta, nuper in Latinum sermonem versa a N. de Comitibus.* Basle: Petrus Perna. (Latin translation only)

1555-58 Johannes Sturm et al. Ἑρμογένους τέχνε ῥητορική. Strassburg: Josias Richel. (Greek only. Yale University Library has the part of this edition containing the περὶ ἰδεῶν, dated 1555)

1569   Franciscus Portus, ed. Οἱ ἐν τῇ Ῥητορικῇ τέχνη χορυφαῖοι.
Reissued 'Αφθόνιος, Ἑρμογένης, Δ. Λονγῖνος . . . *Francisci Porti,*
1570   *Cretensis opera industrique illustrati atque expoliti.* Geneva: I. Crispinus. (Greek only)

1570-71 Johannes Sturm, ed. and tr. *Hermogenis ars rhetorica . . . Latinate donati et scholis explicati atque illustrati.* Strassburg. (Greek with Latin translation, and Latin commentary under separate pagination)

1590   Gabriele Zinano, tr. *Sommarii Di Varie Retoriche Greche,*

Bibliography

Latine, Et Volgari . . . Reggio: H. Bartholi. (Italian paraphrase: "Sommario d'Hermogene," pp. 191-215)

1594 Giulio Camillo Delminio, tr. *Le Idee, overo forme della oratione considerate & ridotte in questa lingua.* Udine: Gio. Battista Natolini. (Italian)

1608 ———. *Modo del ben orare et de comporre le Orationi, cavato dalle Idee del dottissimo Ermogene.* Venice: Bernardo Giunta. (Italian, second edition of the above)

1614 Gaspar Laurentius, ed. and tr. Ερμογενους τέχνη ῥητορική τελειοτατη *cum nova Versione Latina e regione Contextus Graeci, & Commentariis Gasparis Laurentii.* Geneva: Petrus Aubertus. (Greek and Latin, with Latin commentary)

1643 *Autori classici Italiani. Degli autori ben parlare per secolari, e religiosi opere diverse.* Venice: G. degli Aromatari. (Part III, Vol. V contains Gaspar Laurentius' translations and commentaries for the περὶ ἰδεῶν and the περὶ μεθόδον δεινότητος.)

1644 *Operum Graecorum, Latinorum, et Italorum Rhetorum.* Venice. (Vol. III contains Delminio's *Discorso sopra l'Idee di Hermogene,* and the translations and commentaries by Laurentius for all four parts of the *Art of Rhetoric*)

General Bibliography

Ariosto, Orazio. *Risposte ad alcuni luoghi del dialogo dell'epica poesia del Signor Cammillo Pellegrino* (1585). In Torquato Tasso, *Opere*, x. Pisa: Niccolo Capurro, 1823.

Arundel Harington Manuscript of Tudor Poetry, The. Ed. Ruth Hughey. 2 vols. Columbus: Ohio State University Press, 1960.

Ascham, Roger. *The Scholemaster* (1570). In *Elizabethan Critical Essays*, i, ed. G. Gregory Smith. London: Oxford University Press, 1964.

Auden, W. H. *The Collected Poetry.* New York: Random House, 1945.

Auerbach, Erich. *Literary Language and Its Public in Late Latin Antiquity and in the Middle Ages.* Tr. Ralph Manheim. Bollingen Series LXXIV. New York: Pantheon, 1965.

Bacon, Francis. *Works.* Ed. J. Spedding et al. 7 vols. London: Longmans, 1876-1883.

Baldwin, C. S. *Medieval Rhetoric and Poetic to 1400.* Gloucester, Mass.: Peter Smith, 1959.

——. *Renaissance Literary Theory and Practice.* Ed. D. L. Clark. New York: Columbia University Press, 1939.

Barclay, Alexander. *Ship of Fools.* Ed. T. H. Jamieson. Edinburgh: W. Paterson, 1874.

Barksted, William. *Mirrha, the Mother of Adonis: or Lustes Prodegies* (1607). In *Seven Minor Epics of the English Renaissance (1596-1624)*, ed. Paul W. Miller. Gainesville, Fla.: Scholars' Facsimiles, 1967.

Barnfield, Richard. *Poems.* Ed. Montague Summers. London: Fortune Press, 1936.

Bembo, Pietro. *Prose nellequali si ragiona della volgar Lingua.* Venice, 1525.

Betjeman, John. *Collected Poems.* London: John Murray, 1958.

Bolgar, R. R. *The Classical Heritage and Its Beneficiaries.* Cambridge: Cambridge University Press, 1958.

Brand, C. P. *Torquato Tasso: A Study of the Poet and of His Contribution to English Literature.* Cambridge: Cambridge University Press, 1965.

Bunyan, John. *Works.* Ed. Henry Stebbing. 4 vols. Toronto: Virtue, Yorston and Co. (n.d.).

Burton, Robert. *The Anatomy of Melancholy* (1621). Ed. F. Dell and P. Jordan Smith. New York: Tudor Publishing, 1955.

Bibliography

Cambridge University. *Statutes for the University and Colleges of Cambridge.* London: Wm. Clowe, 1840.

Camoens, Luis de. *Os Lusiadas.* Ed. J.D.M. Ford. Cambridge: Harvard University Press, 1946.

———. *The Lusiads.* Tr. Leonard Bacon. New York: Hispanic Society of America, 1950.

Campion, Thomas. *Songs and Masques with Observations in the Art of English Poesy.* Ed. A. H. Bullen. London, 1903.

Caplan, Harry. "Classical Rhetoric and the Mediaeval Theory of Preaching," in *Historical Studies of Rhetoric and Rhetoricians.* Ithaca: Cornell University Press, 1961.

Caputi, A. F. *John Marston, Satirist.* Ithaca: Cornell University Press, 1961.

Castiglione, Baldassare. See Thomas Hoby, tr.

Cicero, Marcus Tullius(?) *Ad C. Herennium, De Ratione Dicendi.* (*Rhetorica ad Herennium*) Ed. and tr. Harry Caplan. Cambridge: Harvard University Press (Loeb Classical Library No. 403), 1964.

———. *Orator.* Ed. and tr. H. M. Hubbell. Cambridge: Harvard University Press, 1939.

Clark, D. L. "John Milton and 'the fitted stile of lofty, mean, or lowly,'" *Seventeenth-Century News,* xi (1953), 5-9.

Clements, R. J. *Critical Theory and Practice of the Pléiade.* Cambridge: Harvard University Press, 1942.

Constable, Henry. *Poems.* Ed. Joan Grundy. Liverpool: Liverpool University Press, 1960.

Crane, William G. *Wit and Rhetoric in the Renaissance.* New York: Columbia University Press, 1937.

Curtius, E. R. *European Literature and the Latin Middle Ages.* Tr. W. R. Trask. London: Routledge and Kegan Paul, 1953.

Daniel, Samuel. *Complete Works.* Ed. Alexander B. Grosart. 4 vols. New York: Russell and Russell, 1963.

———. *Poems, and A Defence of Ryme.* Ed. A. C. Sprague. Cambridge: Harvard University Press, 1930.

Davies, John. *Complete Poems.* Ed. Alexander B. Grosart. 2 vols. London: Chatto and Windus, 1876.

Delminio, Giulio Camillo. *Discorso sopra l'Idee di Hermogene,* in *Tutte l'opere di M. Giulio Camillo Delminio,* ed. Thomaso Porcacchi. Venice: Gabriel Gioliti de' Ferrari, 1567. (Second edition, the first, as recorded by Weinberg, having been published in 1560)

222

Bibliography

Demetrius. *A Greek Critic: Demetrius on Style.* Tr. G.M.A. Grube. Toronto: University of Toronto Press, 1961. (*The Phoenix,* Supp. IV)

Dobson, E. J. *English Pronunciation, 1500-1700.* 2 vols. Oxford: Clarendon Press, 1957.

Dolce, Ludovico. *Osservationi Nella Volgar Lingua.* Venice, 1550.

Donne, John. *Poems.* Ed. H.J.C. Grierson. 2 vols. Oxford: Clarendon Press, 1963.

————. *Sermons.* Ed. George R. Potter and Evelyn M. Simpson. 10 vols. Berkeley and Los Angeles: University of California Press, 1953—62.

Drayton, Michael. *Works.* Ed. J. William Hebel. 5 vols. Oxford: Basil Blackwell, 1931—41.

Dryden, John. *A Discourse Concerning the Original and Progress of Satire,* in *Poetical Works,* IV, ed. Joseph Warton, 1811.

Dyer, Edward. *At the Court of Queen Elizabeth: The Life and Lyrics of Sir Edward Dyer.* Ed. R. M. Sargent. London and New York: Oxford University Press, 1935.

Elizabethan Critical Essays. Ed. G. Gregory Smith. 2 vols. Oxford: Clarendon Press, 1959.

Elyot, Thomas. *The Governour* (1531). Ed. Foster Watson. London: J. M. Dent, 1907.

Empson, William. *Collected Poems.* London: Chatto & Windus, 1955.

England's Helicon (1600). Ed. Hugh Macdonald. London: Routledge and Kegan Paul, 1962.

Fairfax, Edward, tr. *Godfrey of Bouloigne* (1600). Ed. as *Jerusalem Delivered* by J. C. Nelson. New York: Capricorn, 1963.

Fanshawe, Richard, tr. *The Lusiad, or Portugals Historicall Poem* (1655). Ed. J.D.M. Ford. Cambridge: Harvard University Press, 1940.

Faral, E. *Les Arts poétiques du XIIe et du XIIIe siècle.* Paris: H. Champion, 1924.

Farnaby, Thomas. *Index Rhetoricus, Scholis et Institutioni tenerioris aetatis accommodatus.* London, 1625.

French, J. Milton. "Milton as Satirist," *PMLA,* LI (1936), 414-429.

Fuhr, Karl. "Zwei Hermogeneskommentatoren," *Rheinisches Museum für Philologie,* LI (1896), 45-51.

Gil, Alexander. *Logonomia Anglica* (1621). Ed. R. C. Alston. Menston, Eng.: Scolar Press Facsimiles, 1968.

Bibliography

Gentili, Scipio. *Annotationi sopra la Gierusalemme Liberata Di Torquato Tasso.* Leyden, 1586.

Greville, Fulke. *Poems and Dramas.* Ed. Geoffrey Bullough. 2 vols. Edinburgh and London: Oliver and Boyd, 1939.

Grube, G.M.A. See Demetrius.

Guarini, Battista. *Il Verrato Ovvero Difesa Di Quanto Ha Scritto M. Giason Denores Contra Le Tragicomedie, Et Le Pastorali, In Un Suo Discorso Di Poesia* (1588), in *Opere.* Verona: Tumermani, 1737.

Guilpin, Everard. *Skialetheia or A Shadowe of Truth* (1598). London: Humphrey Milford, 1931. (Shakespeare Association Facsimiles, No. 2)

Gunn, Thom. *Fighting Terms.* London: Faber and Faber, 1962.

Hagedorn, Dieter. *Zur Ideenlehre des Hermogenes.* Göttingen: Vandenhoeck and Ruprecht, 1964.

Hall, Joseph. *Poems.* Ed. Arnold Davenport. Liverpool: Liverpool University Press, 1949.

Hall, Vernon. *Renaissance Literary Criticism.* New York: Columbia University Press, 1945.

Harris, Bernard. "Men Like Satyrs," in *Elizabethan Poetry.* London: Edwin Arnold, 1960. (Stratford-on-Avon Studies II, 175-201)

Harvey, Gabriel. *Against Thomas Nashe* (1593), in *Elizabethan Critical Essays,* II, ed. G. Gregory Smith. Oxford: Clarendon Press, 1959.

———. *Rhetor, vel duorum dierum Oratio, De Natura, Arte, & Exercitatione Rhetorica.* London, 1577.

——— and Edmund Spenser. *Three Proper, and wittie, familiar Letters* (1580). In Edmund Spenser, *The Prose Works,* ed. Rudolf Gottfried, Baltimore: Johns Hopkins Press, 1949.

Hathaway, Baxter. *The Age of Criticism: The Late Renaissance in Italy.* Ithaca: Cornell University Press, 1962.

Heinsius, Daniel. *Quintus Horatius Flaccus accedunt nunc Danielis Heinsii De Satyra Horatiana Libri duo.* Leyden, 1629.

Hendrickson, G. L. "The Origin of the Three Characters of Style," *American Journal of Philology,* XXVI (1905), 249-290.

Herbert, George. *Works.* Ed. F. E. Hutchinson. Oxford: Clarendon Press, 1941.

Hermogenes. *Opera.* Ed. Hugo Rabe. Leipzig: Bibliotheca Scriptorum Graecorum et Romanorum Teubneriania, 1913.

Bibliography

———. *Ars Rhetorica.* Ed. L. Spengel. Leipzig: B. G. Teubner, 1854. (In *Rhetores graeci*, II)

———. *Ars Rhetorica.* Ed. C. Walz. Stuttgart and Tubingen: J. G. Cotta, 1834. (In *Rhetores graeci*, III)

Herrick, Robert. *Poetical Works.* Ed. L. C. Martin. Oxford, Clarendon, 1956.

Hieatt, A. Kent. *Short Time's Endless Monument: The Symbolism of the Numbers in Edmund Spenser's "Epithalamion."* New York: Columbia University Press, 1960.

Hoby, Thomas, tr. *The Book of the Courtier* (1561), translated from Baldassare Castiglione, *Il Cortegiano* (1528). In *Three Renaissance Classics*, ed. B. A. Milligan. New York: Charles Scribner, 1953.

Howell, W. S. *Logic and Rhetoric in England, 1500-1700.* New York: Russell and Russell, 1961.

John, L. C. *The Elizabethan Sonnet Sequences.* New York: Columbia University Press, 1938.

Jonson, Ben. *Works.* Ed. C. H. Herford and Percy and Evelyn Simpson. 11 vols. Oxford: Clarendon Press, 1925-1952. Reissued 1965.

Kalstone, David. *Sidney's Poetry: Contexts and Interpretations.* Cambridge: Harvard University Press, 1965.

Kennedy, George. *The Art of Persuasion in Greece.* Princeton: Princeton University Press, 1963.

Kernan, Alvin. *The Cankered Muse: Satire of the English Renaissance.* New Haven: Yale Studies in English, 1959.

Kökeritz, Helge. *Shakespeare's Pronunciation.* New Haven: Yale University Press, 1953.

Kranidas, Thomas. "Decorum and the Style of Milton's Anti-Prelatical Tracts," *Studies in Philology*, LXII (1945), 176-187.

———. *The Fierce Equation: A Study of Milton's Decorum.* The Hague: Mouton, 1965.

———. "Milton and the Rhetoric of Zeal," *Texas Studies in Literature and Language*, VI (1965), 423-432.

Kroll, W. "Rhetorik," in Pauly-Wissowa, *Real-Encylopädie der classischen Altertumswissenschaft*, Supplementband VII, 1125-1128. Stuttgart, 1940.

Krumbacher, Karl. *Geschichte der Byzantinischen Literatur.* Munich: Oskar Beck, 1891.

Kustas, G. L. "The Function and Evolution of Byzantine Rhetoric," I (1970) *Viator* (published by the University of California Press).

225

Bibliography

————. "The Literary Criticism of Photius: A Christian Definition of Style," Ἑλληνικά, XVII (1960), 132-169.

Lawrence, N. G. "A Study of Taffeta Phrases and Honest Kersey Noes," in *Sweet Smoke of Rhetoric*, ed. N. G. Lawrence and J. A. Reynolds. Florida: University of Miami Press, 1964.

Leishman, James B. *Themes and Variations in Shakespeare's Sonnets*. London: Hutchinson, 1961.

Lemnius, Levinus. *The Touchstone of Complexions*. Tr. Henry Newton. London, 1581.

Leopardi, Giacomo. *De vita et scriptis Hermogenis commentarius*. In *Opere Inedite*, 2 vols. Halle, 1878, 1. 105ff. (Not seen)

Lever, Julius W. *The Elizabethan Love Sonnet*. London: Methuen, 1956.

Lodge, Thomas. *Complete Works*. Hunterian Club Reprint. 4 vols. New York: Russell and Russell, 1963.

Lullius, Antonius. *De Oratione Libri septem. Quibus non modò ipse totus, verumetiam quicquid ferè à reliquis Graecis ac Latinis de Arte dicendi traditum est, suis locis aptissime explicatur*. Basle, 1558.

Lynche, Richard. *The Love of Dom Diego and Ginevra* (1596). In *Seven Minor Epics of the English Renaissance (1596-1624)*, ed. Paul W. Miller. Gainesville, Fla.: Scholars' Facsimiles, 1967.

Marston, John. *Poems*. Ed. Arnold Davenport. Liverpool: Liverpool University Press, 1961.

Marvell, Andrew. *Poems and Letters*. 2 vols. Oxford: Ed. H. M. Margoliouth. Clarendon Press, 1927.

Milton, John. *Works*. New York: Columbia University Press, 1931.

Minturno, Antonio (Sebastiani). *L'Arte Poetica . . . Nella Quale Si Contengono i precetti Heroici, Tragici, Comici, Satyrici, e d'ogni altra Poesia: Con La Dottrina De' Sonetti, Canzoni, & ogni sorte di Rime Thoscane, dove s'insegna il modo, che tenne il Petrarca nelle sue opere . . .* Venice, 1564.

Mirror for Magistrates, The. Ed. Lily B. Campbell. New York: Barnes and Noble, 1960.

Montgomery, R. L. *Symmetry and Sense: The Poetry of Sir Philip Sidney*. Austin: University of Texas Press, 1961.

Nashe, Thomas. *Works*. Ed. Ronald B. McKerrow. Oxford: Basil Blackwell, 1958.

Oxford University. *Statuta Antiqua Universitatis Oxoniensis*. Ed. Strickland Gibson. 1931.

Pagano, Pietro. *Discorso . . . sopra il secondo sonetto del Petrarca*

Bibliography

dove si scopre l'artificio usato dal Poeta. B.M. MS. Add. 33.470. (Not seen)

Panofsky, Erwin. *Idea: A Concept in Art Theory.* Tr. Joseph J. S. Peake. Columbia: University of South Carolina Press, 1968.

Paolini, Fabio. *Hebdomades, sive septem de septenario libri . . . in unius Virgilii versus explicatione.* Venice, 1589.

Parthenio, Bernadino. *Della Imitatione Poetica.* Venice, 1560.

Peacham, Henry. *The Garden of Eloquence Conteyning the Figures of Grammer and Rhetorick.* London: H. Jackson, 1577. See also W. G. Crane's facsimile edition of the revised 1593 version (Gainesville, Fla.: Scholars' Facsimiles, 1954).

Peletier du Mans, Jacques. *L'Art poétique* (1555). Ed. André Boulanger. Paris: Faculté des Lettres de L'Université de Strasbourg, No. 53, 1930.

Pellegrino, Camillo. *Del concetto poetico* (1598), in Angelo Borzelli, *Il Cavalier Giovan Battista Marino (1569-1625).* Naples, 1898, pp. 325-359. (Not seen)

Peter, John. *Complaint and Satire in Early English Literature.* Oxford: Clarendon Press, 1956.

Petrarch, Francis. *Rime, Trionfi e Poesie Latine.* Ed. Ferdinando Neri. Milan and Naples: La Letteratura italiana. Storia e testi, VI, 1951.

Portus, Franciscus. *Commentarius in Longinum.* In *Dionysii Longini De Sublimitate Commentarius, Quem Nova Versione donavit . . . Zacharias Pearce, A.M. . . . . Accessit Fr. Porti Cretensis in Longinum Commentarius integer, nunc primum editus.* Amsterdam: R. and J. Wetstenios and G. Smith, 1733, pp. 279-360. (Not seen)

Prince, F. T. *The Italian Element in Milton's Verse.* Oxford: Clarendon Press, 1962.

————. "The Sonnet from Wyatt to Shakespeare," in *Elizabethan Poetry.* London: Edwin Arnold, 1960. (Stratford-on-Avon Studies II, 10-29)

Provot, E. M. *De Hermogenis Tarsensis dicendi genere.* Dissertation. Leipzig, 1910.

Puttenham, George. *The Arte of English Poesie* (1589). Ed. Gladys D. Willcock and Alice Walker. Cambridge: Cambridge University Press, 1936.

Quintilianus, Marcus Fabius. *Institutio Oratoria.* Ed. and tr. H. E. Butler. London and New York: Loeb Classical Library, 1933.

Rhetorica ad Herennium. See Cicero, Marcus Tullius.

227

Bibliography

Rabe, Hugo. "Aus Rhetoren-Handschriften," *Rheinisches Museum für Philologie*, LXII (1907), 247-264. (See also under Hermogenes)

Radermacher, L. "Hermogenes," in Pauly-Wissowa, *Real-Encyclopädie der classischen Altertumswissenschaft*, VIII, 861-881.

Rainolde, Richard. *A Booke called the Foundacion of Rhetorike* (1563). Ed. Francis R. Johnson. New York: Scholars' Facsimiles, 1945.

Raleigh, Walter. *Poems*. Ed. Agnes Latham. London: Routledge and Kegan Paul, 1962. (Muses Library)

Ransom, John Crowe. *Selected Poems*. New York: Alfred A. Knopf, 1947.

Rébitté, Dominique. *De Hermogene, atque in universum de scriptarum a technicis, apud Graecos, artius utilitate, vel inutilitate disquisitio*. Paris: Dezobry and Magdeleine, 1845.

Rees, D. G. "Italian and Italianate Poetry," in *Elizabethan Poetry*. London: Edwin Arnold, 1960. (Stratford-on-Avon Studies II, 52-69)

Rich, Barnaby. *Faultes Faults And Nothing Else But Faultes* (1606). Ed. Melvin H. Wolf. Gainesville, Fla.: Scholars' Facsimiles, 1965.

Ricks, C. B. *Milton's Grand Style*. Oxford: Clarendon Press, 1963.

Robortello, Francesco. *In librum Aristotelis de arte poetica explicationes*. Florence, 1548. (Not seen)

Røstvig, M.-S. *The Hidden Sense*. New York: Humanities Press, 1963.

Rudenstine, Neil. "Sidney and Energia" in *Elizabethan Poetry: Modern Essays in Criticism*. Ed. Paul J. Alpers. New York: Oxford University Press, 1967.

————. *Sidney's Poetic Development*. Cambridge: Harvard University Press, 1967.

Ryan, Lawrence V. *Roger Ascham*. London: Oxford University Press, 1963.

Scaliger, Julius Caesar. *Poetices Libri Septem*. Lyons: Antonius Vincentius, 1561. See also the facsimile edition by A. Buck, Stuttgart: Faksimile-Neudruck, 1964.

Sells, A. L. *The Italian Influence in English Poetry from Chaucer to Southwell*. London: Allen and Unwin, 1955.

Ševčenko, Igor. *Etudes sur la polémique entre Théodore Métochite et Nicéphore Choumnos*. Brussells, 1962. (Not seen)

Shakespeare, William. *A Casebook on Shakespeare's Sonnets*. Ed.

Bibliography

Gerald Willen and Victor B. Reed. New York: Thomas Crowell, 1964.

Sherry, Richard. *A Treatise of Schemes and Tropes* (1550). Gainesville, Fla.: Scholars' Facsimiles, 1961.

Sidney, Philip. *Defence of Poesie* (1595). Ed. G. Shepherd under alternative title of *An Apology for Poetry*. London and Edinburgh: Thomas Nelson, 1965.

————. *Poems.* Ed. William A. Ringler, Jr. Oxford: Clarendon Press, 1962.

Skelton, John. *Complete Poems of John Skelton, Laureate.* Ed. Philip Henderson. London: J. M. Dent, 1959.

Smith, G. Gregory. See *Elizabethan Critical Essays.*

Smith, Hallet. *Elizabethan Poetry.* Cambridge: Harvard University Press, 1952.

Spenser, Edmund. *Works.* Ed. Edwin Greenlaw et al. Baltimore: Johns Hopkins Press, 1932-1957.

———— and Gabriel Harvey. *Three Proper, and wittie, familiar Letters* (1580). In *The Prose Works,* ed. Rudolf Gottfried. Baltimore: Johns Hopkins Press, 1949.

Spingarn, J. E. *A History of Literary Criticism in the Renaissance.* New York: Harcourt, Brace, 1963.

Stein, Arnold. *George Herbert's Lyrics.* Baltimore: Johns Hopkins Press, 1968.

Summers, J. H. *George Herbert: His Religion and Art.* Cambridge: Harvard University Press, 1954.

Summo, Faustino. *Discorsi Poetici, Ne quali si discorreno le piu principali questioni di Poesia, & si dichiarano molti luoghi dubi & difficili intorno all'arte del poetare. Secondo la mente di Aristotile, di Platone, e di altri buoni Auttori.* Padua, 1600.

Tasso, Torquato. *Opere.* 33 vols. Pisa: Niccolo Capurro, 1821-1832.

Trimpi, Wesley. *Ben Jonson's Poems: A Study of the Plain Style.* Stanford: Stanford University Press, 1962.

Tuve, Rosemond. *Elizabethan and Metaphysical Imagery.* Chicago: University of Chicago Press, 1947.

————. *A Reading of George Herbert.* London: Faber and Faber, 1952.

Vaughan, Henry. *Works.* Ed. L. C. Martin. 2 vols. Oxford: Clarendon Press, 1914.

Wallace, K. R. *Francis Bacon on Communication and Rhetoric.* Chapel Hill: University of North Carolina Press, 1943.

Watson, Thomas. *The Hekatompathia or Passionate Centurie of*

Bibliography

Love (1582). Ed. S. K. Heninger, Jr. Gainesville, Fla.: Scholars' Facsimiles, 1964.

Weever, John. *Faunus and Melliflora, or, the original of our English Satyres* (1600). Ed. A. Davenport. London: Hodder and Stoughton, 1948. (Liverpool Reprints, No. 2)

Weinberg, Bernard. *A History of Literary Criticism in the Italian Renaissance.* 2 vols. Chicago: University of Chicago Press, 1961.

Williamson, George. *The Senecan Amble.* London: Faber and Faber, 1951.

Willobie, George. *Willobie his Avisa or The True picture of a modest Maide and of a chast and constant wife* (1594). Ed. A. B. Grosart. Occasional Issues. 1880.

Wilson, Thomas. *Wilson's Arte of Rhetorique, 1560.* Ed. G. H. Mair. Oxford: Clarendon Press, 1909.

Yeats, William Butler. *Collected Poems.* London: Macmillan, 1963.

———. *Essays and Introductions.* New York: Macmillan, 1961.

Young, Bartholomew, tr. *Diana of George of Montemayor.* London, 1598.

Zepheria (1594). Ed. Edward Arber, in *An English Garner* (*Elizabethan Sonnets*, ii). London: Constable, 1904.

INDEX

231

Index

232

Index

Demosthenes, 17n, 22, 34-37, 177-78

Desportes, Philippe, 147-48

diaporesis, figure of, 64, 127, 128n, 144

diction
  in the Seven Ideas: in Beauty, 54, 124; in Clarity, 46; in Gravity, 179; in Magnificence, 27, 71-72, 74; in Speed, 57, 157-58; in Vehemence and Asperity, 105-06; in Verity, 64, 127
  in the Three Styles, 29n, 31, 80-81

Diligence, as an alternative name for Beauty, 123, 126

Dionysius of Halicarnassus, 48

disposition, as a part of rhetoric, 14

Dobson, E. J., 86n

Dolce, Ludovico, Osservationi Nella Volgar Lingua, 72

dolce stil nuovo, 69

Donne, John, Holy Sonnets, 108, 171; Satires, 102, 105, 109-10, 171-72; speed in Elegy XVI, 163; on vehemence in sermons, 114-16

donysis, 132n

Drayton, Michael: The Barons Warres, 176, 198-200, 203; Mortimeriados, 198-200; odes, 79-81, 92, 94; Robert, Duke of Normandy, 198

δριμύτης, see Hermogenes, Idea of Subtlety

Dryden, John, 107; Original and Progress of Satire, 101, 104

Du Bartas, Guillaume de Salluste, Sepmaines, 71

Dyer, Sir Edward, 95

ecphonisis, figure of, 128n

E. K., 59, 83-85, 128n, 172

Eliot, T. S., The Wasteland, 176n

elocution, as a part of rhetoric, 14

Eloquence, as an alternative name for Gravity, 45, 177, 179, 201

Elyot, Sir Thomas, The Governour, 23

enargia, 131-33

energia, 131-33

England's Helicon, 81, 168-69

enjambement, 166-73, 174, 197

Empson, William, Courage Means Running, 153-54, 169, 175

epanalepsis, figure of, 74, 89

epanaphora, figure of, 54, 124, 125n, 129, 142, 157

epanastrophe, figure of, 54, 124, 125n

epanorthosis, figure of, 128n

epic and the High Style, 29, 31; and the Idea of Beauty, 55, 189, 191-92, 200, 211; and the Idea of the hero, 20-21, 37, 204-05; mixture of Ideas in, 66-68, 117-18, 176-213; perfect Idea of, in Tasso's criticism, 20, 38, 40, 42; stanzas suitable for, 93, 176, 199; stronger than complaint, in Drayton, 198-99

epicope, figure of, 125n

epidiorthosis, figure of, 128, 141

ἐπιείκεια, see Hermogenes, Idea of Modesty

epigram, 61

ἐπιμέλεια, 53

epithalamia, 71, 82-83, 85-87

Erasmus, Desiderius, 5n

erotema, figure of, 127, 128n, 140, 149

εὐκρίνεια, 46

ἦθος, see Hermogenes, Idea of Ethos

exclamatio, figure of, 128n

Fairfax, Edward, 163, 189n

Fanshawe, Richard, 50n, 182n, 185n, 187

Faral, E., 30n

Ficino, Marsilio, 8, 38, 41n, 190, 215

233

Index

234

Index

235

Index

118, 124, 157, 162-67, 174, 195
Menander, 59
merismus, figure of, 128n
metaphor, 27, 61, 71, 77, 78
method, as one of the Eight Parts
  of analysis, 27, 46, 74, 105,
  107, 179
Metochites, Theodore, 49
metonymy, figure of, 61
Metropanes of Phrygia, 7n
Meun, Jean de, 125n
Milton, John, 216
  Apology for Smectymnuus: on
  Ideas of style, 26, 48, 118,
  212; on Modesty and Vehemence
  in controversy, 63-64, 111n,
  112; on the style of satire, 104
  epic style, 73, 78-79, 117-18,
  156; Hermogenes in *Of Education*,
  25, 112, 212; on the low
  style, 28
  Paradise Lost, 200; attitude to
  rhetoric in, 212; as an influence
  on Bunyan, 156; and Magnificent
  subjects, 71; style of, 78-79,
  117-18

  Paradise Regained, 200, 212;
  pronunciation of R, 107n;
  Pro Se Defensio, 113n, 118-19;
  Reason of Church Government,
  112-13, 116
Minturno, Antonio, 6, 21, 28,
  140, 216
  Arte Poetica: on Beauty, 55,
  124, 129, 130; on Clarity, 48n,
  49-50; on Circumlocution, 77-78;
  on decorum, 13-15; on Grandeur,
  52-53, 90; on Gravity, 66, 179,
  181, 192; on the Ideas in Italian
  poetry, 67-68; on Magnificence,
  72, 74-76, 80, 89; on mixing
  Ideas, 33; on Modesty, 62; on
  Simplicity, 59; on Speed, 57,
  155-59, 167, 173; on Splendor,

76-77; on the style of satire,
100, 104-05; on Verity, 64-65,
123, 127, 130; on Vigor, 107-08
  De Poeta, 14n, 100; as an
  influence in England, 21
Mirandola, Pico della, 8, 41n
Mirror for Magistrates, 11, 163
Modest Confutation, A, 63, 111n
Mulcaster, Richard, 86n
myth, classical, 60, 70, 123-24, 148

Nashe, Thomas, 216; *Christ's
  Teares over Jerusalem*, 113-14;
  and Gabriel Harvey, 22, 25;
  *Have With You to Saffron
  Walden*, 22; *Nashes Lenten
  Stuffe* and the style of satire, 102
Navagero, Andrea, 191n
Neoplatonism, *see* Platonism
Newdigate, B., 198n
Newton, Henry, 4n
Nicephorus, 7n
number, as one of the Eight Parts
  of analysis, 72, 74, 80, 124,
  130, 133, 135, 140, 144, 157,
  165, 167, 179, 208

obliquitas, figure of, 46, 48
obticentia, figure of, 128n
occultatio, figure of, 128n
odes, Elizabethan, 68, 73, 179;
  appropriate subjects of, 71;
  of Drayton, 79-81; fusion with
  canzone, 79-81; of Herrick,
  59-60; Horatian, 80; of Jonson,
  87-89, 92; lofty compared to
  light, 92-93; Pindaric, 70,
  74, 80, 87-89; of Spenser, 83-87
officia oratoris, 33
oictros, 132n
onomatopoeia, 12-13, 31, 131-32,
  144, 160, 166
ὀρθότης, figure of, 46, 48
ottava rima, 84n, 176, 193, 199
Ovid, 60, 166

236

Index

Index

Index